Library of
Davidson College

Criminology in Literature

Longman English and Humanities Series
Series Editor: Lee Jacobus

Criminology in
Literature

Paul E. Dow
Moravian College

LONGMAN
NEW YORK AND LONDON

Criminology in Literature

Longman Inc., New York
Associated companies, branches, and representatives
throughout the world.

Copyright © 1980 by Longman Inc.

All rights reserved. No part of this publication may be
reproduced, stored in a retrieval system, or transmitted
in any form or by any means, electronic, mechanical,
photocopying, recording, or otherwise, without the prior
permission of the publisher.

Developmental Editor: Gordon T. R. Anderson
Editorial and Design Supervisor: Judith Hirsch
Interior Design: Pencils Portfolio, Inc.
Cover Design: Charles C. Fellows
Manufacturing and Production Supervisor: Kris Becker
Composition: A & S Graphics
Printing and binding: Fairfield Graphics

Manufactured in the United States of America

9 8 7 6 5 4 3 2 1

Library of Congress Cataloging in Publication Data

Dow, Paul E.
   Criminology in literature.

  (Longman English and humanities series)
  Bibliography: p.
  1. Detective and mystery stories.   2. Crime and
criminals.   3. Deviant behavior.   I. Title.
II. Series.
PZ1.D6518Cr   [PN6071.D45]   813'.0872   79-21758
ISBN 0-582-28164-4

Contents

Preface   vii

Part I. The Classical School   1

    George Bernard Shaw, *On the Entirely Reasonable Murder of A Police Constable*   3
    Ormond Greville, *The Perfect Crime*   6

Part II. The Positive School   17

    James T. Farrell, *Big Jeff*   25
    Stephen Crane, *The Blue Hotel*   29

Part III. Culture Conflict Theory   55

    James T. Farrell, *The Fastest Runner on Sixty-First Street*   58
    Robert Penn Warren, *The Patented Gate and the Mean Hamburger*   68
    Theodore Dreiser, *Nigger Jeff*   79

Part IV. Anomie Theory   95

    Willa Cather, *Paul's Case*   99
    Willa Cather, *The Bookkeeper's Wife*   115
    George Garrett, *Thus the Early Gods*   125

Part V. Psychiatric Theories   137

    Flannery O'Connor, *A Good Man Is Hard to Find*   141
    Edgar Allan Poe, *The Tell-Tale Heart*   154
    Edgar Allan Poe, *The Cask of Amontillado*   158

Part VI. Labeling Theory   167

    Bret Harte, *The Outcasts of Poker Flat*   172
    Sondra Spatt Olsen, *Hoods I Have Known*   181
    John Berryman, *The Imaginary Jew*   192

Part VII. Radical Criminology   **203**

    James T. Farrell, *Young Convicts*   208
    Heinrich Böll, *The Balek Scales*   213
    Art Buchwald, *The Trial of Jack the Ripper*   219

Part VIII. Differential Association   **223**

    Hugh Allyn Hunt, *Acme Rooms and Sweet Marjorie Russell*   227
    Shirley Jackson, *The Lottery*   240

Part IX. Predicting Deviant Behavior   **251**

    The Queen v. Dudley and Stephens   255
    Nathaniel Hawthorne, *The Minister's Black Veil*   261

Bibliography   274

Preface

For over two hundred years criminologists have conducted research in the hope of discovering the causes of criminal behavior. Their work is available in many textbooks outlining in painstaking detail the research, findings, and criticism of their theories. This book has been designed for courses in criminology and criminal justice dealing with the nature and problems of the study of crime causation. The anthology provides a unique alternative approach to the field of criminology: fiction is employed to illustrate, clarify, supplement, and summarize the major statements about the etiologies of crime. The short stories enable the student of criminology to understand the causes of crime by relating the plight of the protagonists and antagonists to the particular theory under discussion.

The book is divided into nine parts. Each section begins with a brief yet comprehensive overview of a particular crime theory and is followed by illustrative stories. Issues for discussion conclude each part, relating the story line to the theory being described. The first eight parts present contributions of the classical, positive, culture conflict, anomie, psychiatric, labeling, radical, and differential association theorists. The final part, "Predicting Deviant Behavior: A Critique," puts into perspective the existing state of the art of criminology and proposes alternative goals for future theorists. The arrangement of the sections closely approximates the chronological order in which the theories gained prominence among criminologists. In cases where competing theories appeared almost simultaneously, the order has been rather arbitrarily decided.

Several key terms are used throughout the book. *Criminology* is defined as the systematic study of the causes of criminal behavior. *School of thought* refers to any collection of thoughts, impressions, statements, or theories about crime causation. A *statement* is distinguished from *theory* in that a statement is not adequately supported by empirical data or sufficiently developed to allow for testing, verification, or modification of its principal premise. And because of its imprecise nature, the statement does not provide the basis for prediction. The expression *deviant* characterizes the person who has committed a criminal act, whereas *deviance* refers to the criminal behavior (activity). *Asocial* behavior describes activity that is legally permissible (does not transcribe formal legal codes) yet offends some group or community's informal code of conduct (e.g., folkways, customs, or mores).

I have called upon the assistance of many individuals for their aid and comfort in developing this anthology. Ruth C. D'Aleo, the reference librarian at Moravian College, spent many hours gathering the short stories for my use. Gordon T. R. Anderson, senior editor of Longman and Janet Polster, also of Longman, provided the technical and editorial expertise in an astute, candid, and cordial manner. Thomas West Gregory of Richmond University unselfishly and freely gave suggestions allowing me to avoid many time-consuming pitfalls associated with projects of this nature. Mrs. Margaret Boyer is especially deserving of commendation for her flawless and tireless typing and retyping of the manuscript. I am especially grateful to three colleagues at Moravian College, Jack Dilendik, Judy Blau, and particularly Bettie Smolansky. All were given the seemingly thankless task of editing the introductory essays. Their help and reassurances were always appreciated.

Finally, this publication, like all others before it, is dedicated to Jo-Anne Sessa. She continually and unselfishly provided the understanding and patience that was so often needed.

Acknowledgments

"On the Entirely Reasonable Murder of a Police Constable," from *Crude Criminology* by George Bernard Shaw. Copyright 1932 by George Bernard Shaw. Reprinted by permission of The Society of Authors on behalf of the Bernard Shaw Estate.

"The Perfect Crime" by Ormond Greville. First appeared in *Pearson's Magazine* in 1932. Reprinted by permission of A.P. Watt Ltd.

"Big Jeff" by James T. Farrell. Reprinted from *The Short Stories of James T. Farrell* by permission of the publisher, Vanguard Press, Inc. Copyright 1937; copyright © renewed 1964 by James T. Farrell.

"The Fastest Runner on Sixty-First Street" by James T. Farrell. Reprinted from *An American Dream Girl* by James T. Farrell by permission of the publisher, Vanguard Press, Inc. Copyright 1950; copyright © renewed 1977 by James T. Farrell.

"The Patented Gate and the Mean Hamburger" by Robert Penn Warren. Copyright 1947, 1975 by Robert Penn Warren. Reprinted from his volume *The Circus in the Attic and Other Stories* by permission of Harcourt Brace Jovanovich, Inc.

"Paul's Case" by Willa Cather. Reprinted from *Youth and the Bright Medusa*, by Willa Cather. Courtesy of Alfred A. Knopf, Inc.

"The Bookkeeper's Wife" by Willa Cather. Copyright 1916 by The Century Company renewed 1943 by Willa Cather. Reprinted by permission of Charles E. Cather, trustee.

"Thus the Early Gods," from *In the Briar Patch* by George Garrett. Published by the University of Texas Press. Copyright © 1961 by George Garrett. Reprinted by permission of the author.

"A Good Man Is Hard to Find" by Flannery O'Connor. Copyright 1953 by Flannery O'Connor. Reprinted from her volume *A Good Man Is Hard to Find and Other Stories* by permission of Harcourt Brace Jovanovich, Inc.

"Hoods I Have Known" by Sondra Spatt Olsen. Copyright © 1956 by Street and Smith, Inc. Originally appeared in *Mademoiselle*. Reprinted by permission of Sondra Spatt Olsen.

"The Imaginary Jew," from *Recovery* by John Berryman. Copyright 1945 by

John Berryman. Copyright renewed © 1973 by Kate Berryman. Reprinted by permission of Farrar, Straus & Giroux, Inc.

"Young Convicts" by James T. Farrell. Reprinted from *An Omnibus of Short Stories* by James T. Farrell by permission of the publisher, Vanguard Press, Inc. Copyright © 1956 by James T. Farrell.

"The Balek Scales" by Heinrich Böll From *18 Stories* by Heinrich Böll. Copyright © 1966 by Heinrich Böll. Used with permission of McGraw-Hill Book Company.

"The Trial of Jack the Ripper" by Art Buchwald. Reprinted by permission of G.P. Putnam's Sons from *Son of the Great Society* by Art Buchwald. Copyright © 1965, 1966, by Art Buchwald.

"Acme Rooms and Sweet Marjorie Russell" by Hugh Allyn Hunt. Copyright © 1966 by *Transatlantic Review*. Reprinted by permission of *Transatlantic Review*.

"The Lottery," from *The Lottery* by Shirley Jackson. Copyright 1948, 1949 by Shirley Jackson. Copyright renewed © 1976, 1977 by Laurence Hyman, Barry Hyman, Mrs. Sarah Webster, and Mrs. Joanne Schnurer. "The Lottery" appeared originally in *The New Yorker*. Reprinted by permission of Farrar, Straus & Giroux, Inc.

"Differential Association" by Donald R. Cressey. From pp. 80–82 in *Criminology*, 10th edition by Edwin H. Sutherland and Donald R. Cressey. Copyright © 1978 by J. B. Lippincott Company. Reprinted by permission of Harper & Row, Publishers, Inc. and the author.

PART I

The Classical School

The earliest systematic statements about what has come to be called criminology is attributed to the Italian scholar Cesare Beccari. Although he received his formal education in mathematics, Beccari's study of the leading political, economic, and social writers of his era affected his perceptions about crime and justice.[1] In 1764, at the age of twenty-six, he anonymously published a then revolutionary treatise *Dei delitte e delle pene (On Crime and Punishment).*[2] This work was generally well received by other criminologists and reportedly provided the framework for Jeremy Bentham's philosophies about the utility of punishment.[3]

From Beccari's work emerged the basic statement of the classical school of criminology: *let the punishment fit the crime.* This statement directly related to two other concepts central to the classical school: *free will* and *hedonism.* Classical theorists believe that human behavior is not guided by "invisible" or inexplicable phenomena such as psychological, biological, or economic hardships. Rather, a person *consciously* chooses to engage in acceptable (legal) or unacceptable (illegal) behavior. Hedonism suggests

---

1. Beccari's awareness about the injustices endured by the disadvantaged are attributed to the works of St. Thomas Aquinas, Martin Luther, Jean Bodin, Thomas Hobbes, John Locke, Charles de Montesquieu, Francois Voltaire, Jean Jacques Rousseau, and contemporary supporters Alessandro and Pietro Verri. See Marcello T. Maestro, *Voltaire and Beccari as Reformers of Criminal Law* (New York: Columbia University Press, 1942).

2. See Colman Phillipson, *Three Criminal Law Reformers: Beccari, Bentham, and Romilly* (New York: Dutton, 1923).

3. See Léon Radzinowicz, *A History of English Criminal Law and Its Administration from 1750,* vol. 1 (New York: Macmillan, 1948).

that humans wittingly attempt to maximize pleasure and minimize pain. Classical thinkers believe that the punishment for violating the law should be designed to produce more pain than the potential pleasure to be realized from not obeying the law. They would subject persons, regardless of their status (e.g., minors, the insane, or politically or socially prominent individuals) to equal punishment for violating the same law.[4] Since they attribute criminal behavior solely to hedonistic tendencies, classical theorists need no further explanation of why a person engages in criminal behavior.[5]

Statements by classical school thinkers have had a lasting influence on American jurisprudence, particularly regarding appropriate punishment and its effect on crime prevention. Specifically, many U.S. jurisdictions employ policies designed to deter the offender from future criminal conduct. The concept of retribution, of punishing solely for the purpose of "paying the criminal back," is perceived as being without merit or utility. Moreover, the efficacy of punishment is generally not measured in terms of its severity. Rather, the deterrent value of punishment depends on the certainty and swiftness of it execution.

George Bernard Shaw's "On the Entirely Reasonable Murder of a Police Constable" and Ormond Greville's "The Perfect Crime" describe criminal events easily rationalized by their perpetrators. The acts of violence seem logical, even natural, to the criminals because they have more to gain by committing them than by refraining from the criminal behavior. The hedonistic tendencies of these individuals seem to be the controlling force. Moreover, each criminal has ample opportunity to calculate the deed and then rationally select the appropriate course of action.

---

4. The "neo-classical" school modified the philosophies of the classical school. Neoclassicists believe that behavior is affected by pathology, incompetence, or insanity. Further, there may be mitigating circumstances for criminal behavior, such as mental incompetence. If mitigation exists, the punishment should be lessened accordingly. See George B. Vold, *Theoretical Criminology* (New York: Oxford University Press, 1958), pp. 25–26.

5. An excellent overview and analysis of the classical school appears in Ian Taylor et al., *The New Criminology* (New York: Harper & Row, 1973), pp. 1–30.

ON THE ENTIRELY REASONABLE MURDER OF A POLICE CONSTABLE

George Bernard Shaw

From *The Sunday Express*, 13 May 1928

I have been asked to give my opinion "on the popular point of view that a particularly brutal and callous murder of this kind [the reference is to the murder of Police Constable Gutteridge] is one of the cases in which capital punishment is justified."

Now the first thing I have to observe is that the adjectives "brutal and callous" are wildly inappropriate, and represent simply the popular loss of temper over the murder, and the customary English resort to vituperation to relieve the strain.

The murder of Constable Gutteridge was an entirely reasonable one; the work, apparently, of an out-and-out Rationalist. Further, the person who committed it was one of those sensitive people to whom the condition of a criminal under punishment is unbearable.

Also it was the work of someone who was credulous as to "the marvels of science," which take the same place in modern life as miracles did in that of the Ages of Faith.

Reasonable murders practically all fall into the same class: they are murders committed by criminals to escape detection and capture. The reasoning is simple. Our police statistics show the number of murders committed every year, and the proportion of them that are never brought to justice. That is, they show the odds for and against impunity for the murderer.

A robber surprised in the act by a police officer or a householder has to consider that if he surrenders he will certainly spend several years in penal servitude. If he shoots, this certainty is replaced by a risk of being hanged, and a chance of escape.

Such was the situation created by the encounter with the unfortunate Constable Gutteridge, who, though very likely an amiable and humane person, confronted his murderer not as a man, but as a representative of all the terrors and cruelties of the law. The criminal was rational enough to decide to shoot. There is no ground for suspecting him of any animosity to the man: he shot the law.

He had a sufficient smattering of physiology to know that the last picture that was focused on the constable's retina was a picture of himself; and his modern superstitious credulity as to the possibility of this picture, or rather these two coordinated pictures, being photographed in the laboratory and used to identify him led him to destroy the dead man's eyes with two more careful shots.

These shots were not an outrage: they were a precautionary operation. They complete the impression of the murderer's character. He (or she) was most certainly not the Bill Sikes of the popular imagination.

He (I will assume the male sex) was a murderer not from malice, but solely in the way of business, and therefore conceivably a good husband and a kind father. He was sensitive and imaginative, because only sensitive and imaginative people risk hanging to avoid penal servitude.

He had brains enough to be able to calculate his chances, and strength of mind enough to act on his calculation. He was an habitual criminal, because such calculations are not made on the spur of the moment: he must have thought it all out before he armed himself with a loaded revolver.

He had lost the ordinary squeamishness about bloodshed and death that disables the man of peace in such emergencies; but this gives no special clue to him, because the war has left millions of men in that condition.

These reasonable murders are very dangerous, partly because they serve us right for making our criminal law more "brutal and callous" (if we must sling adjectives) than any criminal ever was or could ever possibly be; so that the criminal feels a natural right to do his worst to us to prevent us from doing our worst to him; and partly because they threaten not only the police force, but the whole body of citizens whose only resource when confronted with a criminal is to call in the police.

Their peculiarity has also an important bearing on the question of the death penalty. There is only one excuse for the official slaughter of a man (or woman) in cold blood; and that is that he gives more trouble to the community than he is worth. The same excuse, that is, that we have for killing a tiger or a mad dog.

If we could get this into our heads, and get the wicked and stupid idea of retaliative punishment (murdering the murderer) and the superstitious idea of expiatory punishment (the blood sacrifice) out of them, we should spare some murderers and kill quite a number of intolerable nuisances whom we now only torment in a cowardly and spiteful way, because, let us say, instead of murdering women they pass their lives in entrapping them into bogus marriages and deserting them after spending all their money.

In Scotland they hang people very properly for throwing vitriol; in England the vitriol thrower is sacred because vitriol blinds but does not kill. Such a distinction is absurd. We should calculate as coolly as the murderer of Constable Gutteridge, and refuse to sacrifice the lives of useful people to caging and guarding mischievous ones, simply turning on our convenient domestic gas when it becomes apparent that any individual is not suited for life in a civilized community. There should be no vindictiveness nor punishment nor any other sort of sentimentality in the matter: our attitude at the execution should be apologetic and regretful.

Now a criminal who shoots to escape detection as a matter of business may be no more homicidal by nature than any soldier. The remedy in his case may be to give up our cruel punishments, and to give him a better chance for the honest enployment of his talents than our present system offers.

I have dealt with the general subject pretty fully elsewhere, and must leave it at this. But as somebody is pretty sure to fall back on the official theory that punishment is deterrent—I call it official because it is the judicial theory, and the recent impudent attempts to revive the vindictive theory have not yet had any judicial confirmation—I may as well remind my readers that there are two conclusive objections to it.

The first is that no severity of punishment deters when detection is uncertain, as it must always be.

When pickpokets were hanged, pockets were picked under the gallows. Now that the penalty is comparatively trifling, pockets are still picked, but never when a policeman is looking on.

The second is that the deterrence theory leads to the conclusion that somebody must be punished for every crime to deter others from committing it. Whether that somebody has committed the crime or not is of no consequence: an innocent person will do as well as a guilty one for the purpose.

As the gentleman in Bleak House said, "Much better hang wrong feller than hang no feller."

THE PERFECT CRIME
Ormond Greville

Farmer Greenwood, a big, stout, red-faced man, was in a disputatious mood, and the other men in the billiard room of the Parish Hall, though they never allowed themselves to smile, were thoroughly enjoying the fun. He had had a glass, as the saying is, and had finished a very erratic game of billiards, and now he was expressing his opinions more freely than usual.

"You chaps all think Parson's a saint. Jumping Jehoshaphat! I'll lay he's much like the rest of us, and we aren't saints that I know of—not even you, Dick Burge, not by a long chalk!"

Dick Burge, who was, amongst other things, parish clerk, undertaker and a contractor in a small way, winked at the others and said, "Don't know as I ever set up to be, Mr. Greenwood. But Parson's nigher to being a saint that anyone *I* ever see." He puffed at his pipe and added, "And I've seen a lot of men who ought to have been—three bishops, two deans, and a score of archdeacons, canons and suchlike. Lor' bless me, when it becomes a matter of a talk with St. Peter, they'll have more to explain away than Parson, and you may lay your shirt on that!"

"You're just like a lot of females," said the farmer contemptuously, "taken in by a good-looking face. You're like my missus, who talks to me about his health and says he don't eat enough. Why, I've heard her chatter to my Jane about his lovely voice and eyes and his beautiful smile! She says he's like St. Paul! Pah! Why he's as strong as a young horse, and no more like St. Paul than I am."

Joe Harris, the blacksmith and motor-agent, remarked here:

"I never heard that St. Paul was as strong as Samson. But what have you got against Parson, anyway, Mr. Greenwood?"

Greenwood finished his glass before replying.

"Well," he said, "I've not got nothin' agin him, except that ever since he came to Oldthorpe, nine years ago come midsummer, everyone in the parish talks as if he was perfect, and as for the women, they're clean daft about him!"

Dick Burge put in, "But he never gives any of them a look, for all the eyes they make at him—you'll allow that, although he hasn't a wife to look after him, like you have, Mr. Greenwood!"

"Confound the man!" said the farmer, "I know that. He can't be caught out in anything, drat him, that's what makes me mad. It's not human nature for a man not to smoke, *nor* drink, *nor* swear, *nor* have his bit of fun with the girls, nor do nothin' at all. I've always found that the men who set up to be plaster saints have a secret somewhere! Jumping Jehoshaphat! I'll lay this one's the same. . . ."

But Bill Hackett, who was a retired builder and said to be the warmest man in the village, broke in here, and told Greenwood that he ought to be ashamed of himself.

"That's as may be," said Greenwood. "I'm no plaster saint!" And as some reminiscence in proof of that assertion smote him, he began to roll about with laughter.

He then ordered drinks for all of them, still highly amused with his thoughts, the nature of which the others seemed to understand, for one of them observed: "We all know what you were, Jim Greenwood, in the time of Parson Gregory."

"Why," said Joe Harris, "look at the words you used to rap out." He proceeded to point out that since Parson Quaile got at him, his favorite oath had taken the place of a much more blasphemous one. This accusation was met by Greenwood with gusts of laughter and the assertion that he didn't mind obliging anyone who was civil, even a parson.

"But he gets you to church," said Dick Burge.

"When it's too wet to get about the farm," said Greenwood, and added, "but I don't deny he can preach. What a gift for talking! It's as good as a play to listen to him."

And then Bill Hackett interposed by asking Burge whether there would be anything said by the parson at the funeral of Joshua Pook the next day.

They all had known Joshua Pook, who had recently died at his comfortable house in the parish. He was an auctioneer and estate agent, with offices in the Cathedral town, only three or four miles from Oldthorpe.

"I don't know," replied Burge. "What could he say about him, anyway, though he was once a sidesman, to be sure?"

And then they proceeded to make comments on Mr. Pook, from which it became apparent that they none of them had either liked or respected him, for all the many years he had lived among them. Mr. Hackett observed that his reputation for honesty in the town was such that no man trusted him a yard.

"He's no loss to anyone so far as I can see."

"And I don't think Parson cared for him much," said Dick Burge. "I saw them talking a short time ago after Church, and I thought to myself that Parson couldn't abide him."

And this brought them to the old topic, and they were still discussing it when closing time came, and they all went out into the windy night.

The subject of this discussion, the Reverend George Theophilus Quaile, was peacefully writing in his study at the Oldthorpe Rectory. He had long been engaged on a life of Julian the Apostate, but it was advancing slowly owing to the many demands of his parish on his time. For there was never a more conscientious rector, and it was quite unusual for him to find that he could give two consecutive hours to his history.

The work had been started originally as a kind of sedative. It kept away distressing thoughts: it occupied any spare time before he felt the need of sleep: it helped him to secure peaceful slumber. The interest of the subject had taken possession of his mind, and he sometimes blamed himself for thinking of the complex character and perplexing motives of the Roman Emperor when he ought to have been thinking of his next sermon.

It was a simply furnished room, with a low ceiling, which Quaile could touch with his hand, when he stood upright, for he was over six feet in height. The only remaining work of the builders was a beautiful Queen Anne fireplace. The windows had been converted into Gothic by a clerical disciple of Horace Walpole. The walls were completely covered with books in every sort of binding and every kind of condition. There were a couple of old oars fastened against the cornice, evidence of successes on the Cam twenty years before. Almost the only furniture was a very long, narrow table of oak, littered with books, papers, two heavy inkstands, an ebony ruler, a couple of candlesticks, a lamp and a Bible-box.

A log fire was burning in the grate and there was a pile of logs beside it. The Rector's reputation for strength in the neighborhood was largely due to the fact that he was accustomed to fell and trim his own trees in a wood which formed part of the glebe, and it was a subject of talk in the parish, not unmixed with pride, that he could wield a woodman's ax as well or better than any professional.

It was nearly midnight when he gave a sigh and rose to his feet. He had finished the important chapter dealing with the massacre of Alexandria, and the behavior of Julian to Athanasius. He threw a few more logs on the fire, for he still had an hour's work before him on the parish accounts, and, lighting an old pipe, gave himself up to reflection.

Unexpectedly, he found he was happier than he had been since his university days. He had got the parish into something like reasonable order. There were no crying scandals and the poor were decently housed. He had as many offers of assistance and of money as he could do with. The Bishop, a man chary of praise, had been more than complimentary of late. The parish church was crowded on Sundays, and he was accustomed to preach, either there or elsewhere, including the Cathedral, to a rapt congregation. His reputation in the diocese was spotless. Indeed, he could not help knowing that he was talked of by enthusiasts as if he were a saint.

His lips, at this thought, formed a sardonic smile. For the Reverend Theophilus Quaile had not always been a pattern among men. At Cambridge, and for a few years afterwards, he had been more than gay, if not worse. The hedonist had become an ascetic suddenly, as the result of a tragic occurrence which had nearly driven him to suicide; and he was only just able, now, after fifteen years, to think calmly of the terrible incident of the death of Margaret Powell in his rooms after a Covent Garden Ball. He saw her again in the eyes of the mind with all her remarkable loveliness and charm, and he was still filled with love, pity and remorse.

No one could condemn him as severely as he condemned himself. A lifetime of devotion to others could hardly, he thought to himself, atone. The coroner's inquest was still a nightmare in the retrospect, and the bribing of three Press reporters to suppress their copy was a distasteful close to a horrible morning. . . . And then, after some long weeks of misery, when death would have been welcome, he found peace in religion and social service. If this is to be called a conversion, he had experienced it. . . .

And then, some years later, after taking Orders, and after he had become Rector of Oldthorpe, and when he had thought confidently that the past was buried except in his own heart, Joshua Pook came on the scene. He had become an inhabitant of the parish and was accustomed to drive daily into the town to conduct a doubtful, if not a disreputable business as an auctioneer. The Rector, who had heard of his reputation, had tried to avoid him as far as possible: but one day Joshua Pook had sought a private interview, and then a blow had fallen on poor Quaile.

By what seemed a most untoward chance, Pook was a half-brother of Margaret, and he had made it his business to know the whole terrible story. His arrival and settlement in Oldthorpe was not an accident. He was in great straits for money, and partly by appeals to the Rector's feelings, and partly by putting his claim as one for compensation, he had induced him to pay him money. In some strange and illogical way the Rector felt that he was making atonement and expiation.

Once this fatal step was taken the rest was easy. More pressure was brought to bear, and more money was paid. Finally the Rector, who wanted every penny of his income for his parish, struck, and said he would pay no more. Pook then resorted to the open method of blackmail. The story he was in a position to tell was a scandalous one: with his own embellishments it would sound terrible.

The Rector cared little for himself; but his influence in the parish was as necessary to him as life itself. After a struggle, he gave in on the terms of paying an annual sum to Pook. And now Pook was dead, and he was to be buried next day.

The Rector felt that a cloud had been lifted from his brain. The secret was to be buried with the auctioneer. The book was getting on. He loved his work. He felt younger and stronger than he had felt for years.

He sat down at his table, and taking the ebony ruler, he had just drawn a line along a sheet of foolscap paper when he heard a tap at the window.

He looked up, fancying that it might be caused by the wind; but it was repeated. He went to the window and, drawing back the curtain, opened it. He saw a man dimly made visible by the light of the room.

The man said, "It's Longhurst, James Longhurst," and added, "Mr. Pook's clerk."

"What do you want here at this time of night? Is it something to do with the funeral?"

"Nothing to do with that, at least, not exactly, governor; but it's something private, deadly private, and I've come at this hour to make sure of a private interview."

The Rector paused. He could not imagine what the man wanted. But late as it was, it might be of importance. He was not a man to feel any fear, or to be swayed by considerations of prudence, so he said: "Well, I'll let you in, though you might have come earlier."

And in a few moments he was back in his room, loking at an undersized, rat-like man, with ferrety eyes and ginger hair.

"Sit down," said the Rector, "and tell me what I can do for you."

Longhurst looked round the room, twisting a cloth cap in his hands, as if uncertain how to begin.

"It's perishing cold outside," he said, looking at the fire.

"Well," said the Rector, "warm yourself at the fire and tell me your private business."

Longhurst went to the fire, which was blazing, and after cramming his cap into a pocket, held his hands to it, looking back over his shoulder towards the Rector.

"Pretty snug here," he said; "there isn't such a thing as a drink handy, I suppose?"

"You can have a glass of water," was the reply. "I don't drink either beer or spirits myself, and there are, I believe, none in the house."

"Gosh!" said the man. "Water? I don't call that a drink."

"Well," said the Rector with a smile, "the sooner you tell me your business, the sooner you will be back home where I suppose there is what you would call a drink. So speak on!"

"It's deadly private, governor! That's why I've walked out at this time of night, unbeknownst to a living soul."

"The servants have been in bed and asleep for about three hours, and there's no one to listen. Come! What is it about?"

"It's about Josh Pook, whom you're burying to-morrow."

"Well, what about him?" said the Rector.

"You used to pay him a hundred and fifty a year," said the man, looking quickly over his left shoulder to see how the Rector would take this statement.

There was a long pause.

"And what has that to do with you?" said the Rector at last.

"I know what you paid it for."

The blow had fallen, and a number of wholly unpleasant thoughts raced through the Rector's mind.

"Well?" he said.

Longhurst did not at first reply. He seemed to be in doubt as to how to continue the interview. At last he turned round from the fire and said, "There's nothing extra to be gained by beating about the bush! You've got to continue the annuity to me."

"Why should I?"

"For the same reason."

"And what is that?"

"Silence, I guess," said Longhurst.

The Rector rose to his feet quickly and advanced towards the man who, shrinking back and putting a hand in his pocket, cried out, "Don't touch me! I've a revolver in my pocket."

The Rector stopped.

"You worm!" he said. "Did you think I was going to dirty my hands on you?"

"Now, now," said the man, "there's nothing to be gained by that kind of talk. You're up against it and you'd better take it quietly."

The Rector sat down again.

"Go on," he said, "I'm listening." And taking up the ruler, he began ruling some fresh lines for his accounts.

Longhurst produced from his inside pocket some flimsy paper.

"I found these while turning out a private drawer of Mr. Pook's yesterday. They seemed interesting and I read them. Golly! Oh, what a surprise! Scandal about the Reverend Theophilus Quaile! Spicy stuff, too! And all ready for the newspapers. And all about Reverend Quaile who preaches religion and moral sob-stuff in the Cathedral, and who hobnobs with the Bishop. I've seen him myself. Why, the copy's worth a guinea a line to the P——*Gazette* or to the *True Briton*! But more to you, governor, a precious sight more!"

The Rector made no reply.

"Come," said the man, "I'll read you a bit," and he proceeded to read a sensational account of the tragedy, full of imaginary conversations and inaccurate detail.

The Rector paused for a moment in his work, holding the ruler tightly in his right hand.

Longhurst went on reading extracts here and there. He came to a description of Margaret, and smacked his lips over it.

"Be quiet!" said the Rector, in a low, emphatic voice.

Longhurst went on with a coarse laugh. The Rector rose to his feet.

"She seems to have been hot stuff," said Longhurst, "and I'll bet a monkey you and she . . ."

The sentence was never finished.

The Rector never knew exactly how it happened. The act was instinctive. With the ruler he had struck, as if to fell the man to the earth. He moved his head and received the blow on his temple. He sank down, a heap of dirty clothes.

The Rector stood looking at the body for a long time without touching it.

He then stooped and found with his hand that the heart had ceased to beat. He got a small mirror and placed it before the man's open mouth. There was no sign of moisture on the glass. It was true, then; he had killed the blackmailer.

He felt no regret, but an enormous disquietude. What was to be done?

The Rector was a man with great powers of imagination. As he sat down again at his table, he visualized in a series of scenes—as if he were looking at a film, all that would follow if he straightway informed the police of everything that had happened. He saw the embarrassed village policemen arriving, the sergeant coming later, the questions put to him and his answers, his arrest, his interview with the inspector of police in the town, the inside of the jail! Would they allow him bail? He thought not. And then he saw himself as the principal figure at the inquest, with hundreds of curious people of both sexes staring at him, and he heard his own answers to the pitiless questions put to him by a hatchet faced counsel, who seemed not to understand his terrible anxiety not to say anything which might tarnish the reputation of Margaret.

His mind made a jump to his trial in the assize court by a small, red-faced judge, before a jury of men (and two women), who looked like half-wits. He heard his conviction for manslaughter; for his mind refused to think of another possibility, and then the sentence of the judge, in solemn tones. The warder touched him on the shoulder and he walked down some stairs to a prison van.

And then he was in prison for an interminable time, with degraded fellow-prisoners, callous warders, and—a curious freak of his mind—a low-church prison chaplain who cordially disliked him, the exact counterpart of the only clergyman with whom the Rector had ever had a quarrel. The chaplain's visits and conversation were almost more than the Rector could bear. . . .

And then he saw himself having a final interview with the governor of the prison, and walking out of the gates. . . .

One or two sympathetic friends came to meet him, but their honest sympathy showed him the depth to which he had fallen. . . He was given to understand that he had no future as one of the working clergy in England. His only chance was to begin life over again; preferably in the colonies.

The Rector at this point struck the table with the fatal ruler, and exclaimed aloud, "By Heaven, I will not give up my work here. I would sooner die!"

He turned his gaze to the untidy object between him and the fireplace. The body, the body! The only obstacle! How could it be made to disappear—and disappear forever?

He drew nearer to it and, turning it over, looked steadily at the weak, futile, vicious face. His imagination pictured for him the man's life. He thought, as he had often thought of others, "Poor foolish wretch! Perhaps he never in all his life had a single decent friend." His anger left him and was replaced by his accustomed sympathy for erring mankind.

He paused, and then said in a low, determined tone, "He must have Christian burial!"

And upon this thought, all things became clear to the priest, and his further acts seemed to follow an inevitable course, as if, indeed, they were those of an automaton guided by an exterior will.

Taking the body in his arms as easily as if it were a child, he walked with it to the front door and let himself out.

The wind had got up, and the many elms in the garden were moaning in the gale; but it was not raining. He walked to the garage and placed the body in the back of the old car. He covered it with a rug.

He drove out of the door, and then stopped. He shut the door and got from the neighboring tool-house and potting-shed a spade, a pick, a piece of rope and two sacks.

The churchyard was little more than a hundred yards away. He drove slowly without lights. The lane was completely desolate. He parked the car in a dark lane under some overhanging trees and entered the churchyard.

The wind was still rising and seemed to threaten the stability of the trees, and the clouds, fitfully visible by the light of a setting moon, were scudding across the sky. The Rector took his tools and walked quickly to the side of the newly dug grave destined to receive, in a few hours, the mortal remains of Joshua Pook. It was close to a row of elms, and the place was so dark that, except at moments when the moon gave a faint light, the Rector could scarcely see the ancient and lofty church spire thirty or forty yards away. The sexton had covered the opening with planks, which the Rector removed. He took one, however, and placed it across the middle of the opening, and with its assistance lowered himself into the grave and began to dig.

Fortunately, digging was an occupation to which he was accustomed, or strong as he was, he would soon have been exhausted. As it was, the thought occurred to him, after half an hour's work, that the sexton was not overpaid. For the first time since the fatal interview he smiled.

At one end of the opening he was much troubled with the roots of a tree, and he was glad he had brought the pick. He worked hard, and it did not seem to him very long before he had excavated about two feet of soil. With the aid of the plank he swung himself up. The keen air seemed to go through him, and he wiped his forehead and put on the coat which he had removed.

When he reached the car, he found that the body was beginning to get stiff; but he managed, without much difficulty, to place it at full length beside the grave. He went back for the rope and the stable lantern. He tied the rope under the arms of the body and, standing at one end of the grave, he carefully lowered it down. Taking the stable lantern he went down himself, untied the rope and arranged the corpse in its final resting place.

It did not take more than a few minutes to shovel the soil down, so that the body was covered to the extent of over a foot. He trod the soil firmly down over it and smoothed it over with the spade. After a careful examination, by the light of the lantern, he hoisted himself out, filled the two sacks with excavated soil, and rearranged the planks and the earth, leaving everything around the grave just as he had found it. He carried his two sacks to the car.

There was a running stream close to the road side, and there he emptied his sacks of soil. He drove home very slowly, for he thought there might be trees down across the road, but he only encountered some moderate sized branches.

The gale was dropping when he reached the Rectory garage. He cleaned out the car, replaced the sacks and the rope, and returned to the house. By the old clock in the hall he noted that it was quarter-past four. Except for its loud ticking the house was silent, as silent as the grave. When the trite phrase crossed his mind, he shuddered.

He entered the sitting-room, where the lamp was still burning; everything was as he left it, except that there were only a few bright embers in the hearth. Its familiar appearance gave him a sense of tightening at the heart; it seemed to him that he had been away a year and was returning a different man. He tidied up his desk and carefully wiped the ebony ruler. The hearth-rug showed no signs of any unusual happening. He removed some dirt from his shoes and brushed his clothes before going to bed.

He slept a dreamless sleep.

The funeral of Joshua Pook, which took place at midday, attracted a large congregation. Nearly every adult in the parish came, for the dead man, though not a favorite, had been a resident among them for a long time and, moreover, there was curiosity to hear what the Rector could find to say about him.

He said nothing beyond the words of the service for the burial of the dead, which he uttered in his magnificent voice and in his usual impressive manner. The female members of the assembly noticed, however, that he looked paler and more ascetic than ever; and Mrs. Greenwood and several others wished that they were allowed to look after him. When he came to the words, "Thou knowest, O Lord, the secrets of our hearts," he made an unusual pause. The men present thought that he was reflecting on the guilty secrets of the deceased sinner; but in this they were mistaken. When the coffin was brought to the grave the Rector, standing at the head of it, was noticed to look down into the opening—as if there were something to be seen at the bottom. But, of course, there was nothing! The coffin was lowered down in the customary way. "Earth to earth, dust to dust, ashes to ashes...."

That night, a little after eleven, Farmer Greenwood, Bill Hackett, Joe Harris and Dick Burge were walking homewards together from the parish room. Their way led past the churchyard and not very far from the spot where they had attended the burial of Joshua Pook and where there was now an oblong mound of soil. Not unnaturally they looked towards the spot, and to their surprise they saw beside it a kneeling figure. They stopped and gazed, open-mouthed.

"It's the Parson," said Joe Harris.

"Praying, begad!" said Greenwood.

"Beside the grave of Pook," said Hackett.

They were silent while they took in the fact; and then they made their respective comments, which were terse.

"Holy Moses!" said Hackett.

"That scalawag!" said Joe Harris.

"That's why!" said Dick Burge.

"Jumping Jehoshaphat!" said the farmer.

And they walked on, ruminating on the incident.

How were they to know that the Reverend Theophilus Quaile had committed the perfect crime, never to be discovered by man, and was now praying to God for forgiveness?

Issues for Discussion

1. In the Shaw and Greville short stories presented in this chapter, the protagonists have committed murder. Read the following quotations (from "On the Entirely Reasonable Murder of a Police Constable" and "The Perfect Crime") and explain how they reflect the classical school's explanation of criminal behavior in terms of free will and hedonism.

   The murder of Constable Gutteridge was an entirely reasonable one; the work, apparently, of an out-and-out Rationalist. Further, the person who committed it was one of those sensitive people to whom the condition of a criminal under punishment is unbearable.

   The criminal was rational enough to decide to shoot. There is no ground for suspecting him of any animosity to the man: he shot the law.

   The Rector [Reverend Theophilus Quaile] never knew exactly how it happened. The act was instinctive.

   He felt no regret, but an enormous disquietude. What was to be done?

   The Rector at this point struck the table with the fatal ruler, and exclaimed aloud, "By Heaven, I will not give up my work here. I would sooner die!"

2. The motives for the murder of Constable Gutteridge and the murder committed by Reverend Quaile are similar. What were these motives and how do they confirm the suspicions of disciples of the classical school about human likelihood for acting in a deviant manner?

3. The founder of the classical school of criminology, Cesare Beccari, believed that "punishment should fit the crime." He also believed that punishment would serve as a deterrent only when it produced more hardship than the potential pleasure derived from committing the crime. What kind of punishment for Constable Gutteridge's murderer and for Reverend Quaile would "fit the crime" and "produce more hardship than the pleasure" derived from the act?

PART II

The Positive School

Over one hundred years passed between the beginning of the classical school and the development of the positive school of criminology. To proponents of the positive school, behavior was determined by *environmental* forces. The term *positivism* relates to methods of inquiry used in developing and proving the school's statements. The positivists elevated criminology to a "science" by using empirical techniques for collecting, observing, measuring, and experimenting with data. According to Stephen Schafer, the positivists' "emergence symbolized clearly that the era of faith was over and the scientific age had begun."[1]

The writing of Cesare Lombroso (1836–1909) provided the foundation for the positive school.[2] Central to Lombroso's theories is *biological determinism,* which claims that individual abnormalities are indicators of potential criminal conduct.[3] According to George B. Vold,

> Back of all physical type theories is the general idea of biological differences in behavior. All biological explanations rest on the basic

---

1. *Theories of Criminology* (New York: Random House, 1969), p. 123.

2. Although Lombroso is often referred to as the father of criminology, scholars predating Lombroso made minor contributions concerning the predictability of deviance. See C. Bernaldo de Quiros, *Modern Theories of Criminality* (Boston: Little, Brown, 1911), pp. 4–5, for a description of several pre-Lombrosian "positivist" criminologists. Lombroso's most famous work, *The Criminal Man,* was first published in pamphlet form in Torina, Italy (1876).

3. Even though Lombroso's contributions centered on biological determinism, he also espoused the importance of environmental and economic conditions (e.g., poverty and unemployment) on behavior. Enrico Ferri, a later positivist, is credited with a more systematic study of these criteria.

logic that *structure determines function*. Individuals behave differently owing to the fundamental fact that they are somehow structurally different. Presumably, too, if there could be complete observation, or complete measurement, all differences between individuals would reduce to some kind of biological, structural difference—and all differences in behavior would be due to some kind of individual structural difference.[4]

Lombroso's work was influenced by some eminent thinkers, especially Charles Darwin with his theories of evolution (*Descent of Man*, 1871). Lombroso speculated that criminals possessed less developed or primitive physical characteristics and thus behaved in a primitive (i.e., deviant) manner. He tested his theories by examining the physiques of prison inmates. Among the criteria he claimed indicated a "primitive" physique were swollen or protruding lips, a slanting forehead, eye defects, no earlobes or long earlobes, excessively long arms, a large jaw with underdeveloped chin, or an excessively hairy or hairless body. He termed persons with these characteristics *atavists,* or throwbacks, who for some inexplicable reason had not reached the evolutionary development of law-abiding citizens.[5]

Lombroso classified three types of criminals: (1) *born criminals,* whom he believed constituted approximately one third of the criminal population; (2) *insane criminals,* a group that included imbeciles, idiots, paranoiacs, and those suffering from paraylsis, alcoholism, or epilepsy; and (3) *criminaloids,* persons who did not possess distinguishing atavistic (physical) qualities but were mentally "inferior" and haphazardly engaged in violent criminal behavior.[6]

Several of Lombroso's disciples made important modifications of positivist statements. In his *Criminal Sociology*, Enrico Ferri (1856–1928) extended Lombroso's theories and also illustrated the conflicting thought of positivists and classical theorists:

> The general opinion of classic criminalists and of the people at large is that crime involves a moral guilt, because it is due to the free will of the individual who leaves the path of virtue and chooses the path of crime, and therefore it must be suppressed by meeting it with a proportionate quantity of punishment. This is to this day the current

---

4. *Theoretical Criminology* (New York: Oxford University Press, 1958), p. 43.

5. Lombroso revised his theory of biological determinism when he discovered no significant physical qualities after he compared physical attributes of incarcerated persons and the public at large. See Alfred A. Lindesmith and Yale Levin, "The Lombrosian Myth in Criminology," *American Journal of Sociology,* March 1937, pp. 653–71.

6. For an evaluation of Lombroso's classifications, see Maurice Parmelee, *Criminology* (New York: Macmillan, 1918), pp. 188–90.

conception of crime. And the illusion of a free human will (the only miraculous factor in the eternal ocean of cause and effect) leads to the assumption that one can choose freely between virtue and vice. How can you still believe in the existence of a free will when modern psychology, armed with all the instruments of positive modern research, denies that there is any free will and demonstrates that every act of a human being is the result of an interaction between the personality and the environment of man?[7]

Ferri postulated that crime was caused by environmental conditions (climate, geographic location, seasonal effects), anthropological factors (age, sex, psychological make-up), and social and economic conditions (population density, custom, folkways, mores and the governmental structure). From his observations, Ferri felt that crime might be prevented by abolishing monopolies, providing birth control information and recreation facilities to the public, and instituting more lenient marriage and divorce laws.[8]

A third leader of the positive school, Raffaele Garofalo (1852–1934), wrote *Criminology,* in which he emphasized the importance of the relationship between psychological infirmities and criminal behavior.[9] Garofalo believed that deviance resulted from an improper "development of the altruistic sensibility"[10] and that criminal behavior was partly attributable to personal organic disabilities. In short, criminal behavior was inherited. Garofalo, like Ferri, offered suggestions for preventing criminal activity. Unlike classical theorists, Garofalo believed there was merit in retribution. The death penalty, for example, eliminated the potential for additional deviance by the offender. Further, capital punishment served the public good by assuring that offenders would sire no future generations of criminals.[11]

Physiological Theories

A close kinship exists between statements presented by positivists and by adherents of the "physiological" schools. Evident parallels involve the

---

7. Boston: Little, Brown, 1901.

8. Vold, *Theoretical Criminology,* p. 34.

9. Boston: Little, Brown, 1914, p. 79.

10. Ibid., pp. 91–96.

11. Compare Charles Goring, *The English Convict: A Statistical Study* (London: His Majesty's Stationery Office, 1913); and Ernest A. Hooton, *Crime and the Man* (Cambridge, Mass.: Harvard University Press, 1937).

concept of biological determinism. Because of these similarities, statements from *phrenology, endocrinology, genetic defects,* and *somatology* theorists can be discussed in conjunction with the positive school.

Phrenology

Phrenology, or what the Viennese founder of the theory, Dr. Franz Gall (1758–1828), preferred to call craniology, involves the study of the external shape of the skull, which Gall believed indicated a person's character. As summarized by one criminologist,

> the three main propositions supporting the discipline were: (1) the exterior conformation of the skull corresponded to its interior and to the conformation of the brain; (2) the mind could be analyzed into faculties and functions; and (3) these faculties were related to the shape of the skull. Corollaries to these propostions held that . . . certain areas of the brain contain organisms to which there corresponded an equal number of psychological characters or powers.[12]

An "irregular" skull shape or size reputedly indicated potential "irregular" (i.e., criminal) behavior. One of Gall's students, John Gaspar Spurzheim (1776–1832), listed thirty-five mental faculties and diagrammed their location in the brain. The list of faculties and corresponding likely criminal offenses include (1) destructiveness (arson, attempt to poison, and manslaughter), (2) combativeness (manslaughter, assault and battery to kill, highway robbery), and (3) amativeness (rape, assault and battery to commit rape, and attempt to ravish).

Endocrinology

In the early nineteenth century a German chemist named Frederich Wöhler posited a relationship between the bodily secretion of various chemical substances and human behavior.[13] Nearly one hundred years later, Louis Berman,[14] and Max G. Schlapp and Edward H. Smith[15] linked Wöhler's work to crime causation: "The reader will find as he proceeds that the glandular theory of crime accounts for all the discrepancies, errors,

---

12. Arthur Fink, *Causes of Crime* (Philadelphia: University of Pennsylvania Press, 1938), pp. 2–3.

13. Vold, *Theoretical Criminology,* p. 102.

14. *The Gland Regulating Personality* (New York: Macmillan, 1921).

15. *The New Criminology* (New York: Boni and Liveright, 1928.)

oversights and inadequacies of the earlier explanations."[16] Specifically, theories about endocrinology suggest that an imbalance in the glandular system and the subsequent abnormal secretion of chemical agents is responsible for deviant behavior. Hormonal imbalance continues to play a suspect role in criminology, particularly in cases of deviate sexual activity. For instance, in child abuse and rape cases, injecting the offender with the female hormones estrogen and progesterone reduces the sex drive, thus decreasing the likelihood of continued similar behavior.[17]

Genetic Theories

Theories relating behavior to inherited genetic qualities came about as a logical extension of theories about biological determinism. Sons and daughters often inherit physical characteristics of their parents. But what if a parent were a thief or murderer? Would the offspring inherit these behavioral characteristics? Proponents of various genetic theories suggest this is the case.

Early support for heredity theories emerged from studies of family trees. In the Dugdale and Estabrook examinations of the Jukes family, over 1200 family members were studied, of whom 140 had criminal records.[18] Because these figures represent a high rate of criminality in one family line, the authors considered their hypotheses were validated.

Related hypotheses involve the behavioral patterns of identical and fraternal twins. With identical twins, behavior should be the same. The German psychiatrist Johannes Lange studied male twins who had been incarcerated and suggested that when comparing the criminal behavior of identical and fraternal twins, the former group more often act alike.[19] Similar studies by K. O. Christiansen[20] lent support to Lange's findings.[21]

More recent research concerning genetic infirmities involves

---

16. Ibid., p. 72.

17. See Saleem A. Shah and Loren H. Roth, "Biological and Psychophysiological Factors in Criminality," in *Handbook of Criminology*, ed. Daniel Glaser (Chicago: Rand McNally, 1974), pp. 101, 123. See also Nicholas N. Kittrie, *The Right to Be Different* (Baltimore: Johns Hopkins University Press, 1971), p. 301.

18. Richard Dugdale, *The Jukes: A Study in Crime, Pauperism, and Heredity* (New York: Putnam, 1877); and A. H. Estabrook, *The Jukes in 1915* (Washington, D.C.: Carnegie Institution, 1916).

19. J. Lange, *Crime as Destiny*, trans. C. Haldane (London: George Allen and Unwin, 1931).

20. "Threshold of Tolerance in Various Population Groups Illustrated from the Danish Criminologic Study," in *The Mentally Abnormal Offender*, ed. A. U. S. de Reuch and R. Porter (Boston: Little, Brown, 1968).

21. An excellent critique of these findings appears in Richard R. Korn and Lloyd W. McCorkle, *Criminology and Penology* (New York: Holt, Rinehart and Winston, 1959), pp. 98–106, 202–4.

chromosome composition. A typical male has an XY chromosome pattern, and a typical female an XX pattern. A small percentage of males have been found to possess an extra Y chromosome (XYY). This discovery meant little until a study of inmates in a Scottish prison revealed that a significantly large percentage of the 197 males investigated possessed the XYY pattern.[22] The additional Y chromosome has also been linked with uncontrollably violent behavior.[23]

The first court case involving the extra chromosome was the murder trial of Daniel Hugon, a Frenchman, who was spared the guillotine because of his chromosome composition. An Australian court in a similar case reduced the sentence of a defendant who possessed the XYY syndrome. No American jurisdiction has yet accepted the argument that the existence of the extra chromosome justifies criminal behavior.[24]

Somatology

Somatologists suggest there is a positive relationship between physique and temperament.[25] The pioneer of somatology, Ernst Kretschmer, categorized four main constitutional body types in 1926: leptosomes (long and skinny), athletic (well developed and muscular), pyknic (small, round, and fat), and dysplastic (mixed characteristics).[26] In a later work, Kretschmer studied 4414 criminals and found that leptosomes typically engaged in petty thievery and fraud; athletic types were violence prone; pyknics engaged in fraud, deception, and, to a lesser extent, crimes of violence; and dysplastics favored various sexual offenses.[27]

American scholars who have promoted body-type theories are Ernest Hooton, William Sheldon, and Sheldon and Eleanor Glueck. Hooton believed Lombroso's failure to verify the relationship between criminality and physical characteristics resulted from his inability to identify a specific type of crime with a particular body physique. Hooton developed a body-type–crime schema as follows:

22. See P. A. Jacobs et al., "Aggressive Behavior, Mental Subnormality, and the XYY Males," *Nature* 208 (December 1965): 1351. See also A. A. Sandburg et al., "XYY Genotype," *New England Journal of Medicine* 268 (March 1963): 585.

23. See Richard S. Fox, "The XYY Offender: A Modern Myth?" *Journal of Criminal Law, Criminology and Police Science* 62 (1971): 59–73.

24. For a discussion of these cases, see Note: "The XYY Syndrome: A Challenge to Our System of Criminal Responsibility," *New York Law Forum* 16 (Spring 1970): 232.

25. For an overview of body type theory, see William A. Lessa, "An Appraisal of Constitutional Types," *Memoirs of the American Anthropological Society*, 45, no. 4 (1943).

26. *Physique and Character*, trans. W. T. H. Sprott (New York: Harcourt, Brace, 1926).

27. *Körperbau und Charakter*, 21/22 Auflage, Springer-Verlag (Berlin: Göttingen und Heidelberg, 1955), pp. 331–57.

It is a remarkable fact that tall, thin men tend to murder and to rob, tall heavy men to kill and commit forgery and fraud, undersized thin men to steal and to burglarize, short heavy men to assault, to rape, and to commit other sex crimes, whereas men of mediocre body build tend to break the law without obvious discrimination or preference.[28]

Sheldon's conclusions about physiques differ significantly from Kretschmer's, though his typology is similar. The ectomorph has a tall, skinny body; the endomorph has a short, fat body; and the mesomorph is strong and lean.[29] However, Sheldon does not suggest that body structure alone can indicate a particular criminal activity. Sheldon contends that somatotyping is a "kind of temporary scaffolding, for the description of the individual."[30] Environmental variables also have to be classified and systematically applied before somatotyping can be effectively employed.[31]

The most methodologically sound research involving body structure and its relationship to behavior was conducted by the Gluecks.[32] Using Sheldon's typologies of body physique, they examined the behavior of 500 delinquent boys and a control group of 500 nondelinquent boys. Variables such as age, intelligence, and socioeconomic status were closely matched between the two groups. Their findings supported Sheldon's hypothesis that a statistical relationship exists between mesomorphy and delinquency. The Gluecks argue that though "it is quite apparent that physique alone does not adequately explain delinquent behavior, it is nevertheless clear that in conjunction with other forces, it does bear a relationship to delinquency."[33]

"Big Jeff" by James T. Farrell depicts notions of crime causation held by early positivists. Jeff has a large physique and, coincidentally, engages in deviant acts. Arguing from the positive school perspective, Jeff's physique (i.e., structure) determines or controls his behavior (i.e., function); his

28. *Crime and the Man* (Cambridge, Mass.: Harvard University Press, 1939), p. 376.

29. *The Varieties of Human Physique: An Introduction to Constitutional Psychology* (New York: Harper & Row, 1940), p. 1.

30. *Atlas of Men* (New York: Harper & Row, 1942), p. 15.

31. Ibid.

32. See *Unravelling Juvenile Delinquency* (New York: Commonwealth Fund, 1950).

33. *Physique and Delinquency* (New York: Harper & Row, 1956), p. 249. But S. L. Washburn states the Gluecks have only developed a "new Phrenology in which the bumps of the buttocks take the place of the bumps on the skull" ("Review of W. H. Sheldon, *Varieties of Delinquent Youth*," *American Anthropologist* 53 [1951]: 561–63. For other critiques of somatology, see W. Norwood East, "Physical Factors in Criminal Behavior," *Journal of Clinical Psychopathy* 8 (1976): 7–36; and Edwin H. Sutherland, "Critique of Sheldon's *Varieties of Delinquent Youth*," *American Sociological Review* 16 (1951): 10–14.

motivating force, then, has nothing to do with the treatment accorded him by his "friends," or with his need to survive. A compelling argument might be presented attributing Jeff's conduct to the later positivist belief that biological determinism may be supplemented or completely replaced by the effects of environmental determinism.

Stephen Crane's "The Blue Hotel" illustrates the positive school concept that behavior is affected by environment. The Swede perceives his predicament to be something other than it is. He behaves in a manner that may have been suitable for another era but is clearly out of place in the existing milieu. His idiosyncratic behavior eventually affects everyone around him until he transforms the environment more in accordance with his own fantasies.

BIG JEFF
James T. Farrell

Jeff the fat Jewboy . . . Jeff the fatass of Fifty-eighth Street . . . his mother looked like a blown-up balloon . . . with Jeff in her womb . . . Jeff's birth . . . like the bursting of a balloon . . . Jeff weighed too much from the start . . . Jeff grew heavier and heavier and heavier . . . Jeff went to *Chedar* . . . knew his lessons . . . and still his ass was whaled black and blue . . . Jeff was always easy to laugh at . . . Jeff, the fat Jewboy . . . Jeff the fatass of Fifty-eight Street . . . Big Fat Jeff who waved his fanny through life . . . Big Fat Jeff.

Every day Jeff waddled to Carter School . . . every day his fanny grew bigger and bigger and bigger . . . the kids all told him how fat an ass he had . . . Jeff wanted to be like the other kids . . . wanted to be one of them . . . he was too big and fat . . . Jeff tried to play marbles . . . he knelt down to shoot . . . got a dozen boots in the tuchas . . . Jeff stole money from home . . . bought the little girls candy . . . Jeff loved little Clara Schmaltz . . . Jeff stuck his hands in the old man's pocket . . . the old man caught him . . . gave Jeff a hell of a beating . . . Jeff loved little Clara Schmaltz . . . Jeff walked down the hall at school . . . Jeff heard little Clara talking . . . Denny Dennis says Jeff is a big fatass hehehe . . . Jeff heard Clara . . . Jeff waddled away . . . Jeff lugged his heavy fanny by Bathcellar's poolroom . . . the big guys gave him the horse laugh . . . Jeff had too much fanny . . . too much of a load to carry . . . Jeff was slow . . . lazy . . . dopey . . . crazy . . . Jeff helped clean house . . . ran the oil mop over the floor in two hours . . . his old lady cursed his big tuchas . . . Jeff tried to play ball in the playground . . . Jeff was always kicked out of the game . . . too much lead in his fanny when he ran bases . . . You got too much lead in your ass Jeff . . . Jeff tried to play baby-in-the-hole . . . the kids always let him . . . Jeff ran out of the circle like a steamroller . . . Jeff was always hit . . . got ten babies first . . . Jeff was placed against a wall . . . what a target . . . each kid threw at him six times . . . smack-whack . . . you couldn't miss that Jewish tuchas . . . Jeff played blue-my-blackberry in Washington Park . . . he was tagged . . . he was down . . . Denny Dennis didn't try to guard him . . . the kids put stones in their caps . . . blued his blackberry . . . Jesus it was funny . . . and Jeff's can stayed blue for three weeks . . . Jeff walked through Washington Park . . . Jeff's pudgy face lit with a smile . . . Jeff smiled a lot . . . Jeff waddled through the park . . . Big Schmaltz the wolf saw him . . . Big Schmaltz got hot . . . Big Schmaltz took him in the bushes . . . Coady the flatfooted cop saw them . . . Big Schmaltz ran . . . Jeff tried to run . . . got caught . . . there was hell to pay . . . it cost the old man something . . .

and Big Jeff got saved from reform school . . . anyway Jeff's can was good for something . . . Jeff never passed in school . . . he got bigger and bigger . . . and his classmates got smaller and smaller . . . the teachers wanted to sock him . . . they said he would end up in jail . . . maybe on the gallows . . . but Jeff smiled . . . nobody knew what made Jeff smile so much . . . the punk kids picked fights with him . . . he fought like an ox . . . the kids socked him and retreated . . . socked him and retreated again . . . Jeff was always waddling along Fifty-eighth Street with a pair of shiners . . . and Jeff's fanny kept swelling and swelling.

Big Jeff got wise . . . Big Jeff started using his Jewish noodle . . . Big Jeff started gyping everybody . . . he stole marbles . . . candy . . . money . . . anything he could . . . he devised schemes . . . talked the kids out of their money . . . somebody was always laying for Jeff . . . to punch hell out of him . . . Jeff was always working his Jewish noodle to gyp hell out of somebody . . . Jeff stole everything and his ass kept swelling . . . and he kept smiling through life.

Jeff was easy to laugh at all right . . . Jeff, you'll make a fat man in a circus . . . Jeff you'd make a mint in a peg house . . . Jeff, you're a dirty louse . . . but you're funny . . . Jeff, how old are you . . . sa-ay you couldn't get that fat in fourteen years . . . and Jeff kept right on bloating and bloating . . . until he had more ass than a dozen Negro mammies.

Big Jeff got kicked out of school . . . put on long pants . . . yards of long pants . . . he didn't get a job . . . who the hell would hire him anyway . . . Big Jeff sold things . . . he sold baseball pool tickets . . . where there was no pool . . . he took bets on horses . . . when the nags never ran . . . he sold French postcards . . . he sold post-war gin . . . he sold bonded stuff . . . and never delivered . . . he sold everything . . . and he made good jack.

He walked down Fifty-eighth Street . . . turned down a side street . . . walked smiling along . . . he fell down a manhole . . . Jesus it was as funny as a Keystone Comedy . . . Jeff groaned from a manhole . . . they needed a derrick to pull him out . . . and they damn neared needed a horse doctor for his broken leg . . . holy Jesus it was funny . . . Big Jeff came out of the hospital and started pimping . . . Big Jeff stood on street corners in the Black Belt . . . hailing the boys . . . married men . . . farm boys . . . blushing high school kids . . . hailing business . . . he waddled up to them . . . want a little nooky lad . . . want a girl to make you glad . . . want a three-way broad . . . want a frail that'll love you like a French frog . . . come on, lad, I got the nigger whore that's going to change your luck . . . Big Jeff led many a lad to heaven . . . and many a lad to syphilis, clap and the Chicago Public Health Institute . . . Big Jeff took in the shekels . . . and Big Jeff spent his money on the whores . . . sweet cookie . . . he liked his nooky . . . he liked his gals . . . and he paid them hard iron men . . . Jeff came around the poolroom at Fifty-eighth Street . . . described the frails he had . . . Jeff that's bad . . . Jeff how can you get in the saddle . . . listen brother if you slept with the peach I had last night . . . listen brother she was a blonde and she wasn't tight . . . B.S. Jeff . . . all right brother but that means nothin'. . . that don't take away the lovin' ah gets . . . Big Jeff . . . gyping . . . pimping . . . rimming . . . jazzing . . . doping himself up . . . waving his fanny along . . . Big Jeff made his dough pimping . . . took a course in reducing . . . got fatter and fatter . . . don't worry Jeff the first ton is the hardest . . . but Big Jeff kept using his noodle . . . he always caught the boys from the poolroom on a new racket . . . he had to . . . the whores soaked him twenty-five and fifty bucks . . . Big Jeff paid a hundred grafted dollars for a new suit . . . hey Jeff who's your tailor . . . Omar the tentmaker . . . listen brother this is a suit . . . hundred berries good goods . . . Jeff you're a wagon-load of manure . . . all right brother but you can't shell out a hundred bucks for a suit of cloth like this . . . B.S. . . . listen brother I got a scheme now and I can get you some prewar stuff . . . Big Jeff on another racket.

Big Jeff went swimming to Fifty-fourth Street beach . . . where there was no bath house . . . and he wore his suit under his clothes . . . Big Jeff took his pants off in a half hour . . . mother look at the fat man . . . hey see the big ham . . . boy is he fat . . . if he goes in the water there'll be a flood and we'll all row home . . . the lake must be that boy's bathtub . . . Big Jeff lumbering into the water . . . everybody watching him . . . Jesus he couldn't sink if he wanted to . . . Big Jeff on the beach . . . pinching girls' legs . . . Big Jeff putting on his pants . . . for a half hour . . . Big Jeff just waddling his fanny through life . . . listen brother do you want me to fix you up with a real broad . . . a three-way doll . . . and what she don't know about lovin' . . . well I don't either.

Big Jeff kept on pimping . . . good dough in it . . . he pimped for black babies in the Black Belt . . . made and spent his shekels . . . led many a boy to heaven and many a boy to syphilis, clap and the Chicago Public Health Institute . . . Big Jeff paid big for his women . . . and got the syph . . . he gyped too many people . . . had to blow town or get his old tomato pumped full of bullets . . . shoved off with a thousand bucks in his kick . . . Big Jeff spent his money in New Orleans . . . then Big Jeff didn't go so well there . . . Big Jeff was sick with the syph . . . Big Jeff walked the streets broke . . . Big Jeff kept smiling along . . . and the rackets got goddamn tough . . . Big Jeff panhandled . . . pimped for two-bit whores . . . but Big Jeff didn't hit it off so well in New Orleans . . . the load was too heavy . . . too much lead in his pants . . . too much syphilis . . . too much of Big Jeff for one world . . . Big Jeff slept with his last whore . . . diseased her . . . and smilingly pretended to sleep . . . stole her money . . . bought a gun . . . and the gravediggers cursed all holy hell when they lowered his crated body . . . they said they needed a derrick.

And then the maggots got busy . . . they rubbed their paws together . . . smiled sleekly, said . . . well I'm eating with my feet under the table tonight . . . the maggots said well this is a feed you don't get every day . . . the maggots said this is real meat . . . the maggots said I ain't never had grub like this . . . the maggots said we'll put some flesh on our bones now . . . the maggots thanked Jesus for having put so much ass on one corpse.

And the guys from Fifty-eighth Street stood in front of the poolroom . . . he was no good anyway . . . the cheap grafter he should have been killed long ago . . . good riddance to bad rubbage . . . he was one big load of garbage . . . they must have had a crate or a steamship for a coffin . . . the stiffs will sue him for taking up so much room in the morgue . . . he should have been sent to a booby hatch . . . well anyway Jeff had the world's biggest ass . . . he was a sonofabitch . . . cheated his own mother . . . he'll make enough fertilizer for the fields of all Russia . . . when he shot himself he should have blown the lead out of his pants.

THE BLUE HOTEL
Stephen Crane

I

The Palace Hotel at Fort Romper was painted a light blue, a shade that is on the legs of a kind of heron, causing the bird to declare its position against any background. The Palace Hotel, then, was always screaming and howling in a way that made the dazzling winter landscape of Nebraska seem only a gray swampish hush. It stood alone on the prairie and when the snow was falling the town two hundred yards away was not visible. But when the traveller alighted at the railway station he was obliged to pass the Palace Hotel before he could come upon the company of low clapboard houses which composed Fort Romper, and it was not to be thought that any traveller could pass the Palace Hotel without looking at it. Pat Scully, the proprietor, had proved himself a master of strategy when he chose his paints. It is true that on clear days, when the great transcontinental expresses, long lines of swaying Pullmans, swept through Fort Romper, passengers were overcome at the sight, and the cult that knows the brown-reds and the subdivisions of the dark greens of the East expressed shame, pity, horror, in a laugh. But to the citizens of this prairie town and to the people who would naturally stop there, Pat Scully had performed a feat. With this opulence and splendor, these creeds, classes, egotisms, that streamed through Romper on the rails day after day, they had no color in common.

As if the display delights of such a blue hotel were not sufficiently enticing, it was Scully's habit to go every morning and evening to meet the leisurely trains that stopped at Romper and work his seductions upon any man that he might see wavering, gripsack in hand.

One morning, when a snow-crusted engine dragged its long string of freight cars and its one passenger coach to the station, Scully performed the marvel of catching three men. One was a shaky and quick-eyed Swede, with a great shining cheap valise; one was a tall bronzed cowboy, who was on his way to a ranch near the Dakota line; one was a little silent man from the East, who didn't look it, and didn't announce it. Scully practically made them prisoners. He was so nimble and merry and kindly that each probably felt it would be the height of brutality to try to escape. They trudged off over the creaking board sidewalks in the wake of the eager little Irishman. He wore a heavy fur cap squeezed tightly down on his head. It caused his two red ears to stick out stiffly, as if they were made of tin.

At last, Scully, elaborately, with boisterous hospitality, conducted them through the portals of the blue hotel. The room which they entered was small. It seemed to be merely a proper temple for an enormous stove, which, in the center, was humming with godlike violence. At various points on its surface the iron had become luminous and glowed yellow from the heat. Beside the stove Scully's son Johnnie was playing High-Five[1] with an old farmer who had whiskers both gray and sandy. They were quarrelling. Frequently the old farmer turned his face toward a box of sawdust—colored brown from tobacco juice—that was behind the stove, and spat with an air of great impatience and irritation. With a loud flourish of words Scully destroyed the game of cards, and bustled his son upstairs with part of the baggage of the new guests. He himself conducted them to three basins of the coldest water in the world. The cowboy and the Easterner burnished themselves fiery red with this water, until it seemed to be some kind of metal polish. The Swede, however, merely dipped his fingers gingerly and with trepidation. It was notable that throughout this series of small ceremonies the three travellers were made to feel that Scully was very benevolent. He was conferring great favors upon them. He handed the towel from one to another with an air of philanthropic impulse.

Afterward they went to the first room, and, sitting about the stove, listened to Scully's officious clamor at his daughters, who were preparing the midday meal. They reflected in the silence of experienced men who tread carefully amid new people. Nevertheless, the old farmer, stationary, invincible in his chair near the warmest part of the stove, turned his face from the sawdust-box frequently and addressed a glowing commonplace to the strangers. Usually he was answered in short but adequate sentences by either the cowboy or the Easterner. The Swede said nothing. He seemed to be occupied in making furtive estimates of each man in the room. One might have thought that he had the sense of silly suspicion which comes to guilt. He resembled a badly frightened man.

Later, at dinner, he spoke a little, addressing his conversation entirely to Scully. He volunteered that he had come from New York, where for ten years he had worked as a tailor. These facts seemed to strike Scully as fascinating, and afterward he volunteered that he had lived at Romper for fourteen years. The Swede asked about the crops and the price of labor. He seemed barely to listen to Scully's extended replies. His eyes continued to rove from man to man.

Finally, with a laugh and a wink, he said that some of these Western communities were very dangerous; and after his statement he straightened his legs under the table, tilted his head, and laughed again, loudly. It was plain that the demonstration had no meaning to the others. They looked at him wondering and in silence.

1. A card game popular in the nineties throughout the country, called "cinch" or "double pedro" in the far West.

II

As the men trooped heavily back into the front room, the two little windows presented views of a turmoiling sea of snow. The huge arms of the wind were making attempts—mighty, circular, futile—to embrace the flakes as they sped. A gate-post like a still man with a blanched face stood aghast amid this profligate fury. In a hearty voice Scully announced the presence of a blizzard. The guests of the blue hotel, lighting their pipes assented with grunts of lazy masculine contentment. No island of the sea could be exempt in the degree of this little room with its humming stove. Johnnie, son of Scully, in a tone which defined his opinion of his ability as a card-player, challenged the old farmer of both gray and sandy whiskers to a game of High-Five. The farmer agreed with a contemptuous and bitter scoff. They sat close to the stove, and squared their knees under a wide board. The cowboy and the Easterner watched the game with interest. The Swede remained near the window, aloof, but with a countenance that showed signs of an inexplicable excitement.

The play of Johnnie and the gray-beard was suddenly ended by another quarrel. The old man arose while casting a look of heated scorn at his adversary. He slowly buttoned his coat, and then stalked with fabulous dignity from the room. In the discreet silence of all the other men the Swede laughed. His laughter rang somehow childish. Men by this time had begun to look at him askance, as if they wished to inquire what ailed him.

A new game was formed jocosely. The cowboy volunteered to become the partner of Johnnie, and they all then turned to ask the Swede to throw in his lot with the little Easterner. He asked some questions about the game, and, learning that it wore many names, and that he had played it when it was under an alias, he accepted the invitation. He strode toward the men nervously, as if he expected to be assaulted. Finally, seated, he gazed from face to face and laughed shrilly. This laugh was so strange that the Easterner looked up quickly, the cowboy sat intent and with his mouth open, and Johnnie paused, holding the cards with still fingers.

Afterward there was a short silence. Then Johnnie said, "Well let's get at it. Come on now!" They pulled their chairs forward until their knees were bunched under the board. They began to play, and their interest in the game caused the others to forget the manner of the Swede.

The cowboy was a board-whacker. Each time that he held superior cards he whanged them, one by one, with exceeding force, down upon the improvised table, and took the tricks with a glowing air of prowess and pride that sent thrills of indignation into the hearts of his opponents. A game with a board-whacker in it is sure to become intense. The countenances of the Easterner and the Swede were miserable whenever the cowboy thundered down his aces and kings, while Johnnie, his eyes gleaming with joy, chuckled and chuckled.

Because of the absorbing play none considered the strange ways of the Swede. They paid strict heed to the game. Finally, during a lull caused by a new deal, the Swede suddenly addressed Johnnie: "I suppose there have been a good many men killed in this room." The jaws of the others dropped and they looked at him.

"What in hell are you talking about?" said Johnnie.

The Swede laughed again his blatant laugh, full of a kind of false courage and defiance. "Oh, you know what I mean all right," he answered.

"I'm a liar if I do!" Johnnie protested. The card was halted, and the men stared at the Swede. Johnnie evidently felt that as the son of the proprietor he should make a direct inquiry. "Now, what might you be drivin' at, mister?" he asked. The Swede winked at him. It was a wink full of cunning. His fingers shook on the edge of the board. "Oh, maybe you think I have been to nowheres. Maybe you think I'm a tenderfoot?"

"I don't know nothin' about you," answered Johnnie, "and I don't give a damn where you've been. All I got to say is that I don't know what you're driving at. There hain't never been nobody killed in this room."

The cowboy, who had been steadily gazing at the Swede, then spoke: "What's wrong with you, mister?"

Apparently it seemed to the Swede that he was formidably menaced. He shivered and turned white near the corners of his mouth. He sent an appealing glance in the direction of the little Easterner. During these moments he did not forget to wear his air of advanced pot-valor.[2] "They say they don't know what I mean," he remarked mockingly to the Easterner.

The latter answered after prolonged and cautious reflection. "I don't understand you," he said, impassively.

The Swede made a movement then which announced that he thought he had encountered treachery from the only quarter where he had expected sympathy, if not help. "Oh, I see you are all against me. I see—"

The cowboy was in a state of deep stupefaction. "Say," he cried, as he tumbled the deck violently down upon the board, "say, what are you gittin' at, hey?"

The Swede sprang up with the celerity of a man escaping from a snake on the floor. "I don't want to fight!" he shouted. "I don't want to fight!"

The cowboy stretched his long legs indolently and deliberately. His hands were in his pockets. He spat into the sawdust-box. "Well, who the hell thought you did?" he inquired.

The Swede backed rapidly toward a corner of the room. His hands were out protectingly in front of his chest, but he was making an obvious

---

2. "Pot-valiant" means "brave when drunk."

struggle to control his fright. "Gentlemen," he quavered, "I suppose I am going to be killed before I can leave this house! I suppose I am going to be killed before I can leave this house!" In his eyes was the dying-swan look. Through the windows could be seen the snow turning blue in the shadow of dusk. The wind tore at the house, and some loose thing beat regularly against the clapboards like a spirit tapping.

A door opened, and Scully himself entered. He paused in surprise as he noted the tragic attitude of the Swede. Then he said, "What's the matter here?"

The Swede answered him swiftly and eagerly: "These men are going to kill me."

"Kill you!" ejaculated Scully. "Kill you! What are you talkin'?"

The Swede made the gesture of a martyr.

Scully wheeled sternly upon his son. "What is this, Johnnie?"

The lad had grown sullen. "Damned if I know," he answered. "I can't make no sense to it." He began to shuffle the cards, fluttering them together with an angry snap. "He says a good many men have been killed in this room, or something like that. And he says he's goin' to be killed here too. I don't know what ails him. He's crazy, I shouldn't wonder."

Scully then looked for explanation to the cowboy, but the cowboy simply shrugged his shoulders.

"Kill you?" said Scully again to the Swede. "Kill you? Man, you're off your nut."

"Oh, I know," burst out the Swede. "I know what will happen. Yes, I'm crazy—yes. Yes, of course, I'm crazy—yes. But I know one thing—" There was a sort of sweat of misery and terror upon his face. "I know I won't get out of here alive."

The cowboy drew a deep breath, as if his mind was passing into the last stages of dissolution. "Well, I'm doggoned," he whispered to himself.

Scully wheeled suddenly and faced his son. "You've been troublin' this man!"

Johnnie's voice was loud with its burden of grievance. "Why, good Gawd, I ain't done nothin' to 'im."

The Swede broke in. "Gentlemen, do not disturb yourselves. I will leave this house. I will go away, because"—he accused them dramatically with his glance—"because I do not want to be killed."

Scully was furious with his son. "Will you tell me what is the matter, you young divil? What's the matter, anyhow? Speak out!"

"Blame it!" cried Johnnie in despair, "don't I tell you I don't know? He—he says we want to kill him, and that's all I know. I can't tell what ails him."

The Swede continued to repeat: "Never mind, Mr. Scully; never mind. I will leave this house. I will go away, because I do not wish to be killed. Yes, of course, I am crazy—yes. But I know one thing! I will go away. I will leave this house. Never mind, Mr. Scully; never mind. I will go away."

"You will not go 'way," said Scully. "You will not go 'way until I hear the reason of this business. If anybody has troubled you I will take care of him. This is my house. You are under my roof, and I will not allow any peaceable man to be troubled here." He cast a terrible eye upon Johnnie, the cowboy, and the Easterner.

"Never mind, Mr. Scully; never mind. I will go away. I do not wish to be killed." The Swede moved toward the door which opened upon the stairs. It was evidently his intention to go at once for his baggage.

"No, no," shouted Scully peremptorily; but the white-faced man slid by him and disappeared. "Now," said Scully severely, "what does this mane?"

Johnnie and the cowboy cried together: "Why, we didn't do nothin' to 'im!"

Scully's eyes were cold. "No," he said, "you didn't?"

Johnnie swore a deep oath. "Why, this is the wildest loon I ever see. We didn't do nothin' at all. We were jest sittin' here playin' cards, and he—"

The father suddenly spoke to the Easterner. "Mr. Blane," he asked, "what has these boys been doin'?"

The Easterner reflected again. "I didn't see anything wrong at all," he said at last, slowly.

Scully began to howl. "But what does it mane?" He stared ferociously at his son. "I have a mind to lather you for this, my boy."

Johnnie was frantic. "Well, what have I done?" he bawled at his father.

III

"I think you are tongue-tied," said Scully finally to his son, the cowboy, and the Easterner; and at the end of this scornful sentence he left the room.

Upstairs the Swede was swiftly fastening the straps of his great valise. Once his back happened to be half turned toward the door, and, hearing a noise there, he wheeled and sprang up, uttering a loud cry. Scully's wrinkled visage showed grimly in the light of the small lamp he carried. This yellow effulgence, streaming upward, colored only his prominent features, and left his eyes, for instance, in mysterious shadow. He resembled a murderer.

"Man! man!" he exclaimed, "have you gone daffy?"

"Oh, no! Oh, no!" rejoined the other. "There are people in this world who know pretty nearly as much as you do—understand?"

For a moment they stood gazing at each other. Upon the Swede's deathly pale cheeks were two spots brightly crimson and sharply edged, as if they had been carefully painted. Scully placed the light on the table and sat himself on the edge of the bed. He spoke ruminatively. "By cracky, I never heard of such a thing in my life. It's a complete muddle. I can't, for the soul of me, think how you ever got this idea into your head." Presently he lifted his eyes and asked: "And did you sure think they were going to kill you?"

The Swede scanned the old man as if he wished to see into his mind. "I did," he said at last. He obviously suspected that this answer might precipitate an outbreak. As he pulled on a strap his whole arm shook, the elbow wavering like a bit of paper.

Scully banged his hand impressively on the footboard of the bed. "Why, man, we're goin' to have a line of ilictric street-cars in this town next spring."

" 'A line of electric street-cars,' " repeated the Swede, stupidly.

"And," said Scully, "there's a new railroad goin' to be built down from Broken Arm to here. Not to mintion the four churches and the smashin' big brick schoolhouse. Then there's the big factory, too. Why, in two years Romper'll be a met-tro-*pol*-is."

Having finished the preparation of his baggage, the Swede straightened himself. "Mr. Scully," he said, with sudden hardihood, "how much do I owe you?"

"You don't own me anythin'," said the old man, angrily.

"Yes, I do," retorted the Swede. He took seventy-five cents from his pocket and tendered it to Scully; but the latter snapped his fingers in disdainful refusal. However, it happened that they both stood gazing in a strange fashion at three silver pieces on the Swede's open palm.

"I'll not take your money," said Scully at last. "Not after what's been goin' on here." Then a plan seemed to strike him. "Here," he cried, picking up his lamp and moving toward the door. "Here! Come with me a minute."

"No," said the Swede, in overwhelming alarm.

"Yes," urged the old man. "Come on! I want you to come and see a picter—just across the hall—in my room."

The Swede must have concluded that his hour was come. His jaw dropped and his teeth showed like a dead man's. He ultimately followed Scully across the corridor, but he had the step of one hung in chains.

Scully flashed the light high on the wall of his own chamber. There was revealed a ridiculous photograph of a little girl. She was leaning against a balustrade of gorgeous decoration, and the formidable bang to her hair was prominent. The figure was as graceful as an upright sled-stake, and withal, it was of the hue of lead. "There," said Scully tenderly, "that's the picter of my little girl that died. Her name was Carrie. She had the purtiest hair you ever saw! I was that fond of her, she—"

Turning then, he saw that the Swede was not contemplating the picture at all, but, instead, was keeping keen watch on the gloom in the rear.

"Look, man!" cried Scully, heartily. "That's the picter of my little gal that died. Her name was Carrie. And then here's the picter of my oldest boy. Michael. He's a lawyer in Lincoln, an' doin' well. I gave that boy a grand eddication, and I'm glad for it now. He's a fine boy. Look at 'im now. Ain't he bold as blazes, him there in Lincoln, an honored an' respicted gintleman! An honored and respicted gintleman," concluded Scully with a flourish. And, so saying, he smote the Swede jovially on the back.

The Swede faintly smiled.

"Now," said the old man, "there's only one more thing." He dropped suddenly to the floor and thrust his head beneath the bed. The Swede could hear his muffled voice. "I'd keep it under me piller if it wasn't for that boy Johnnie. Then there's the old woman— Where is it now? I never put it twice in the same place. Ah, now come out with you!"

Presently he backed clumsily from under the bed, dragging with him an old coat rolled into a bundle. "I've fetched him," he muttered. Kneeling on the floor, he unrolled the coat and extracted from its heart a large yellow-brown whiskey bottle.

His first maneuver was to hold the bottle up to the light. Reassured, apparently, that nobody had been tampering with it, he thrust it with a generous movement toward the Swede.

The weak-kneed Swede was about to eagerly clutch this element of strength, but he suddenly jerked his hand away and cast a look of horror upon Scully.

"Drink," said the old man affectionately. He had risen to his feet, and now stood facing the Swede.

There was a silence. Then again Scully said: "Drink!"

The Swede laughed wildly. He grabbed the bottle, put it to his mouth; and his lips curled absurdly around the opening and his throat worked, he kept his glance, burning with hatred, upon the old man's face.

IV

After the departure of Scully the three men, with the card-board still upon their knees, preserved for a long time an astounded silence. Then Johnnie said: "That's the doddangedest Swede I ever see."

"He ain't no Swede," said the cowboy, scornfully.

"Well, what is he then?" cried Johnnie. "What is he then?"

"It's my opinion," replied the cowboy deliberately, "he's some kind of a Dutchman." It was a venerable custom of the country to entitle as Swedes all light-haired men who spoke with a heavy tongue. In consequence the idea of the cowboy was not without its daring. "Yes, sir," he repeated. "It's my opinion this feller is some kind of a Dutchman."

"Well, he says he's a Swede, anyhow," muttered Johnnie, sulkily. He turned to the Easterner: "What do you think, Mr. Blane?"

"Oh, I don't know," replied the Easterner.

"Well, what do you think makes him act that way?" asked the cowboy.

"Why, he's frightened." The Easterner knocked his pipe against a rim of the stove. "He's clear frightened out of his boots."

"What at?" cried Johnnie and the cowboy together.

The Easterner reflected over his answer.

"What at?" cried the others again.

"Oh, I don't know, but it seems to me this man has been reading dime novels, and he thinks he's right out in the middle of it—the shootin' and stabbin' and all."

"But," said the cowboy, deeply scandalized, "this ain't Wyoming, ner none of them places. This is Nebrasker."

"Yes," added Johnnie, "an' why don't he wait til he gits *out West?*"

The travelled Easterner laughed. "It isn't different there even—not in these days. But he thinks he's right in the middle of hell."

Johnnie and the cowboy mused long.

"It's awful funny," remarked Johnnie at last.

"Yes," said the cowboy. "This is a queer game. I hope we don't git snowed in, because then we'd have to stand this here man bein' around with us all the time. That wouldn't be no good."

"I wish pop would throw him out," said Johnnie.

Presently they heard a loud stamping on the stairs, accompanied by ringing jokes in the voice of old Scully, and laughter, evidently from the Swede. The men around the stove stared vacantly at each other. "Gosh!" said the cowboy. The door flew open, and old Scully, flushed and anecdotal, came into the room. He was jabbering at the Swede, who followed him, laughing bravely. It was the entry of two roisterers from a banquet hall.

"Come now," said Scully sharply to the three seated men, "move up and give us a chance at the stove." The cowboy and the Easterner obediently sidled their chairs to make room for the newcomers. Johnnie, however, simply arranged himself in a more indolent attitude, and then remained motionless.

"Come! Git over, there," said Scully.

"Plenty of room on the other side of the stove," said Johnnie.

"Do you think we want to sit in the draught?" roared the father.

But the Swede here interposed with a grandeur of confidence. "No, no. Let the boy sit where he likes," he cried in a bullying voice to the father.

"All right! All right!" said Scully, deferentially. The cowboy and the Easterner exchanged glances of wonder.

The five chairs were formed in a crescent about one side of the stove. The Swede began to talk; he talked arrogantly, profanely, angrily. Johnnie, the cowboy, and the Easterner maintained a morose silence, while old

Scully appeared to be receptive and eager, breaking in constantly with sympathetic ejaculations.

Finally the Swede announced that he was thirsty. He moved in his chair, and said that he would go for a drink of water.

"I'll git it for you," cried Scully at once.

"No," said the Swede, contemptuously. "I'll get it for myself." He arose and stalked with the air of an owner off into the executive parts of the hotel.

As soon as the Swede was out of hearing Scully sprang to his feet and whispered intensely to the others: "Upstairs he thought I was tryin' to poison 'im."

"Say," said Johnnie, "this makes me sick. Why don't you throw 'im out in the snow?"

"Why, he's all right now," declared Scully. "It was only that he was from the East, and he thought this was a tough place. That's all. He's all right now."

The cowboy looked with admiration upon the Easterner. "You were straight," he said. "You were onto that there Dutchman."

"Well," said Johnnie to his father, "he may be all right now, but I don't see it. Other time he was scared, but now he's too fresh."

Scully's speech was always a combination of Irish brogue and idiom, Western twang and idiom, and scraps of curiously formal diction taken from the story-books and newspapers. He now hurled a strange mass of language at the head of his son. "What do I keep? What do I keep?" he demanded, in a voice of thunder. He slapped his knee impressively, to indicate that he himself was going to make reply, and that all should heed. "I keep a hotel," he shouted. "A hotel, do you mind? A guest under my roof has sacred privileges. He is to be intimidated by none. Not one word shall he hear that would prijudice him in favor of goin' away. I'll not have it. There's no place in this here town where they can say they iver took in a guest of mine because he was afraid to stay here." He wheeled suddenly upon the cowboy and the Easterner. "Am I right?"

"Yes, Mr. Scully," said the cowboy, "I think you're right."

"Yes, Mr. Scully," said the Easterner, "I think you're right."

V

At six-o'clock supper, the Swede fizzled like a fire-wheel. He sometimes seemed on the point of bursting into riotous song, and in all his madness he was encouraged by old Scully. The Easterner was encased in reserve; the cowboy sat in wide-mouthed amazement, forgetting to eat, while Johnnie wrathily demolished great plates of food. The daughters of the house, when they were obliged to replenish the biscuits, approached as warily as Indians, and, having succeeded in their purpose, fled with ill-concealed trepidation. The Swede domineered the whole feast, and he gave it the appearance of a cruel bacchanal. He seemed to have grown suddenly taller, he gazed, brutally disdainful, into every face. His voice rang through the room. Once when he jabbed out harpoon-fashion with his fork to pinion a biscuit, the weapon nearly impaled the hand of the Easterner, which had been stretched quietly out for the same biscuit.

After supper, as the men filed toward the other room, the Swede smote Scully ruthlessly on the shoulder. "Well, old boy, that was a good, square meal." Johnnie looked hopefully at his father; he knew that shoulder was tender from an old fall; and, indeed, it appeared for a moment as if Scully was going to flame out over the matter, but in the end he smiled a sickly smile and remained silent. The others understood from his manner that he was admitting his responsibility for the Swede's new viewpoint.

Johnnie, however, addressed his parent in an aside. "Why don't you license somebody to kick you downstairs?" Scully scowled darkly by way of reply.

When they were gathered about the stove, the Swede insisted on another game of High-Five. Scully gently deprecated the plan at first, but the Swede turned a wolfish glare upon him. The old man subsided, and the Swede canvassed the others. In his tone there was always a great threat. The cowboy and the Easterner both remarked indifferently that they would play. Scully said that he would presently have to go to meet the 6.58 train, so the Swede turned menacingly upon Johnnie. For a moment their glances crossed like blades, and then Johnnie smiled and said, "Yes, I'll play."

They formed a square, with the little board on their knees. The Easterner and the Swede were again partners. As the play went on, it was noticeable that the cowboy was not board-whacking as usual. Meanwhile, Scully, near the lamp, had put on his spectacles and, with an appearance curiously like an old priest, was reading a newspaper. In time he went out to meet the 6.58 train, and, despite his precautions, a gust of polar wind whirled into the room as he opened the door. Besides scattering the cards, it chilled the players to the marrow. The Swede cursed frightfully. When Scully returned, his entrance disturbed a cosy and friendly scene. The Swede again cursed. But presently they were once more intent, their heads bent forward and their hands moving swiftly. The Swede had adopted the fashion of board-whacking.

Scully took up his paper and for a long time remained immersed in matters which were extraordinarily remote from him. The lamp burned badly, and once he stopped to adjust the wick. The newspaper, as he turned from page to page, rustled with a slow and comfortable sound. Then suddenly he heard three terrible words: "You are cheatin'!"

Such scenes often prove that there can be little of dramatic import in environment. Any room can present a tragic front; any room can be comic. This little den was now hideous as a torture-chamber. The new faces of the men themselves had changed it upon the instant. The Swede held a huge fist in front of Johnnie's face, while the latter looked steadily over it into the blazing orbs of his accuser. The Easterner had grown pallid; the cowboy's jaw had dropped in that expression of bovine amazement which was one of his important mannerisms. After the three words, the first sound in the room was made by Scully's paper as it floated forgotten to his feet. His spectacles had also fallen from his nose, but by a clutch he had saved them in air. His hand, grasping the spectacles, now remained poised awkwardly and near his shoulder. He stared at the card-players.

Probably the silence was while a second elapsed. Then, if the floor had been suddenly twitched out from under the men they could not have moved quicker. The five had projected themselves headlong toward a common point. It happened that Johnnie, in rising to hurl himself upon the Swede, had stumbled slightly because of his curiously instinctive care for the cards and the board. The loss of the moment allowed time for the arrival of Scully, and also allowed the cowboy to give the Swede a great push which sent him staggering back. The men found tongue together, and hoarse shouts of rage, appeal, or fear burst from every throat. The cowboy pushed and jostled feverishly at the Swede, and the Easterner and Scully clung wildly to Johnnie; but through the smoky air, above the swaying bodies of the peace-compellers, the eyes of the two warriors ever sought each other in glances of challenge that were at once hot and steely.

Of course the board had been overturned, and now the whole company of cards was scattered over the floor, where the boots of the men trampled the fat and painted kings and queens as they gazed with their silly eyes at the war that was waging above them.

Scully's voice was dominating the yells. "Stop now! Stop, I say! Stop, now—"

Johnnie, as he struggled to burst through the rank formed by Scully and the Easterner, was crying, "Well, he says I cheated! He says I cheated! I won't allow no man to say I cheated! If he says I cheated, he's a — —!"

The cowboy was telling the Swede, "Quit, now! Quit, d'ye hear—"

The screams of the Swede never ceased: "He did cheat! I saw him! I saw him—"

As for the Easterner, he was importuning in a voice that was not heeded: "Wait a moment, can't you? Oh, wait a moment. What's the good of a fight over a game of cards? Wait a moment—"

In this tumult no complete sentences were clear. "Cheat"—"Quit"—"He says"—these fragments pierced the uproar and rang out sharply. It was remarkable that, whereas Scully undoubtedly made the most noise, he was the least heard of any of the riotous band.

Then suddenly there was a great cessation. It was as if each man had paused for breath; and although the room was still lighted with the anger of men, it could be seen that there was no danger of immediate conflict, and at once Johnnie, shouldering his way forward, almost succeeded in confronting the Swede. "What did you say I cheated for? What did you say I cheated for? I don't cheat, and I won't let no man say I do!"

The Swede said, "I saw you! I saw you!"

"Well," said Johnnie, "I'll fight any man what says I cheat!"

"No, you won't," said the cowboy. "Not here."

"Ah, be still, can't you?" said Scully, coming between them.

The quiet was sufficient to allow the Easterner's voice to be heard. He was repeating, "Oh, wait a moment, can't you? What's the good of a fight over a game of cards? Wait a moment!"

Johnnie, his red face appearing above his father's shoulder, hailed the Swede again. "Did you say I cheated?"

The Swede showed his teeth. "Yes."

"Then," said Johnnie, "we must fight."

"Yes, fight," roared the Swede. He was like a demoniac. "Yes, fight! I'll show you what kind of a man I am! I'll show you who you want to fight! Maybe you think I can't fight! Maybe you think I can't! I'll show you, you skin, you card-sharp! Yes, you cheated! You cheated! You cheated!"

"Well, let's go at it, then, mister," said Johnnie, coolly.

The cowboy's brow was beaded with sweat from his efforts in intercepting all sorts of raids. He turned in despair to Scully. "What are you goin' to do now?"

A change had come over the Celtic visage of the old man. He now seemed all eagerness; his eyes glowed.

"We'll let them fight," he answered, stalwartly. "I can't put up with it any longer. I've stood this damned Swede till I'm sick. We'll let them fight."

VI

The men prepared to go out-of-doors. The Easterner was so nervous that he had great difficulty in getting his arms into the sleeves of his new leather coat. As the cowboy drew his fur cap down over his ears his hands trembled. In fact, Johnnie and old Scully were the only ones who displayed no agitation. These preliminaries were conducted without words.

Scully threw open the door. "Well, come on," he said. Instantly, a terrific wind caused the flame of the lamp to struggle at its wick, while a puff of black smoke sprang from the chimney-top. The stove was in mid-current of the blast, and its voice swelled to equal the roar of the storm. Some of the scarred and bedabbled cards were caught up from the floor and dashed helplessly against the farther wall. The men lowered their heads and plunged into the tempest as into a sea.

No snow was falling, but great whirls and clouds of flakes, swept up from the ground by the frantic winds, were streaming southward with the speed of bullets. The covered land was blue with the sheen of an unearthly satin, and there was no other hue save where, at the low, black railway station—which seemed incredibly distant—one light gleamed like a tiny jewel. As the men floundered into a thigh-deep drift, it was known that the Swede was bawling out something. Scully went to him, put a hand on his shoulder, and projected an ear. "What's that you say?" he shouted.

"I say," bawled the Swede again, "I won't stand much show against this gang. I know you'll all pitch on me."

Scully smote him reproachfully on the arm. "Tut, man!" he yelled. The wind tore the words from Scully's lips and scattered them far alee.

"You are all a gang of—" boomed the Swede, but the storm also seized the remainder of this sentence.

Immediately turning their backs upon the wind, the men had swung around a corner to the sheltered side of the hotel. It was the function of the little house to preserve here, amid this great devastation of snow, an irregular V-shape of heavily encrusted grass, which crackled beneath the feet. One could imagine the great drifts piled against the windward side. When the party reached the comparative peace of this spot it was found that the Swede was still bellowing.

"Oh, I know what kind of thing this is! I know you'll all pitch on me. I can't lick you all!"

Scully turned upon him panther-fashion. "You'll not have to whip all of us. You'll have to whip my son Johnnie. An' the man what troubles you durin' that time will have me to dale with."

The arrangements were swiftly made. The two men faced each other, obedient to the harsh commands of Scully, whose face, in the subtly luminous gloom, could be seen set in the austere impersonal lines that are pictured on the countenances of the Roman veterans. The Easterner's teeth were chattering, and he was hopping up and down like a mechanical toy. The cowboy stood rocklike.

The contestants had not stripped off any clothing. Each was in his ordinary attire. Their fists were up, and they eyed each other in a calm that had the elements of leonine cruelty in it.

During the pause, the Easterner's mind, like a film, took lasting impressions of three men—the iron-nerved master of the ceremony; the Swede, pale, motionless, terrible; and Johnnie, serene yet ferocious, brutish yet heroic. The entire prelude had in it a tragedy greater than the tragedy of action, and this aspect was accentuated by the long, mellow cry of the blizzard, as it sped the tumbling and wailing flakes into the black abyss of the south.

"Now!" said Scully.

The two combatants leaped forward and crashed together like bullocks. There was heard the cushioned sound of blows, and of a curse squeezing out from between the tight teeth of one.

As for the spectators, the Easterner's pent-up breath exploded from him with a pop of relief, absolute relief from the tension of the preliminaries. The cowboy bounded into the air with a yowl. Scully was immovable as from supreme amazement and fear at the fury of the fight which he himself had permitted and arranged.

For a time the encounter in the darkness was such a perplexity of flying arms that it presented no more detail than would a swiftly revolving wheel. Occasionally a face, as if illumined by a flash of light, would shine out, ghastly and marked with pink spots. A moment later, the men might have been known as shadows, if it were not for the involuntary utterance of oaths that came from them in whispers.

Suddenly a holocaust of warlike desire caught the cowboy, and he bolted forward with the speed of a broncho. "Go it, Johnnie! go it! Kill him! Kill him!"

Scully confronted him. "Kape back," he said; and by his glance the cowboy could tell that this man was Johnnie's father.

To the Easterner there was a monotony of unchangeable fighting that was an abomination. This confused mingling was eternal to his sense, which was concentrated in a longing for the end, the priceless end. Once the fighters lurched near him, and as he scrambled hastily backward he heard them breathe like men on the rack.

"Kill him, Johnnie! Kill him! Kill him! Kill him!" The cowboy's face was contorted like one of those agony masks in museums.

"Keep still," said Scully, icily.

Then there was a sudden loud grunt, incomplete, cut short, and Johnnie's body swung away from the Swede and fell with sickening heaviness to the grass. The cowboy was barely in time to prevent the mad Swede from flinging himself upon his prone adversary. "No, you don't," said the cowboy, interposing an arm. "Wait a second."

Scully was at his son's side. "Johnnie! Johnnie, me boy!" His voice had a quality of melancholy tenderness. "Johnnie! Can you go on with it?" He looked anxiously down into the bloody, pulpy face of his son.

There was a moment of silence, and then Johnnie answered in his ordinary voice, "Yes, I—it—yes."

Assisted by his father he struggled to his feet. "Wait a bit now til you git your wind," said the old man.

A few paces away the cowboy was lecturing the Swede. "No, you don't! Wait a second!"

The Easterner was plucking at Scully's sleeve. "Oh, this is enough," he pleaded. "This is enough! Let it go as it stands. This is enough!"

"Bill," said Scully, "git out of the road." The cowboy stepped aside. "Now." The combatants were actuated by a new caution as they advanced toward collision. They glared at each other, and then the Swede aimed a lightning blow that carried with it his entire weight. Johnnie was evidently half stupid from weakness, but he miraculously dodged, and his fist sent the over-balanced Swede sprawling.

The cowboy, Scully, and the Easterner burst into a cheer that was like a chorus of triumphant soldiery, but before its conclusion the Swede had scuffled agilely to his feet and come in berserk abandon at his foe. There was another perplexity of flying arms, and Johnnie's body again swung away and fell, even as a bundle might fall from a roof. The Swede instantly staggered to a little wind-waved tree and leaned upon it, breathing like an engine, while his savage and flame-lit eyes roamed from face to face as the men bent over Johnnie. There was a splendor of isolation in his situation at this time which the Easterner felt once when, lifting his eyes from the man on the ground, he beheld that mysterious and lonely figure, waiting.

"Are you any good yet, Johnnie?" asked Scully in a broken voice.

The son gasped and opened his eyes languidly. After a moment he answered, "No—I ain't—any good—any—more." Then, from shame and bodily ill, he began to weep, the tears furrowing down through the blood-stains on his face. "He was too—too—too heavy for me."

Scully straightened and addressed the waiting figure. "Stranger," he said, evenly "it's all up with our side." Then his voice changed into that vibrant huskiness which is commonly the tone of the most simple and deadly announcements. "Johnnie is whipped."

Without reply, the victor moved off on the route to the front door of the hotel.

The cowboy was formulating new and unspellable blasphemies. The Easterner was startled to find that they were out in a wind that seemed to come direct from the shadowed arctic floes. He heard again the wail of the snow as it was flung to its grave in the south. He knew now that all this time the cold had been sinking into him deeper and deeper, and he wondered that he had not perished. He felt indifferent to the condition of the vanquished man.

"Johnnie, can you walk?" asked Scully.

"Did I hurt—hurt him any?" asked the son.

"Can you walk, boy? Can you walk?"

Johnnie's voice was suddenly strong. There was a robust impatience in it. "I asked you whether I hurt him any!"

"Yes, yes, Johnnie," answered the cowboy, consolingly; "he's hurt a good deal."

They raised him from the ground, and as soon as he was on his feet he went tottering off, rebuffing all attempts at assistance. When the party rounded the corner they were fairly blinded by the pelting of the snow. It burned their faces like fire. The cowboy carried Johnnie through the drift to the door. As they entered, some cards again rose from the floor and beat against the wall.

The Eastener rushed to the stove. He was so profoundly chilled that he almost dared to embrace the glowing iron. The Swede was not in the room. Johnnie sank into a chair and, folding his arms on his knees, buried his face in them. Scully, warming one foot and then the other at the rim of the stove, muttered to himself with Celtic mournfulness. The cowboy had removed his fur cap, and with a dazed and rueful air he was running one hand through his tousled locks. From overhead they could hear the creaking of boards, as the Swede tramped here and there in his room.

The sad quiet was broken by the sudden flinging open of a door that led toward the kitchen. It was instantly followed by an inrush of women. They precipitated themselves upon Johnnie amid a chorus of lamentation. Before they carried their prey off to the kitchen, there to be bathed and harangued with that mixture of sympathy and abuse which is a feat of their sex, the mother straightened herself and fixed old Scully with an eye of stern reproach. "Shame be upon you, Patrick Scully!" she cried. "Your own son, too. Shame be upon you!"

"There, now! Be quiet, now!" said the old man, weakly.

"Shame be upon you, Patrick Scully!" The girls, rallying to this slogan, sniffed disdainfully in the direction of those trembling accomplices, the cowboy and the Easterner. Presently they bore Johnnie away, and left the three men to dismal reflection.

VII

"I'd like to fight this here Dutchman myself," said the cowboy, breaking a long silence.

Scully wagged his head sadly. "No, that wouldn't do. It wouldn't be right. It wouldn't be right."

"Well, why wouldn't it?" argued the cowboy. "I don't see no harm in it."

"No," answered Scully, with mournful heroism. "It wouldn't be right. It was Johnnie's fight, and now we mustn't whip the man just because he whipped Johnnie."

"Yes, that't true enough," said the cowboy; "but—he better not get fresh with me, because I couldn't stand no more of it."

"You'll not say a word to him," commanded Scully, and even then they heard the tread of the Swede on the stairs. His entrance was made theatric. He swept the door back with a bang and swaggered to the middle of the room. No one looked at him. "Well," he cried, insolently, at Scully, "I s'pose you'll tell me now how much I owe you?"

The old man remained stolid. "You don't own me nothin'."

"Huh!" said the Swede, "huh! Don't owe 'im nothin'."

The cowboy addressed the Swede. "Stranger, I don't see how you come to be so gay around here."

Old Scully was instantly alert. "Stop!" he shouted, holding his hand forth, fingers upward, "Bill, you shut up!"

The cowboy spat carelessly into the sawdust-box. "I didn't say a word, did I?" he asked.

"Mr. Scully," called the Swede, "how much do I owe you?" It was seen that he was attired for departure, and that he had his valise in his hand.

"You don't owe me nothin'," repeated Scully in the same imperturbable way.

"Huh!" said the Swede. "I guess you're right. I guess if it was any way at all, you'd owe me somethin'. That's what I guess." He turned to the cowboy. " 'Kill him! Kill him! Kill him!' " he mimicked, and then guffawed victoriously. " 'Kill him!' " He was convulsed with ironical humor.

But he might have been jeering the dead. The three men were immovable and silent, staring with glassy eyes at the stove.

The Swede opened the door and passed into the storm, giving one derisive glance backward at the still group.

As soon as the door was closed, Scully and the cowboy leaped to their feet and began to curse. They trampled to and fro, waving their arms and smashing into the air with their fists. "Oh, but that was a hard minute!" wailed Scully. "That was a hard minute! Him there leerin' and scoffin'! One bang at his nose was worth forty dollars to me that minute! How did you stand it, Bill?"

"How did I stand it?" cried the cowboy in a quivering voice. "How did I stand it? Oh!"

The old man burst into sudden brogue. "I'd loike to take that Swade," he wailed, "and hould 'im down on a shtone flure and bate 'im to a jelly wid a shtick."

The cowboy groaned in sympathy. "I'd like to git him by the neck and ha-ammer him"—he brought his hand down on a chair with a noise like a pistol-shot—"hammer that there Dutchman until he couldn't tell himself from a dead coyote!"

"I'd bate 'im until he—"

"I'd show *him* some things—"

And then together they raised a yearning, fanatic cry—"Oh-o-oh! if we only could—"

"Yes!"

"Yes!"

"And then I'd—"

"O-o-oh!"

VIII

The Swede, tightly gripping his valise, tacked across the face of the storm as if he carried sails. He was following a line of little naked, gasping trees which, he knew, must mark the way of the road. His face, fresh from the pounding of Johnnie's fists, felt more pleasure than pain in the wind and the driving snow. A number of square shapes loomed upon him finally, and he knew them as the houses of the main body of the town. He found a street and made travel along it, leaning heavily upon the wind whenever, at a corner, a terrific blast caught him.

He might have been in a deserted village. We picture the world as thick with conquering and elate humanity, but here, with the bugles of the tempest pealing, it was hard to imagine a peopled earth. One viewed the existence of man then as a marvel, and conceded a glamor of wonder to these lice which were caused to cling to a whirling, fire-smitten, ice-locked, disease-stricken, space-lost bulb. The conceit of man was explained by this storm to be the very engine of life. One was a coxcomb not to die in it. However, the Swede found a saloon.

In front of it an indomitable red light was burning, and the snowflakes were made blood-color as they flew through the circumscribed territory of the lamp's shining. The Swede pushed open the door of the saloon and entered. A sanded expanse was before him, and at the end of it four men sat about a table drinking. Down one side of the room extended a radiant bar, and its guardian was leaning upon his elbows listening to the talk of the men at the table. The Swede dropped his valise upon the floor and, smiling fraternally upon the barkeeper, said, "Gimme some whiskey, will you?" The man placed a bottle, a whiskey-glass and a glass of ice-thick water upon the bar. The Swede poured himself an abnormal portion of whiskey and drank it in three gulps. "Pretty bad night," remarked the bartender, indifferently. He was making the pretension of blindness which is usually a distinction of his class; but it could have been seen that he was furtively studying the half-erased bloodstains on the face of the Swede. "Bad night," he said again.

"Oh, it's good enough for me," replied the Swede, hardily, as he poured himself some more whiskey. The barkeeper took his coin and maneuvered it through its reception by the high nickelled cash-machine. A bell rang; a card labelled "20 cts." had appeared.

"No," continued the Swede, "this isn't too bad weather. It's good enough for me."

"So?" murmured the barkeeper, languildy.

The copious drams made the Swede's eyes swim, and he breathed a trifle heavier. "Yes, I like this weather. I like it. It suits me." It was apparently his design to impart a deep significance to these words.

"So?" murmured the bartender again. He turned to gaze dreamily at the scroll-like birds and bird-like scrolls which had been drawn with soap upon the mirrors in back of the bar.

"Well, I guess I'll take another drink," said the Swede, presently. "Have something?"

"No, thanks; I'm not drinkin'," answered the bartender. Afterward he asked, "How did you hurt your face?"

The Swede immediately began to boast loudly. "Why, in a fight. I thumped the soul out of a man down here at Scully's hotel."

The interest of the four men at the table was at last aroused.

"Who was it?" said one.

"Johnnie Scully," blustered the Swede. "Son of the man what runs it. He will be pretty near dead for some weeks, I can tell you. I made a nice thing of him, I did. He couldn't get up. They carried him in the house. Have a drink?"

Instantly the men in some subtle way encased themselves in reserve. "No, thanks," said one. The group was of curious formation. Two were prominent local business men; one was the district attorney; and one was a professional gambler of the kind known as "square." But a scrutiny of the group would not have enabled an observer to pick the gambler from the men of more reputable pursuits. He was, in fact, a man so delicate in manner, when among people of fair class, and so judicious in his choice of victims, that in the strictly masculine part of the town's life he had come to be explicitly trusted and admired. People called him a thoroughbred. The fear and contempt with which his craft was regarded were undoubtedly the reason why his quiet dignity shone conspicuous above the quiet dignity of men who might be merely hatters, billiard-markers, or grocery-clerks. Beyond an occasional unwary traveller who came by rail, this gambler was supposed to prey solely upon reckless and senile farmers, who, when flush with good crops, drove into town in all the pride and confidence of an absolutely invulnerable stupidity. Hearing at times in circuitous fashion of the despoilment of such a farmer, the important men of Romper invariably laughed in contempt of the victim, and if they thought of the wolf at all, it was with a kind of pride at the knowledge that he would never dare think of attacking their wisdom and courage. Besides, it was popular that this gambler had a real wife and two real children in a neat cottage in a suburb, where he led an exemplary home life; and when any one even suggested a discrepancy in his character, the crowd immediately vociferated descriptions of this virtuous family circle. Then men who led exemplary home lives, and men who did not lead exemplary home lives, all subsided in a bunch, remarking that there was nothing more to be said.

However, when a restriction was placed upon him—as, for instance, when a strong clique of members of the new Pollywog Club refused to permit him, even as a spectator, to appear in the rooms of the organization—the candor and gentleness with which he accepted the judgment disarmed many of his foes and made his friends more desperately partisan. He invariably distinguished between himself and a respectable Romper man so quickly and frankly that his manner actually appeared to be a continual broadcast compliment.

And one must not forget to declare the fundamental fact of his entire position in Romper. It is irrefutable that in all affairs outside his business, in all matters that occur eternally and commonly between man and man, this thieving card-player was so generous, so just, so moral, that, in a contest, he could have put to flight the consciences of nine tenths of the citizens of Romper.

And so it happened that he was seated in this saloon with the two prominent local merchants and the district attorney.

The Swede continued to drink raw whiskey, meanwhile babbling at the barkeeper and trying to induce him to indulge in potations. "Come on. Have a drink. Come on. What—no? Well, have a little one, then. By gawd, I've whipped a man tonight, and I want to celebrate. I whipped him good, too. Gentlemen," the Swede cried to the men at the table, "have a drink?"

"Ssh!" said the barkeeper.

The group at the table, although furtively attentive, had been pretending to be deep in talk, but now a man lifted his eyes toward the Swede and said, shortly, "Thanks. We don't want any more."

At this reply the Swede ruffled out his chest like a rooster. "Well," he exploded, "it seems I can't get anybody to drink with me in this town. Seems so, don't it? Well!"

"Ssh!" said the barkeeper.

"Say," snarled the Swede, "don't you try to shut me up. I won't have it. I'm a gentleman, and I want people to drink with me. And I want 'em to drink with me now. *Now*—do you understand?" He rapped the bar with his knuckles.

Years of experience had calloused the bartender. He merely grew sulky. "I hear you," he answered.

"Well," cried the Swede, "listen hard then. See those men over there? Well, they're going to drink with me, and don't you forget it. Now you watch."

"Hi!" yelled the barkeeper, "this won't do!"

"Why won't it?" demanded the Swede. He stalked over to the table, and by chance laid his hand upon the shoulder of the gambler. "How about this?" he asked wrathfully. "I asked you to drink with me."

The gambler simply twisted his head and spoke over his shoulder. "My friend, I don't know you."

"Oh, hell!" answered the Swede, "come and have a drink."

"Now, my boy," advised the gambler, kindly, "take your hand off my shoulder and go 'way and mind your own business." He was a little, slim man, and it seemed strange to hear him use this tone of heroic patronage to the burly Swede. The other men at the table said nothing.

"What! You won't drink with me, you little dude? I'll make you, then! I'll make you!" The Swede had grasped the gambler frenziedly at the throat and was dragging him from his chair. The other men sprang up. The barkeeper dashed around the corner of his bar. There was a great tumult, and then was seen a long blade in the hand of the gambler. It shot forward, and a human body, this citadel of virtue, wisdom, power, was pierced as easily as if it had been a melon. The Swede fell with a cry of supreme astonishment.

The prominent merchants and the district attorney must have at once tumbled out of the place backward. The bartender found himself hanging limply to the arm of a chair and gazing into the eyes of a murderer.

"Henry," said the latter, as he wiped his knife on one of the towels that hung beneath the bar rail, "you tell 'em where to find me. I'll be home, waiting for 'em." Then he vanished. A moment afterward the barkeeper was in the street dinning through the storm for help and, moreover, companionship.

The corpse of the Swede, alone in the saloon, had its eyes fixed upon a dreadful legend that dwelt atop of the cash-machine: "This registers the amount of your purchase."

IX

Months later, the cowboy was frying pork over the stove of a little ranch near the Dakota line, when there was a quick thud of hoofs outside, and presently the Easterner entered with the letters and the papers.

"Well," said the Easterner at once, "the chap that killed the Swede has got three years. Wasn't much, was it?"

"He has? Three years?" The cowboy poised his pan of pork, while he ruminated upon the news. "Three years. That ain't much."

"No. It was a light sentence," replied the Easterner as he unbuckled his spurs. "Seems there was a good deal of sympathy for him in Romper."

"If the bartender had been any good," observed the cowboy, thoughtfully, "he would have gone in and cracked that there Dutchman on the head with a bottle in the beginnin' of it and stopped all this here murderin'."

"Yes, a thousand things might have happened," said the Easterner, tartly.

The cowboy returned his pan of pork to the fire, but his philosophy continued. "It's funny, ain't it? If he hadn't said Johnnie was cheatin' he'd be alive this minute. He was an awful fool. Game played for fun, too. Not for money. I believe he was crazy."

"I feel sorry for that gambler," said the Easterner.

"Oh, so do I," said the cowboy. "He don't deserve none of it for killin' who he did."

"The Swede might not have been killed if everything had been square."

"Might not have been killed?" exclaimed the cowboy. "Everythin' square? Why, when he said that Johnnie was cheatin' and acted like such a jackass? And then in the saloon he fairly walked up to git hurt?" With these arguments the cowboy browbeat the Easterner and reduced him to rage.

"You're a fool!" cried the Easterner, viciously. "You're a bigger jackass than the Swede by a million majority. Now let me tell you one thing. Let me tell you something. Listen! Johnnie *was* cheating!"

"'Johnnie,'" said the cowboy, blankly. There was a minute of silence, and then he said, robustly, "Why, no. The game was only for fun."

"Fun or not," said the Easterner, "Johnnie was cheating. I saw him. I know it. I saw him. And I refused to stand up and be a man. I let the Swede fight it out alone. And you—you were simply puffing around the place and wanting to fight. And then old Scully himself! We are all in it! This poor gambler isn't even a noun. He is kind of an adverb. Every sin is the result of a collaboration. We, five of us, have collaborated in the murder of this Swede. Usually there are from a dozen to forty women really involved in every murder, but in this case it seems to be only five men—you, I, Johnnie, old Scully; and that fool of an unfortunate gambler came merely as a culmination, the apex of a human movement, and gets all the punishment."

The cowboy, injured and rebellious, cried out blindly into the fog of mysterious theory: "Well, I didn't do anythin', did I?"

Issues for Discussion

1. In James T. Farrell's "Big Jeff," Jeff has what Kretschner calls a "pyknic body type," or what Sheldon calls "endomorphic." Discuss whether Jeff's deviant behavior conforms to the predictions of the "body type" theorists.
2. Read the following passage from "Big Jeff." Does the quotation provide more support for Lombroso's idea that "structure determines function" or for Ferri's statement that behavior is partly the product of one's social milieu?

   Jeff the fat Jewboy . . . Jeff the fatass of Fifty-eighth Street . . . his mother looked like a blown-up balloon . . . with Jeff in her womb . . . Jeff's birth . . . like the bursting of a balloon . . . Jeff weighed too much from the start . . . Jeff grew heavier and heavier and heavier . . . Jeff went to *Chedar* . . . knew his lessons . . . and still his ass was whaled black and blue . . . Jeff was always easy to laugh at . . . Jeff, the fat Jewboy . . . Jeff the fatass of Fifty-eighth Street . . . Big Fat Jeff who waved his fanny through life . . . Big Fat Jeff.

3. Cesare Lombroso believed indicators of behavior were reflected in a person's physical structure. Enrico Ferri and Raffaele Garofalo extended the positivists' criteria to include such things as mental state and social and economic environment. Read the following quotation from Stephen Crane's "The Blue Motel" and relate how the passage supports the notion that behavior is not the product of free will (as suggested by the classical theorists) but is directed by a person's environment.

   Because of the absorbing play none considered the strange ways of the Swede. They paid strict heed to the game. Finally, during a lull caused by a new deal, the Swede suddenly addressed Johnnie: "I suppose there have been a good many men killed in this room." The jaws of the others dropped and they looked at him.

ISSUES FOR DISCUSSION

"What in hell are you talking about?" said Johnnie.

The Swede laughed again his blatant laugh, full of a kind of false courage and defiance. "Oh, you know what I mean all right," he answered.

"I'm a liar if I do!" Johnnie protested. The card game was halted, and the men stared at the Swede. Johnnie evidently felt that as the son of the proprietor he should make a direct inquiry. "Now, what might you be drivin' at, mister?" he asked. The Swede winked at him. It was a wink full of cunning. His fingers shook on the edge of the board. "Oh, maybe you think I have been to nowheres. Maybe you think I'm a tenderfoot?"

4. It is obvious that the Swede's dime-novel impressions of the West are far out of date with the current atmosphere in Scully's hotel. Yet Crane gives the reader the impression that the Swede's demise cannot be reversed. How do the behaviors of Scully, Johnnie, the Easterner, the cowboy, and, ultimately, the gambler, combine to substantiate the Swede's fears that he has entered a hostile environment?

PART III

Culture Conflict Theory

Culture conflict theory as an explanation of deviance began to gain popularity in the United States in 1938 with the publication of Thorsten Sellin's *Culture Conflict and Crime*.[1] Prevailing views of adherents of conflict theory extend statements presented by the labeling and radical (i.e., Marxist) theorists.[2] Essentially, rules, laws, norms, folkways, customs, and mores arise out of competing *group* interests.[3] Whether rules emerge within the primitive tribe or within the sophisticated setting of a senate or parliament, they nonetheless reflect the interests of the collective group. Relating group activity to criminal behavior, Richard Quinney notes that

> (1) crime is a definition of human conduct that is created by authorized agents in a politically organized society, (2) criminal definitions describe behaviors that conflict with the interests of the segments of society that have the power to shape the enforcement and administration of criminal law.[4]

---

1. New York: Social Science Research Council, 1938.
2. See Parts VIII and IX for fuller discussions of these schools of thought.
3. See Arthur F. Bentley, *The Processes of Government* (Chicago: University of Chicago Press, 1908), pp. 258–96.
4. *The Social Reality of Crime* (Boston: Little, Brown, 1970), pp. 15–18. See also William J. Chambliss, *Functional and Conflict Theories of Crime* (New York: MSS Modular Publications, 1974), pp. 1–23.

The formal source of norm conflict emanates from legal codes that emerge from group conflict and resolution. One function of the formal law is to order behavior. The intent of laws is the modification of behavior currently acceptable to some groups. Nevertheless, outlawing previously acceptable and practiced behavior is likely to bring about intense and prolonged conflict. The Mormon practice of polygamy serves as one illustration. Conflict also may result when developing societies attempt to alter existing rules to coincide with the believed current values of the community. Attempts to modify laws that reflect "popular" current attitudes are extremely difficult in a multicultured society. Competing interests among different ethnic, political, social, racial, or religious groups confound the task of promoting universally acceptable laws. For example, in America a federal law may represent the desires of a particular lobby but conflict with interests of some state or local groups. Moreover, a federal law may be obnoxious to the majority of the citizens of a given state or region. The new law may eventually garner general public support, but the short-term effects contribute to norm conflict and deviant behavior.[5]

The dynamics of group lawmaking also can be seen in less politically charged environments. These rules represent the customs, mores, and folkways indigenous to the clan, tribe, religious sect, union, club, or ethnic community. They emerge just as laws of states and nations do—through a constant flux of group interaction and resolution. But these rules differ from "state sanctioned" laws in that they have no legal effect.[6] Yet their effect on human behavior may be as significant as are formal laws on the general population. A member of the tribe, clan, and so on, may reject informal rules and become the object of peer ostracism and ridicule. Or, unless the individual conforms, self-imposed or group-forced banishment may result.[7]

James T. Farrell's "The Fastest Runner on Sixty-First Street" illustrates the conflict that results from the clash of formal and informal codes. Assault

---

5. Criticism of conflict theory has varied. One seemingly serious flaw of the theory lies in its inability to adequately explain the process of norm acquisition and norm abandonment. Specifically, how are particular norms individually weighted, and why may one eschew a seemingly important value? Moreover, why do similarly situated persons engage in differential behavior? Or how does the theory predict and explain deviance in tribes and groups insulated from infectious alien values? Finally, the causal relation between norm conflict and criminality is vague and imprecise. One is informed only that the likelihood of deviant behavior increases with the infusion of poly norms; the nature and extent of criminality is left to speculation. See *Publisher's Weekly* 18 (February 1974): 70.

6. Although violation of these rules does not amount to criminal behavior as such, it nonetheless amounts to behavior to which informal sanctions that are as punitive as society's sanctions may be applied

7. For a good discussion of group conflict in primitive society, see Bronislaw Malinowski, *Crime and Custom in Savage Society* (Totowa, N.J.: Littlefield, Adams, 1976).

INTRODUCTION   57

and battery is a crime, yet the conduct of Morty and his gang is supported by the norms of the white community. The retribution by the Negroes is also group sanctioned. "The Patented Gate and the Mean Hamburger" by Robert Penn Warren examines the anxiety caused by a changing social and economic milieu. Jeff York struggles for thirty years to acquire "his place." But he has acquired more than a farm. He is the product of the values typified by the hard-working, independent American farmer. Conflict emerges when he must adapt to the culture of the big city.

In Theodore Dreiser's "Nigger Jeff," community members demand that "justice" be swift and certain. Yet the justice accorded Jeff clearly conflicts with the rules of the American court scene: a jury trial, rules of evidence and procedure, an impartial judge, and defense counsel. Although there is little doubt about Jeff's guilt, or about the outcome of a trial had he been given one, the behavior of the outraged community illustrates the power of the "collective conscience" (group will) over "impersonal" legal codes.

THE FASTEST RUNNER ON SIXTY-FIRST STREET
James T. Farrell

Morty Aiken liked to run and to skate. He liked running games and races. He liked running so much that sometimes he'd go over to Washington Park all by himself and run just for the fun of it. He got a kick out of running, and he had raced every kid he could get to run against him. His love of racing and running had even become a joke among many of the boys he knew. But even when they gave him the horse laugh it was done in a good-natured way, because he was a very popular boy. Older fellows liked him, and when they would see him, they'd say, there's a damn good kid and a damned fast runner.

When he passed his fourteenth birthday, Morty was a trifle smaller than most boys of his own age. But he was well known, and, in a way, almost famous in his own neighborhood. He lived at Sixty-first and Eberhardt, but kids in the whole area had heard of him, and many of them would speak of what a runner and what a skater Morty Aiken was.

He won medals in playground tournaments, and, in fact, he was the only lad from his school who had ever won medals in these tournaments. In these events he became the champion in the fifty- and hundred-yard dash, and with this he gained the reputation of being the best runner, for his age, on the South Side of Chicago.

He was as good a skater as he was a runner. In winter, he was to be seen regularly almost every day on the ice at the Washington Park lagoon or over on the Midway. He had a pair of Johnson racers which his father had given him, and he treasured these more than any other possession. His mother knitted him red socks and a red stocking cap for skating, and he had a red-and-white sweater. When he skated, he was like a streak of red. His form was excellent, and his sense of himself and of his body on the ice was sure and right. Almost every day there would be a game of I-Got-It. The skater who was *it* would skate in a wide circle, chased by the pack until he was caught. Morty loved to play I-Got-It, and on many a day this boy in short pants, wearing the red stocking cap, the red-and-white sweater, and the thick, knitted red woolen socks coming above the black shoes of his Johnson racers, would lead the pack, circling around and around and around, his head forward, his upper torso bent forward, his hands behind his back, his legs working with grace and giving him a speed that sometimes seemed miraculous. And in February, 1919, Morty competed in an ice derby, conducted under the auspices of the Chicago *Clarion*. He won two gold medals. His picture was on the first page of the sports section of the Sunday *Clarion*. All in all, he was a famous and celebrated lad. His father and mother were proud of him. His teacher and Mrs. Bixby, the principal of the school, were proud of him. Merchants on Sixty-first Street were proud of him. There was not a lad in the neighborhood who was greeted on the street by strangers as often as Morty.

Although he was outwardly modest, Morty had his dreams. He was graduated from grammar school in 1919, and was planning to go to Park High in the fall. He was impatient to go to high school and to get into high-school track meets. He'd never been coached, and yet look how good he was! Think of how good he would be when he had some coaching! He'd be a streak of lightning, if ever there was one. He dreamed that he would be called the Human Streak of Lightning. And after high school there would be college, college track meets, and the Big Ten championships, and after that he would join an athletic club and run in track meets, and he would win a place on the Olympic team, and somewhere, in Paris or Rome or some European city, he would beat the best runners in the world, and, like Ty Cobb[1] in baseball and Jess Willard[2] in prize fighting, he'd be the world's greatest runner.

And girls would all like him, and the most beautiful girl in the world would marry him. He liked girls, but girls liked him even more than he liked them. In May, a little while before his graduation, the class had a picnic, and they played Post Office. The post office was behind a clump of bushes in Jackson Park. He was called to the post office more than any other of the boys. There was giggling and talking and teasing, but it hadn't bothered him, especially because he knew that the other fellows liked and kind of envied him. To Morty, this was only natural. He accepted it. He accepted the fact that he was a streak of lightning on his feet and on the ice, and that this made him feel somehow different from other boys and very important. Even Tony Rabuski looked at him in this way, and if any kid would have picked on him, Tony would have piled into that kid. Tony was the toughest boy in school, and he was also considered to be the dumbest. He was also the poorest. He would often come to school wearing a black shirt, because a black shirt didn't show the dirt the way that other shirts did, and his parents couldn't afford to buy him many shirts. One day Tony was walking away from school with Morty, and Tony said:

"Kid, you run de fastest, I fight de best in de whole school. We make a crack-up team. We're pals. Shake, kid, we're pals."

Morty shook Tony's hand. For a fourteen-year-old boy, Tony had very

---

1. Tyrus Raymond Cobb (born 1886), famous for his batting and base-stealing.

2. Jess Willard (born 1883), heavyweight champion from 1915 to 1919.

big and strong hands. The other kids sometimes called them "meat hooks."

Morty looked on this handshake as a pledge. He and Tony became friends, and they were often together. Morty had Tony come over to his house to play, and sometimes Tony stayed for a meal. Tony ate voraciously and wolfishly. When Morty's parents spoke of the way Tony ate and of the quantity of food he ate, Morty would reply by telling them that Tony was his friend.

Because he was poor and somewhat stupid, a dull and fierce resentment smoldered in Tony. Other boys out-talked him, and they were often able to plague and annoy him, and then outrun him because he was heavy footed. The kids used to laugh at Tony because they said he had lead, iron, and bricks in his big feet. After Morty and Tony had shaken hands and become pals, Morty never would join the other boys in razzing Tony. And he and Tony doped out a way that would permit Tony to get even with kids who tried to torment him. If some of the boys made game of Tony until he was confused and enraged and went for them, Morty would chase the boys. He had no difficulty in catching one of them. When he caught any of the boys who'd been teasing and annoying Tony, he'd usually manage to hold the boy until Tony would lumber up and exact his punishment and revenge. Sometimes Tony would be cruel, and on a couple of occasions when Tony, in a dull and stupefied rage, was sitting on a hurt, screaming boy and pounding him, Morty ordered Tony to lay off. Tony did so instantly. Morty didn't want Tony to be too cruel. He had come to like Tony and to look on him as a big brother. He'd always wanted a brother, and sometimes he would imagine how wonderful it would be if Tony could even come to live at his house.

The system Morty and Tony worked out, with Morty chasing and catching one of the boys who ragged Tony, worked out well. Soon the kids stopped ragging Tony. Because of their fear, and because they liked and respected Morty and wanted him to play with them, they began to accept Tony. And Tony began to change. Once accepted, so that he was no longer the butt of jokes, he looked on all the boys in Morty's gang as his pals. He would protect them as he would protect Morty. Tony then stopped scowling and making fierce and funny faces and acting in many odd little ways. After he became accepted, as a result of being Morty's pal, his behavior changed, and because he was strong and could fight, the boys began to admire him. At times he really hoped for strange boys to come around the neighborhood and act like bullies so he could beat them up. He wanted to fight and punch because he could feel powerful and would be praised and admired.

II

Ever since he had been a little fellow, Tony had often been called a "Polack" or a "dirty Polack." After he became one of the gang or group around Morty, some of the boys would tell him that he was a "white Polack." In his slow way, he thought about these words and what they meant. When you were called certain words, you were lauged at, you were looked at as if something were wrong with you. If you were a Polack, many girls didn't want to have anything to do with you. The boys and girls who weren't Polacks had fun together that Polacks couldn't have. Being a Polack and being called a Polack was like being called a sonofabitch. It was a name. When you were called a name like this, you were looked at as a different kind of kid from one who wasn't called a name. Morty Aiken wasn't called names. Tony didn't want to be called names. And if he fought and beat up those who called him names, they would be afraid of him. He wanted that. But he also wanted to have as much fun as the kids who weren't called these names. And he worked it out that these kids felt better when they called other kids names. He could fight and he could call names, and if he called a kid a name, and that kid got tough, he could beat him up. He began to call names. And there was a name even worse than Polack—"nigger." If Tony didn't like a kid, he called him a "nigger." And he talked about the "niggers." He felt as good as he guessed these other kids did when he talked about the "niggers." And they could be beat up. They weren't supposed to go to Washington Park because that was a park for the whites. That was what he had often heard.

He heard it said so much that he believed it. He sometimes got a gang of the boys together and they would roam Washington Park, looking for colored boys to beat up. Morty went with them. He didn't particularly like to beat up anyone, but when they saw a colored kid and chased him, he would always be at the head, and he would be the one who caught the colored boy. He could grab or tackle him, and by that time the others would catch up. He worked the same plan that he and Tony had worked against the other boys. And after they caught and beat up a colored boy, they would all talk and shout and brag about what they had done, and talk about how they had gotten in their licks and punches and kicks, and how fast Morty had run to catch that shine, and what a sock Tony had given him, and talking all together and strutting and bragging, they felt good and proud of themselves, and they talked about how the Sixty-first Street boys would see to it that Washington Park would stay a white man's park.

And this became more and more important to Tony. There were those names, "Polack," "dirty Polack," "white Polack." If you could be called a "Polack," you weren't considered white. Well, when he beat them up, was he or wasn't he white? They knew. After the way he clouted these black ones, how could the other kids not say that Tony Rabuski wasn't white? That showed them all. That showed he was a hero. He was a hero as much as Morty Aiken was.

III

Morty was a proud boy on the night he graduated from grammar school in June, 1919. When he received his diploma, there was more applause in the auditorium than there was for any other member of the class. He felt good when he heard this clapping, but, then, he expected it. He lived in a world where he was somebody, and he was going into a bigger world where he would still be somebody. He was fine, clean-looking lad, with dark hair, frank blue eyes, regular and friendly features. He was thin but strong. He wore a blue serge suit with short trousers and a belted jacket, and a white shirt with a white bow tie. His class colors, orange and black ribbons, were pinned on the lapel of his coat. He was scrubbed and washed and combed. And he was in the midst of an atmosphere of gaiety and friendliness. The teachers were happy. There were proud and happy parents and aunts and uncles and older sisters. The local alderman made a speech praising everybody, and speaking of the graduating boys and girls as fine future Americans. And he declared that in their midst there were many promising lads and lassies who would live to enjoy great esteem and success. He also said that among this group there was also one who not only promised to become a stellar athlete but who had already won gold medals and honors.

And on that night, Morty's father and mother were very happy. They kept beaming with proud smiles. Morty was their only son. Mr. Aiken was a carpenter. He worked steadily, and he had saved his money so that the house he owned was now paid for. He and his wife were quiet-living people who minded their own business. Mr. Aiken was tall and rugged, with swarthy skin, a rough-hewn face, and the look and manner of a workman. He was a gentle but firm man, and was inarticulate with his son. He believed that a boy should have a good time in sports, should fight his own battles, and that boyhood—the best time of one's life—should be filled with happy memories.

The mother was faded and maternal. She usually had little to say; her life was dedicated to caring for her son and her husband and to keeping their home clean and orderly. She was especially happy to know that Morty liked running and skating, because these were not dangerous.

After the graduation ceremonies the father and mother took Morty home where they had cake and ice cream. The three of them sat together eating these refreshments, quiet but happy. The two parents were deeply moved. They were filled with gratification because of the applause given their son when he had walked forward on the stage to receive his diploma. They were raising a fine boy, and they could look people in the neighborhood in the eye and know that they had done their duty as parents. The father was putting money by for Morty's college education and hoped that, besides becoming a famous runner, Morty would become a professional man. He talked of this to the son and the mother over their ice cream and cake, and the boy seemed to accept his father's plans. And as the father gazed shyly at Morty he thought of his own boyhood on a Wisconsin farm, and of long summer days there. Morty had the whole summer before him. He would play and grow and enjoy himself. He was not a bad boy, he had never gotten into trouble, he wasn't the kind of boy who caused worry. It was fine. In August there would be his vacation, and they would all go to Wisconsin, and he would go fishing with the boy.

That evening Morty's parents went to bed feeling that this was the happiest day of their lives.

And Morty went to bed, a happy, light-hearted boy, thinking of the summer vacation which had now begun.

IV

The days passed. Some days were better than others. Some days there was little to do, and on other days there was a lot to do. Morty guessed that this was turning out to be as good as any summer he could remember.

Tony Rabuski was working, delivering flowers for a flower merchant, but he sometimes came around after supper, and the kids sat talking or playing on the steps of Morty's house or of another house in the neighborhood. Morty liked to play Run, Sheep, Run, because it gave him a chance to run, and he also liked hiding and searching and hearing the signals called out, and the excitement and tingling and fun when he'd be hiding, perhaps under some porch, and the other side would be near, maybe even passing right by, and he, and the other kids with him, would have to be so still, and he'd even try to hold his breath, and then finally, the signal for which he had been waiting—Run, Sheep, Run—and the race, setting off, tearing away along sidewalks and across streets, running like hell and like a streak of lightning and feeling your speed in your legs and muscles and getting to the goal first.

The summer was going by and it was fun. There wasn't anything to worry about and there were dreams. Edna Purcell, who had been in his class, seemed sweet on him, and she was a wonderful girl. One night she and some other girls came around, and they sat on the steps of Morty's house and played Tin-Tin. Morty had to kiss her. He did, with the kids laughing, and it seemed that something happened to him. He hadn't been shy when he was with girls, but now, when Edna was around, he would be shy. She was wonderful. She was more than wonderful. When he did have the courage to talk to her, he talked about running and iceskating. She told him she knew what a runner and skater he was. A fast skater, such as he was, wouldn't want to think of skating with someone like her. He said that he would, and that next winter he would teach her to skate better. Immediately, he found himself wishing it were next winter already, and he would imagine himself skating with her, and he could see them walking over to the Washington Park lagoon and coming home again. He would carry her skates, and when they breathed they would be able to see their breaths, and the weather would be cold and sharp and would make her red cheeks redder, and they would be alone, walking home, with the snow packed on the park, alone, the two of them walking in the park, with it quiet, so quiet that you would hear nothing, and it would be like they were in another world, and then, there in the quiet park, with white snow all over it, he would kiss Edna Purcell. He had kissed Edna when they'd played Tin-Tin, and Post Office, but he looked forward to the day that he got from her the kiss that would mean that she was his girl, his sweetheart, and the girl who would one day be his wife just like his mother was his father's wife. Everything he dreamed of doing, all the honors he would get, all the medals and cups he dreamed of winning—now all of this would be for Edna. And she was also going to Park High. He would walk to school with her, eat lunch with her, walk her home from school. When he ran in high-school track meets for Park High, Edna would be in the stands. He would give her his medals. He wanted to give her one of his gold skating medals, but he didn't know how to go about asking her to accept it.

No matter what Morty thought about, he thought about Edna at the same time. He thought about her every time he dreamed. When he walked on streets in the neighborhood, he thought of her. When he went to Washington Park or swimming, he thought of Edna. Edna, just to think of her, Edna made everything in the world wonderfully wonderful.

And thus the summer of 1919 was passing for Morty.

V

Morty sat on the curb with a group of boys, and they were bored and restless. They couldn't agree about what game to play, where to go, what to do to amuse themselves. A couple of them started to play Knife but gave it up. Morty suggested a race, but no one would race him. They couldn't agree on playing ball. One boy suggested swimming, but no one would go with him. Several of the boys wrestled, and a fight almost started. Morty sat by himself and thought about Edna. He guessed that he'd rather be with her than with the kids. He didn't know where she was. If he knew that she'd gone swimming, he'd go swimming. He didn't know what to do with himself. If he only could find Edna and if they would do something together, or go somewhere, like Jackson Park Beach, just the two of them, why, then, he knew that today would be the day that he would find a way of giving her one of his *Clarion* gold medals. But he didn't know where she was.

Tony Rabuski came around with four tough-looking kids. Tony had lost his job, and he said that the niggers had jumped him when he was delivering flowers down around Forty-seventh Street, and he wanted his pals to stick by him. He told them what had happened, but they didn't get it, because Tony couldn't tell a story straight. Tony asked them didn't they know what was happening? There were race riots, and the beaches and Washington Park and the whole South Side were full of dark clouds, and over on Wentworth Avenue the big guys were fighting, and the dark clouds were out after whites. They didn't believe Tony. But Morty said it was in the newspapers, and that there were race riots. The bored boys became excited. They bragged about what they would do if the jigs came over to their neighborhood. Tony said they had to get some before they got this far. When asked where they were, Tony said all over. Finally, they went over to Washington Park, picking up sticks and clubs and rocks on the way. The park was calm. A few adults were walking and strolling about. A lad of eighteen or nineteen lay under a tree with his head in the lap of a girl who was stroking his hair. Some of the kids smirked and leered as they passed the couple. Morty thought of Edna and wished he could take her to Washington Park and kiss her. There were seven or eight rowboats on the lagoon, but all of the occupants were white. The park sheep were grazing. Tony threw a rock at them, frightening the sheep, and they all ran, but no cop was around to shag them. They passed the boathouse, talking and bragging. They now believed the rumors which they themselves had made up. White girls and women were in danger, and anything might happen. A tall lad sat in the grass with a nursemaid. A baby carriage was near them. The lad called them over and asked them what they were doing with their clubs and rocks. Tony said they were looking for niggers. The lad said that he'd seen two near the goldfish pond and urged the boys to go and get the sonsofbitches. Screaming and shouting, they ran to the goldfish pond. Suddenly, Tony shouted:

"Dark clouds."

VI

They ran. Two Negro boys, near the goldfish pond, heard Tony's cry, and then the others' cry, and they ran. The mob of boys chased them. Morty was in the lead. Running at the head of the screaming, angry pack of boys, he forgot everything except how well and how fast he was running, and images of Edna flashed in and out of his mind. If she could see him running! He was running beautifully. He'd catch them. He was gaining. The colored boys ran in a northwest direction. They crossed the drive which flanked the southern end of the Washington Park ball field. Morty was stopped by a funeral procession. The other boys caught up with him. When the funeral procession passed, it was too late to try and catch the colored boys they had been chasing. Angry, bragging, they crossed over to the ball field and marched across it, shouting and yelling. They picked up about eight boys of their own age and three older lads of seventeen or eighteen. The older lads said they knew where they'd find some shines. Now was the time to teach them their place once and for all. Led by the older boys, they emerged from the north end of Washington Park and marched down Grand Boulevard, still picking up men and boys as they went along. One of the men who joined them had a gun. They screamed, looked in doorways for Negroes, believed everything anyone said about Negroes, and kept boasting about what they would do when they found some.

"Dark clouds," Tony boomed.

The mob let out. They crossed to the other side of Grand Boulevard and ran cursing and shouting after a Negro. Morty was in the lead. He was outrunning the men and the older fellows. He heard them shouting behind him. He was running. He was running like the playground hundred-yard champion of the South Side of Chicago. He was running like the future Olympic champion. He was running like he'd run for Edna. He was tearing along, pivoting out of the way of shocked, surprised pedestrians, running, really running. He was running like a streak of lightning.

The Negro turned east on Forty-eighth Street. He had a start of a block. But Morty would catch him. He turned into Forty-eighth Street. He tore along the center of the street. He began to breathe heavily. But he couldn't stop running now. He was outdistancing the gang, and he was racing his own gang and the Negro he was chasing. Down the center of the street and about half a block ahead of him, the Negro was tearing away for dear life. But Morty was gaining on him. Gaining. He was now about a half a block ahead of his own gang. They screamed murderously behind him. And they encouraged him. He heard shouts of encouragement.

"Catch 'em, Morty boy!"

"Thata boy, Morty boy!"

He heard Tony's voice. He ran.

The Negro turned into an alley just east of Forestville. Morty ran. He turned into the alley just in time to see the fleeing Negro spurt into a yard in the center of the block. He'd gained more. He was way ahead of the white mob. Somewhere behind him they were coming and yelling. He tore on. He had gained his second wind. He felt himself running, felt the movement of his legs and muscles, felt his arms, felt the sensation of his whole body as he raced down the alley. Never had he run so swiftly. Suddenly Negroes jumped out of yards. He was caught and pinioned. His only thought was one of surprise. Before he ever realized what had happened, his throat was slashed. He fell, bleeding. Feebly, he mumbled just once:

"Mother!"

The Negroes disappeared.

He lay bleeding in the center of the dirty alley, and when the gang of whites caught up with him they found him dead in dirt and his own blood in the center of the alley. No Negroes were in sight. The whites surrounded his body. The boys trembled with fear. Some of them cried. One wet his pants. Then they became maddened. And they stood in impotent rage around the bleeding, limp body of Morty Aiken, the fastest runner on Sixty-first Street.

THE PATENTED GATE AND THE MEAN HAMBURGER
Robert Penn Warren

You have seen him a thousand times. You have seen him standing on the street corner on Saturday afternoon, in the little county-seat towns. He wears blue jean pants, or overalls washed to a pale pastel blue like the color of sky after a shower in spring, but because it is Saturday he has on a wool coat, an old one, perhaps the coat left from the suit he got married in a long time back. His long wrist bones hang out from the sleeves of the coat, the tendons showing along the bone like the dry twist of grapevine still corded on the stove-length of a hickory sapling you would find in his wood box beside his cookstove among the split chunks of gum and red oak. The big hands, with the knotted, cracked joints and the square, horn-thick nails, hang loose off the wrist bone like clumsy, homemade tools hung on the wall of a shed after work. If it is summer, he wears a straw hat with a wide brim, the straw fraying loose around the edge. If it is winter, he wears a felt hat, black once, but now weathered with streaks of dark gray and dull purple in the sunlight. His face is long and bony, the jawbone long under the drawn-in cheeks. The flesh along the jawbone is nicked in a couple of places where the unaccustomed razor has been drawn over the leather-coarse skin. A tiny bit of blood crusts brown where the nick is. The color of the face is red, a dull red like the red clay mud or clay dust which clings to the bottom of his pants and to the cast-iron-looking brogans on his feet, or a red like the color of a piece of hewed cedar which has been left in the weather. The face does not look alive. It seems to be molded from the clay or hewed from the cedar. When the jaw moves, once, with its deliberate, massive motion on the quid of tobacco, you are still not convinced. That motion is but the cunning triumph of a mechanism concealed within.

But you see the eyes. You see that the eyes are alive. They are pale blue or gray, set back under the deep brows and thorny eyebrows. They are not wide, but are squinched up like eyes accustomed to wind or sun or to measuring the stroke of an ax or to fixing the object over the rifle sights. When you pass, you see that the eyes are alive and are warily and dispassionately estimating you from the ambush of the thorny brows. Then you pass on, and he stands there in that stillness which is his gift.

With him may be standing two or three others like himself, but they are still, too. They do not talk. The young men, who will be like these men when they get to be fifty or sixty, are down at the beer parlor, carousing and laughing with a high, whickering laugh. But the men on the corner are long past all that. They are past many things. They have endured and will endure in their silence and wisdom. They will stand on the street corner and reject the world which passes under their level gaze as a rabble passes under the guns of a rocky citadel around whose base a slatternly town has assembled.

I had seen Jeff York a thousand times, or near, standing like that on the street corner in town, while the people flowed past him, under the distant and wary and dispassionate eyes in ambush. He would be waiting for his wife and the three towheaded children who were walking around the town looking into store windows and at the people. After a while they would come back to him, and then, wordlessly, he would lead them to the store where they always did their trading. He would go first, marching with a steady bent-kneed stride, setting the cast-iron brogans down deliberately on the cement; then his wife, a small woman with covert, sidewise, curious glances for the world, would follow, and behind her the towheads bunched together in a dazed, glory-struck way. In the store, when their turn came, Jeff York would move to the counter, accept the clerk's greeting, and then bend down from his height to catch the whispered directions of his wife. He would straighten up and say, "Gimme a sack of flahr, if'n you please." Then when the sack of flour had been brought, he would lean again to his wife for the next item. When the stuff had all been bought and paid for with the grease-thick, wadded dollar bills which he took from an old leather coin purse with a metal catch to it, he would heave it all together into his arms and march out, his wife and towheads behind him and his eyes fixed level over the heads of the crowd. He would march down the street and around to the hitching lot where the wagons were, and put his stuff into his wagon and cover it with an old quilt to wait till he got ready to drive out to his place.

For Jeff York had a place. That was what made him different from the other men who looked like him and with whom he stood on the street corner on Saturday afternoon. They were croppers,[1] but he, Jeff York, had a place. But he stood with them because his father had stood with their fathers and his grandfathers with their grandfathers, or with men like their fathers and grandfathers, in other towns, in settlements in the mountains, in towns beyond the mountains. They were the great-great-great-grandsons of men who, half woodsmen and half farmers, had been shoved into the sand hills, into the limestone hills, into the barrens, two hundred, two hundred and fifty years before and had learned there the way to grabble a life out of the sand and the stone. And when the soil had leached away into the sand or burnt off the stone, they went on west, walking with the bent-kneed stride over the mountains, their eyes squinched warily in the gaunt faces, the rifle over the crooked arm, hunting a new place.

---

1. Sharecroppers: farm tenants who pay a designated share of the crop as rent.

But there was a curse on them. They only knew the life they knew, and that life did not belong to the fat bottom lands, where the cane was head-tall, and to the grassy meadows and the rich swale. So they passed those places by and hunted for the place which was like home and where they could pick up the old life, with the same feel in the bones and the squirrel's bark sounding the same after first light. They had walked a long way, to the sand hills of Alabama, to the red country of North Mississippi and Louisiana, to the Barrens of Tennessee, to the Knobs of Kentucky and the scrub country of West Kentucky, to the Ozarks. Some of them had stopped in Cobb County, Tennessee, in the hilly eastern part of the county, and had built their cabins and dug up the ground for the corn patch. But the land had washed away there, too, and in the end they had come down out of the high land into the bottoms—for half of Cobb County is a rich, swelling country—where the corn was good and the tobacco unfurled a leaf like a yard of green velvet and the white houses stood among the cedars and tulip trees and maples. But they were not to live in the white houses with the limestone chimneys set strong at the end of each gable. No, they were to live in the shacks on the back of the farms, or in cabins not much different from the cabins they had once lived in two hundred years before over the mountains or, later, in the hills of Cobb County. But the shacks and the cabins now stood on somebody else's ground, and the curse which they had brought with them over the mountain trail, more precious than the bullet mold or grandma's quilt, the curse which was the very feeling in the bones and the habit in the hand, had come full circle.

Jeff York was one of those men, but he had broken the curse. It had taken him more than thirty years to do it, from the time when he was nothing but a big boy until he was fifty. It had taken him from sun to sun, year in and year out, and all the sweat in his body, and all the power of rejection he could muster, until the very act of rejection had become a kind of pleasure, a dark, secret, savage dissipation, like an obsessing vice. But those years had given him his place, sixty acres with a house and barn.

When he bought the place, it was not very good. The land was run-down from years of neglect and abuse. But Jeff York put brush in the gullies to stop the wash and planted clover on the run-down fields. He mended the fences, rod by rod. He patched the roof on the little house and propped up the porch, buying the lumber and shingles almost piece by piece and one by one as he could spare the sweat-bright and grease-slick quarters and half-dollars out of his leather purse. Then he painted the house. He painted it white, for he knew that that was the color you painted a house sitting back from the road with its couple of maples, beyond the clover field.

Last, he put up the gate. It was a patented gate, the kind you can ride up to and open by pulling on a pull rope without getting off your horse or out of your buggy or wagon. It had a high pair of posts, well braced and with a high cross-bar between, and the bars for the opening mechanism extending on each side. It was painted white, too. Jeff was even prouder of the gate than he was of the place. Lewis Simmons, who lived next to Jeff's place, swore he had seen Jeff come out after dark on a mule and ride in and out of that gate, back and forth, just for the pleasure of pulling on the rope and making the mechanism work. The gate was the seal Jeff York had put on all the years of sweat and rejection. He could sit on his porch on a Sunday afternoon in summer, before milking time, and look down the rise, down the winding dirt track, to the white gate beyond the clover, and know what he needed to know about all the years passed.

Meanwhile Jeff York had married and had had the three towheads. His wife was twenty years or so younger than he, a small, dark woman, who walked with her head bowed a little and from that humble and unprovoking posture stole sidewise, secret glances at the world from eyes which were brown or black—you never could tell which because you never remembered having looked her straight in the eye—and which were surprisingly bright in that sidewise, secret flicker, like the eyes of a small, cunning bird which surprise you from the brush. When they came to town she moved along the street, with a child in her arms or later with the three trailing behind her, and stole her looks at the world. She wore a calico dress, dun-colored, which hung loose to conceal whatever shape her thin body had, and in winter over the dress a brown wool coat with a scrap of fur at the collar which looked like some tattered growth of fungus feeding on old wood. She wore black high-heeled shoes, slippers of some kind, which she kept polished and which surprised you under that dress and coat. In the slippers she moved with a slightly limping, stealthy gait, almost sliding them along the pavement, as though she had not fully mastered the complicated trick required to use them properly. You knew that she wore them only when she came to town, that she carried them wrapped up in a piece of newspaper until their wagon had reached the first house on the outskirts ot town, and that, on the way back, at the same point, she would take them off and wrap them up again and hold the bundle in her lap until she got home. If the weather happened to be bad, or if it was winter, she would have a pair of old brogans under the wagon seat.

It was not that Jeff York was a hard man and kept his wife in clothes that were as bad as those worn by the poorest of the women of the croppers. In fact, some of cropper women, poor or not, black or white, managed to buy dresses with some color in them and proper hats, and went to the moving picture show on Saturday afternoon. But Jeff still owed a little money on his place, less than two hundred dollars, which he had had to borrow to rebuild his barn after it was struck by lightning. He had, in fact, never been entirely out of debt. He had lost a mule which had got out on the highway and been hit by a truck. That had set him back. One of his towheads had been sickly for a couple of winters. He had not been in deep, but he was not a man, with all those years of rejection behind him, to forget the meaning of those years. He was good enough to his family. Nobody ever said the contrary. But he was good to them in terms of all the years he had lived through. He did what he could afford. He bought the towheads a ten-cent bag of colored candy every Saturday afternoon for them to suck on during the ride home in the wagon, and the last thing before they left town, he always took the lot of them over to the dogwagon to get hamburgers and orange pop.

The towheads were crazy about hamburgers. And so was his wife, for that matter. You could tell it, even if she didn't say anything, for she would lift her bowed-forward head a little, and her face would brighten, and she would run her tongue out to wet her lips just as the plate with the hamburger would be set on the counter before her. But all those folks, like Jeff York and his family, like hamburgers, with pickle and onions and mustard and tomato catsup, the whole works. It is something different. They stay out in the country and eat hog-meat, when they can get it, and greens and corn bread and potatoes, and nothing but a pinch of salt to brighten it on the tongue, and when they get to town and get hold of beef and wheat bread and all the stuff to jack up the flavor, they have to swallow to keep the mouth from flooding before they even take the first bite.

So the last thing every Saturday, Jeff York would take his family over to Slick Hardin's Dew Drop Inn Diner and give them the treat. The diner was built like a railway coach, but it was set on a concrete foundation on a lot just off the main street of town. At each end the concrete was painted to show wheels. Slick Hardin kept the grass just in front of the place pretty well mowed and one or two summers he even had a couple of flower beds in the middle of that shirttail-size lawn. Slick had a good business. For a few years he had been a prelim fighter over in Nashville and had got his name in the papers a few times. So he was a kind of hero, with the air of romance about him. He had been born, however, right in town and, as soon as he had found out he wasn't ever going to be good enough to be a real fighter, he had come back home and started the dogwagon, the first one ever in town. He was a slick-skinned fellow, about thirty-five, prematurely bald, with his head slick all over. He had big eyes, pale blue and slick looking like agates. When he said something that he thought smart, he would roll his eyes around, slick in his head like marbles, to see who was laughing. Then he'd wink. He had done very well with his business, for despite the fact that he had picked up city ways and a lot of city talk, he still remembered enough to deal with the country people, and they were the ones who brought the dimes in. People who lived right there in town, except for school kids in the afternoon and the young toughs from the pool room or men on the night shift down at the railroad, didn't often get around to the dogwagon.

Slick Hardin was perhaps trying to be smart when he said what he did to Mrs. York. Perhaps he had forgotten, just for that moment, that people like Jeff York and his wife didn't like to be kidded, at least not in that way. He said what he did, and then grinned and rolled his eyes around to see if some of the other people present were thinking it was funny.

Mrs. York was sitting on a stool in front of the counter, flanked on one side by Jeff York and on the other by the three towheads. She had just sat down to wait for the hamburger—there were several orders in ahead of the York order—and had been watching in her sidewise fashion every move of Slick Hardin's hands as he patted the pink meat onto the hot slab and wiped the split buns over the greasy iron to make them ready to receive it. She always watched him like that, and when the hamburger was set before her she would wet her lips with her tongue.

That day Slick set the hamburger down in front of Mrs. York and said, "Anybody likes hamburger much as you, Mrs. York, ought to git him a hamburger stand."

Mrs. York flushed up, and didn't say anything, staring at her plate. Slick rolled his eyes to see how it was going over, and somebody down the counter snickered. Slick looked back at the Yorks, and if he had not been so encouraged by the snicker he might, when he saw Jeff York's face, have hesitated before going on with his kidding. People like Jeff York are touchous, and they are especially touchous about the women-folks, and you do not make jokes with or about their women-folks unless it is perfectly plain that the joke is a very special kind of friendly joke. The snicker down the counter had defined the joke as not entirely friendly. Jeff was looking at Slick, and something was growing slowly in that hewed-cedar face, and back in the gray eyes in the ambush of thorny brows.

But Slick did not notice. The snicker had encouraged him, and so he said, "Yeah, if I liked them hamburgers much as you, I'd buy me a hamburger stand. Fact, I'm selling this one. You want to buy it?"

There was another snicker, louder, and Jeff York, whose hamburger had been about half way to his mouth for another bite, laid it down deliberately on his plate. But whatever might have happened at that moment did not happen. It did not happen because Mrs. York lifted her flushed face, looked straight at Slick Hardin, swallowed hard to get down a piece of hamburger or to master her nerve, and said in a sharp, strained voice, "You sellen this place?"

There was complete silence. Nobody had expected her to say anything. The chances were she had never said a word in that diner in the couple of hundred times she had been in it. She had come in with Jeff York and, when a stool had come vacant, had sat down, and Jeff had said, "Gimme five hamburgers, if'n you please, and make 'em well done, and five bottles of orange pop." Then, after the eating was over, he had always laid down seventy-five cents on the counter—that is, after there were five hamburger-eaters in the family—and walked out, putting his brogans down slow, and his wife and kids following without a word. But now she spoke up and asked the question, in that strained, artificial voice, and everybody, including her husband, looked at her with surprise.

As soon as he could take it in, Slick Hardin replied, "Yeah, I'm selling it."

She swallowed hard again, but this time it could not have been hamburger, and demanded, "What you asken fer hit?"

Slick looked at her in the new silence, half shrugged, a little contemptuously, and said, "Fourteen hundred and fifty dollars."

She looked back at him, while the blood ebbed from her face. "Hit's a lot of money," she said in a flat tone, and returned her gaze to the hamburger on her plate.

"Lady," Slick said defensively, "I got that much money tied up here. Look at that there stove. It is a Heat Master and they cost. Them coffee urns, now. Money can't buy no better. And this here lot, lady, the diner sets on. Anybody knows I got that much money tied up here. I got more. This lot cost me more'n . . ." He suddenly realized that she was not listening to him. And he must have realized, too, that she didn't have a dime in the world and couldn't buy his diner, and that he was making a fool of himself, defending his price. He stopped abruptly, shrugged his shoulders, and then swung his wide gaze down the counter to pick out somebody to wink to.

But before he got the wink off, Jeff York had said, "Mr. Hardin."

Slick looked at him and asked, "Yeah?"

"She didn't mean no harm," Jeff York said. "She didn't mean to be messen in yore business."

Slick shrugged. "Ain't no skin off my nose," he said. "Ain't no secret I'm selling out. My price ain't no secret neither."

Mrs. York bowed her head over her plate. She was chewing a mouthful of her hamburger with a slow, abstracted motion of her jaw, and you knew that it was flavorless on her tongue.

That was, of course, on a Saturday. On Thursday afternoon of the next week Slick was in the diner alone. It was the slack time, right in the middle of the afternoon. Slick, as he told it later, was wiping off the stove and wasn't noticing. He was sort of whistling to himself, he said. He had a way of whistling soft through his teeth. But he wasn't whistling loud, he said, not so loud he wouldn't have heard the door open or the steps if she hadn't come gum-shoeing in on him to stand there waiting in the middle of the floor until he turned round and was so surprised he nearly had heart failure. He had thought he was there alone, and there she was, watching every move he was making, like a cat watching a goldfish swim in a bowl.

"Howdy-do," he said, when he got his breath back.

"This place still fer sale?" she asked him.

"Yeah, lady," he said.

"What you asken fer hit?"

"Lady I done told you," Slick replied, "fourteen hundred and fifty dollars."

"Hit's a heap of money," she said.

Slick started to tell her how much money he had tied up there, but before he had got going, she had turned and slipped out of the door.

"Yeah," Slick said later to the men who came into the diner, "me like a fool starting to tell her how much money I got tied up here when I knowed she didn't have a dime. That woman's crazy. She must walked that five or six miles in here just to ask me something she already knowed the answer to. And then turned right round and walked out. But I am selling me this place. I'm tired of slinging hash to them hicks. I got me some connections over in Nashville and I'm gonna open me a place over there. A cigar stand and about three pool tables and maybe some beer. I'll have me a sort of club in the back. You know, membership cards to git in, where the boys will play a little game. Just sociable. I got good connections over in Nashville. I'm selling this place. But that woman, she ain't got a dime. She ain't gonna buy it."

But she did.

On Saturday Jeff York led his family over to the dinner. They ate hamburgers without a word and marched out. After they had gone, Slick said, "Looks like she ain't going to make the invest-mint. Gonna buy a block of bank stock instead." Then he rolled his eyes, located a brother down the counter, and winked.

It was almost the end of the next week before it happened. What had been going on inside the white house out on Jeff York's place nobody knew or was to know. Perhaps she just starved him out, just not doing the cooking or burning everything. Perhaps she just quit attending to the children properly and he had to come back tired from work and take care of them. Perhaps she just lay in bed at night and talked and talked to him, asking him to buy it, nagging him all night long, while he would fall asleep and then wake up with a start to hear her voice still going on. Or perhaps she just turned her face away from him and wouldn't let him touch her. He was a lot older than she, and she was probably the only woman he had ever had. He had been too ridden by his dream and his passion for rejection during all the years before to lay even a finger on a woman. So she had him there. Because he was a lot older and because he had never had another woman. But perhaps she used none of these methods. She was a small, dark, cunning woman, with a sidewise look from her lowered face, and she could have thought up ways of her own, no doubt.

Whatever she thought up, it worked. On Friday morning Jeff York went to the bank. He wanted to mortgage his place, he told Todd Sullivan, the president. He wanted fourteen hundred and fifty dollars, he said. Todd Sullivan would not let him have it. He already owed the bank one hundred and sixty dollars and the best he could get on a mortgage was eleven hundred dollars. That was in 1935 and then farmland wasn't worth much and half the land in the country was mortgaged anyway. Jeff York sat in the chair by Todd Sullivan's desk and didn't say anything. Eleven hundred dollars would not do him any good. Take off the hundred and sixty he owed and it wouldn't be but a little over nine hundred dollars clear to him. He sat there quietly for a minute, apparently turning that fact over in his head. Then Todd Sullivan asked him, "How much you say you need?"

Jeff York told him.

"What you want it for?" Todd Sullivan asked.

He told him that.

"I tell you," Todd Sullivan said, "I don't want to stand in the way of a man bettering himself. Never did. That diner ought to be a good proposition, all right, and I don't want to stand in your way if you want to come to town and better yourself. It will be a step up from that farm for you, and I like a man has got ambition. The bank can't lend you the money, not on that piece of property. But I tell you what I'll do. I'll buy your place. I got me some walking horses I'm keeping out on my father's place. But I could use me a little place of my own. For my horses. I'll give you seventeen hundred for it. Cash."

Jeff York did not say anything to that. He looked slow at Todd Sullivan as though he did not understand.

"Seventeen hundred," the banker repeated. "That's a good figure. For these times."

Jeff was not looking at him now. He was looking out the window, across the alleyway—Todd Sullivan's office was in the back of the bank. The banker, telling about it later when the doings of Jeff York had become for a moment a matter of interest, said, "I thought he hadn't even heard me. He looked like he was half asleep or something. I coughed to sort of wake him up. You know the way you do. I didn't want to rush him. You can't rush those people, you know. But I couldn't sit there all day. I had offered him a fair price."

It was, as a matter of fact, a fair price for the times, when the bottom was out of everything in the section.

Jeff York took it. He took the seventeen hundred dollars and bought the dogwagon with it, and rented a little house on the edge of town and moved in with his wife and the towheads. The first day after they got settled, Jeff

York and his wife went over to the diner to get instructions from Slick about running the place. He showed Mrs. York all about how to work the coffee machine and the stove, and how to make up the sandwiches, and how to clean the place up after herself. She fried up hamburgers for all of them, herself, her husband, and Slick Hardin, for practice, and they ate hamburgers while a couple of hangers-on watched them. "Lady," Slick said, for he had money in his pocket and was heading out for Nashville on the seven o'clock train that night, and was feeling expansive, "lady, you sure fling a mean hamburger."

He wiped the last crumbs and mustard off his lips, got his valise from behind the door, and said, "Lady, git in there and pitch. I hope you make a million hamburgers." Then he stepped out into the bright fall sunshine and walked away whistling up the street, whistling through his teeth and rolling his eyes as though there were somebody to wink to. That was the last anybody in town ever saw of Slick Hardin.

The next day, Jeff York worked all day down at the diner. He was scrubbing up the place inside and cleaning up the trash which had accumulated behind it. He burned all the trash. Then he gave the place a good coat of paint outside, white paint. That took him two days. Then he touched up the counter inside with varnish. He straightened up the sign out front, which had begun to sag a little. He had that place looking spick and span.

Then on the fifth day after they got settled—it was Sunday—he took a walk in the country. It was long toward sunset when he started out, not late, as a matter of fact, for by October the days are shortening up. He walked out the Curtisville pike and out the cut-off leading to his farm. When he entered the cut-off, about a mile from his own place, it was still light enough for the Bowdoins, who had a filling station at the corner, to see him plain when he passed.

The next time anybody saw him was on Monday morning about six o'clock. A man taking milk into town saw him. He was hanging from the main cross-bar of the white patented gate. He had jumped off the gate. But he had propped the thing open so there wouldn't be any chance of clambering back up on it if his neck didn't break when he jumped and he should happen to change his mind.

But that was an unnecessary precaution, as it developed. Dr. Stauffer said that his neck was broken very clean. "A man who can break a neck as clean as that could make a living at it," Dr. Stauffer said. And added, "If he's damned sure it ain't ever his own neck."

Mrs. York was much cut up by her husband's death. People were sympathetic and helpful, and out of a mixture of sympathy and curiosity she got a good starting trade at the diner. And the trade kept right on. She got so she didn't hang her head and look sidewise at you and the world. She would look straight at you. She got so she could walk in high heels without giving the impression that it was a trick she was learning. She wasn't a bad-looking woman, as a matter of fact, once she had caught on how to fix herself up a little. The railroad men and the pool hall gang liked to hang out there and kid with her. Also, they said, she flung a mean hamburger.

NIGGER JEFF
Theodore Dreiser

The city editor was waiting for his good reporter, Eugene Davies. He had cut an item from one of the afternoon papers and laid it aside to give to Mr. Davies. Presently the reporter appeared.

It was one o'clock of a sunny, spring afternoon. Davies wore a new spring suit, a new hat and new shoes. In the lapel of his coat was a small bunch of violets. He was feeling exceedingly well and good-natured. The world seemed worth singing about.

"Read that, Davies," said the city editor, handing him the clipping. "I'll tell you what I want you to do afterward."

The reporter stood by the editorial chair and read:

> "Pleasant Valley, Mo., April 16.
> "A most dastardly crime has just been reported here. Jeff Ingalls, a negro, this morning assaulted Ada Whittier, the nineteen-year-old daughter of Morgan Whittier, a well-to-do farmer, whose home is four miles south of this place. A posse, headed by Sheriff Mathews, has started in pursuit. If he is caught, it is thought he will be lynched."

The reporter raised his eyes as he finished.

"You had better go out there, Davies," said the city editor. "It looks as if something might come of that. A lynching up here would be a big thing."

Davies smiled. He was always pleased to be sent out of town. It was a mark of appreciation. The city editor never sent any of the other boys on these big stories. What a nice ride he would have.

He found Pleasant Valley to be a small town, nestling between green slopes of low hills, with one small business corner and a rambling array of lanes. One or two merchants of St. Louis lived out here, but otherwise it was exceedingly rural. He took note of the whiteness of the little houses, the shimmering beauty of the little creek you had to cross in going from the depot. At the one main corner a few men were gathered about a typical village barroom. Davies headed for this as being the most apparent source of information.

In mingling with the company, he said nothing about his errand. He was very shy about mentioning that he was a newspaper man.

The whole company was craving excitement and wanted to see something come of the matter. They hadn't had such a chance to work up wrath and satisfy their animal propensities in years. It was a fine opportunity and such a righteous one.

He went away thinking that he had best find out for himself how the girl was. Accordingly he sought the old man that kept a stable in the village and procured a horse. No carriage was to be had. Davies was not an excellent rider, but he made a shift of it. The farm was not so very far away, and before long he knocked at the front door of the house, set back a hundred feet from the rough country road.

"I'm from the *Republic*," he said, with dignity. His position took very well with farmers. "How is Miss Whittier?"

"She's doing very well," said a tall, raw-boned woman. "Won't you come in? She's rather feverish, but the doctor says she'll be all right."

Davies acknowledged the invitation by entering. He was anxious to see the girl, but she was sleeping, and under the influence of an opiate.

"When did this happen?" he asked.

"About eight o'clock this morning," said the woman. "She started off to go over to our next neighbor here, Mr. Edmonds, and this negro met her. I didn't know anything about it until she came crying through the gate and dropped down in here."

"Were you the first one to meet her?" asked Davies.

"Yes, I was the only one," said Mrs. Whittier. "The men had gone out in the fields."

Davies listened to more of the details, and then rose to go. He was allowed to have a look at the girl, who was rather pretty. In the yard he met a country chap who had come over to hear the news. This man imparted more information.

"They're lookin' all around south of here," said the man, speaking of the crowd supposed to be in search. "I expect they'll make short work of him if they get him."

"Where does this negro live?" asked Davies.

"Oh, right down here a little way. You follow this road to the next crossing and turn to the right. It's a little log house that sits back off the road—something like this, only it's got a lot of chips scattered about."

Davies decided to go there, but changed his mind. It was getting late. He had better return to the village, he thought.

Accordingly, he rode back and put the horse in the hands of its owner. Then he went over to the principal corner. Much the same company was still present. He wondered what these people had been doing all the time. He decided to ingratiate himself by imparting a little information.

Just then a young fellow came galloping up.

"They've got him," he shouted, excitedly, "they've got him."

A chorus of "whos" and "wheres," with sundry other queries, greeted this information as the crowd gathered about the rider.

"Why, Mathews caught him up here at his own house. Says he'll shoot the first man that dares to try to take him away. He's taking him over to Clayton."

"Which way'd he go?" exclaimed the men.

"Cross Sellers' Lane," said the rider. "The boys think he's going to Baldwin."

"Whoopee," yelled one of the listeners. "Are you going, Sam?"

"You bet," said the latter. "Wait'll I get my horse."

Davies waited no longer. He saw the crowd would be off in a minute to catch up with the sheriff. There would be information in that quarter. He hastened after his horse.

"He's eating," said the man.

"I don't care," exclaimed Davies. "Turn him out. I'll give you a dollar more."

The man led the horse out, and the reporter mounted.

When he got back to the corner several of the men were already there. The young man who had brought the news had dashed off again.

Davies waited to see which road they would take. Then he did the riding of his life.

In an hour the company had come in sight of the sheriff, who, with two other men, was driving a wagon he had borrowed. He had a revolver in each hand and was sitting with his face toward the group, that trailed after at a respectful distance. Excited as every one was, there was no disposition to halt the progress of the law.

"He's in that wagon," Davies heard one man say. "Don't you see they've got him tied and laid down in there?"

Davies looked.

"We ought to take him away and hang him," said one of the young fellows who rode nearest the front.

"Where's old man Whittier?" asked one of the crowd, who felt that they needed a leader.

"He's out with the other crowd," was the reply.

"Somebody ought to go and tell him."

"Clark's gone," assured another, who hoped for the worst.

Davies rode among the company very much excited. He was astonished at the character of the crowd. It was largely impelled to its excited jaunt by curiosity and a desire to see what would happen There was not much daring in it. The men were afraid of the determined sheriff. They thought something ought to be done, but they did not feel like getting into trouble.

The sheriff, a sage, lusty, solemn man, contemplated the recent addition to these trailers with considerable feeling. He was determined to protect his man and avoid injustice. A mob should not have him if he had to shoot, and if he shot, he was going to empty both revolvers, and those of his companions. Finally, since the company thus added to did not dash upon him, he decided to scare them off. He thought he could do it since they trailed like calves.

"Stop a minute," he said to his driver.

The latter pulled up. So did the crowd behind. Then the sheriff stood over the prostrate body of the negro, who lay trembling in the jolting wagon bed and called back to the men.

"Go on away from here, you people," he said. "Go on, now. I won't have you foller after me."

"Give us the nigger," yelled one in a half-bantering, half-derisive tone of voice.

"I'll give you five minutes to go on back out of this road," returned the sheriff grimly. They were about a hundred feet apart.

"If you don't, I'll clear you out."

"Give us the nigger!"

"I know you, Scott," answered the sheriff, recognizing the voice. "I'll arrest every last one of you tomorrow. Mark my word!"

The company listened in silence, the horses champing and twisting.

"We've got a right to follow," answered one of the men.

"I give you fair warning," said the sheriff, jumping from his wagon and leveling his pistols as he approached. "When I count five, I'll begin to shoot."

He was a serious and stalwart figure as he approached, and the crowd retreated.

"Get out o' this now," he yelled. "One, two—"

The company turned completely and retreated.

"We'll follow him when he gets farther on," said one of the men in explanation.

"He's got to do it," said another. "Let him get a little ahead."

The sheriff returned to his wagon and drove on. He knew that he would not be obeyed, and that safety lay in haste alone. If he could only make them lose track of him and get a good start it might be possible to get to Clayton and the strong county jail by morning.

Accordingly he whipped up his horses while keeping his grim lookout.

"He's going to Baldwin," said one of the company of which Davies was a member.

"Where is that?" asked Davies.

"Over west of here, about four miles."

The men lagged, hesitating what to do. They did not want to lose sight of him, and yet cowardice controlled them. They did not want to get into direct altercation with the law. It wasn't their place to hang the man, although he ought to be hanged and it would be a stirring and exciting thing if he were. Consequently, they desired to watch and be on hand—to get old Whittier and his son Jake if they could, who were out looking elsewhere. They wanted to see what the father and brother would do.

The quandary was solved by Dick Hewlitt, who suggested that they could get to Baldwin by going back to Pleasant Valley and taking the Sand River pike. It was a shorter cut than this. Maybe they could beat the sheriff there. Accordingly, while one or two remained to track the sheriff, the rest set off at a gallop to Pleasant Valley. It was nearly dusk when they got there and stopped for a few minutes at the corner store. Here they talked, and somehow the zest to follow departed; they were not certain now of going on. It was supper time. The fires of evening meals were marked by upcurling smoke. Evidently the sheriff had them worsted for tonight. Morg Whittier had not been found. Neither had Jake. Perhaps they had better eat. Two or three had already secretly fallen away.

They were telling the news to the one or two storekeepers, when Jake Whittier, the girl's brother, and several companions came riding up. They had been scouring the territory to the north of the town.

"The sheriff's got him," said one of the company. "He's taking him over to Baldwin in a wagon."

"Which way did he go?" asked young Jake, whose hardy figure, worn, hand-me-down clothes and rakish hat showed up picturesquely as he turned on his horse.

" 'Cross Seller's Lane. You won't get him that way. Better take the short cut."

A babble of voices was making the little corner interesting. One told how he had been caught, another that the sheriff was defiant, a third that men were tracking him, until the chief points of the drama had been spoken, if not heard.

"Come on, boys," said Jake, jerking at the reins and heading up the pike. "I'll get the damn nigger."

Instantly suppers were forgotten. The whole customary order of the evening was neglected. The company started off on another exciting jaunt, up hill and down dale, through the lovely country that lay between Baldwin and Pleasant Valley.

Davies was very weary of his saddle. He wondered when he was to write his story. The night was exceedingly beautiful. Stars were already beginning to shine. Distant lamps twinkled like yellow eyes from the cottages in the valleys on the hillsides. The air was fresh and tender. Some pea fowls were crying afar off and the east promised a golden moon.

Silently the assembled company trotted on—no more than a score in all. It was too grim a pilgrimage for joking. Young Jake, riding silently toward the front, looked as if he meant business. His friends did not like to say anything to him, seeing that he was the aggrieved. He was left alone.

After an hour's riding Baldwin came into view, lying in a sheltering cup of low hills. Its lights were twinkling softly, and there was an air of honest firesides and cheery suppers about it which appealed to Davies in his hungry state. Still, he had no thought but of carrying out his mission.

Once in the village they were greeted by calls of recognition. Everybody knew what they had come for. The local storekeepers and loungers followed the cavalcade up the street to the sherriff's house, for the riders had now fallen into a solemn walk.

"You won't get him, boys," said Seavey, the young postmaster and telegraph operator, as they passed his door. "Mathews says he's sent him to Clayton."

At the first street corner they were joined by several men who had followed the sheriff.

"He tried to give us the slip," they said, excitedly, "but he's got the nigger in the house there, down in the cellar."

"How do you know?"

"I saw him bring him in this way. I think he is, anyhow."

A block from the sheriff's little white cottage the men parleyed. They decided to go up and demand the negro.

"If he don't turn him out, we'll break in the door and take him," said Jake.

"That's right. We'll stand by you, Whittier."

A throng had gathered. The whole village was up in arms. The one street was alive and running with people. Riders pranced up and down, hallooing. A few shot off revolvers. Presently the mob gathered about the sheriff's gate, and Jake stepped forward as leader.

Their coming was not unexpected. Sheriff Mathews was ready for them with a double-barreled Winchester. He had bolted the doors and put the negro in the cellar, pending the arrival of the aid he had telegraphed for to Clayton. The latter was cowering and chattering in the darkest corner of his dungeon against the cold, damp earth, as he hearkened to the voices and the firing of the revolvers. With wide, bulging eyes, he stared into the gloom.

Jake, the son and brother, took the precautionary method of calling to the sheriff.

"Hello, Mathews!"

"Eh, eh, eh," bellowed the crowd.

Suddenly the door flew open, and appearing first in the glow of the lamp came the double barrel of a Winchester, followed by the form of the sheriff, who held his gun ready for a quick throw to the shoulder. All except Jake fell back.

"We want that nigger," said Jake, deliberately.

"He isn't here," said the sheriff.

"Then what you got that gun for?" yelled a voice.

The sheriff made no answer.

"Better give him up, Mathews," called another, who was safe in the crowd, "or we'll come in and take him."

"Lookee here, gentlemen," said the sheriff, "I said the man wasn't here. I say it again. You couldn't have him if he was and you can't come in my house. Now, if you people don't want trouble, you'd better go on away."

"He's down in the cellar," yelled another.

The sheriff waved his gun slightly.

"Why don't you let us see?" said another.

"You'd better go away from here now," cautioned the sheriff.

The crowd continued to simmer and stew, while Jake stood out before. He was very pale and determined, but lacked initiative.

"He won't shoot. Why don't you go in, boys, and get him?"

"He won't, eh?" thought the sheriff. Then he said aloud: "The first man that comes inside that gate takes the consequences."

No one ventured near the gate. It seemed as if the planned assault must come to nothing.

"You'd better go away from here," cautioned the sheriff again. "You can't come in, it'll only mean bloodshed."

There was more chattering and jesting while the sheriff stood on guard. He said no more. Nor did he allow the banter, turmoil and lust for tragedy to disturb him. Only he kept his eye on Jake, on whose movements the crowd hung.

"I'll get him," said Jake, "before morning."

The truth was that he felt the weakness of the crowd. He was, to all intents and purposes, alone, for he did not inspire confidence.

Thus the minutes passed. It became a half hour and then an hour. With the extending time pedestrians dropped out and then horsemen. Some went up the street, several back to Pleasant Valley, more galloped about until there were very few left at the gate. It was plain that organization was lost. Finally Davies smiled and came away. He was sure he had a splendid story.

He began to look for something to eat, and hunted for the telegraph operator.

He found the operator first and told him he wanted to write a story and file it. The latter said there was a table in the little post-office and telegraph station which he could use. He got very much interested in Davies, and when he asked where he could get something to eat, said he would run across the street and tell the proprietor of the only boarding-house to fix him something which he could eat as he wrote.

"You start your story," he said, "and I'll come back and see if I can get the *Republic*."

Davies sat down and started the account.

"Very obliging postmaster," he thought, but he had so often encountered pleasant and obliging people on his rounds, that he soon dropped that thought.

The food was brought and Davies wrote. By eight-thirty the *Republic* answered an often-repeated call.

"Davies at Baldwin," ticked the postmaster, "get ready for quite a story."

"Let 'er go," answered the operator in the *Republic,* who had been expecting this dispatch.

Davies turned over page after page as the events of the day formulated themselves in his mind. He ate a little between whiles, looking out through the smalll windows before him, where afar off he could see a lonely light twinkling in a hillside cottage. Not infrequently he stopped work to see if anything new was happening. The operator also wandered about, waiting for an accumulation of pages upon which he could work, but making sure to catch up with the writer. The two became quite friendly.

Davies finished his dispatch with the caution that more might follow, and was told by the city editor to watch it. Then he and the postmaster sat down to talk.

About twelve o'clock the lights in all the village houses had vanished and the inhabitants had gone to bed. The man-hunters had retired, and the night was left to its own sounds and murmurs, when suddenly the faint beating of hoofs sounded out on the Sand River Pike, which led away toward Pleasant Valley, back of the post-office. The sheriff had not relaxed any of his vigilance. He was not sleeping. There was no sleep for him until the county authorities should come to his aid.

"Here they come back again," exclaimed the postmaster.

"By George, you're right," said Davies.

There was a clattering of hoofs and grunting of saddle girths as a large company of men dashed up the road and turned into the narrow street of the village.

Instantly the place was astir again. Lights appeared in doorways, and windows were thrown open. People were gazing out to see what new movement was afoot. Davis saw that there was none of the hip and hurrah business about this company such as had characterized the previous descent. There was grimness everywhere, and he began to feel that this was the beginning of the end. He ran down the street toward the sheriff's house, arriving a few moments after the crowd, which was in part dismounted.

With the clear moon shining straight overhead, it was nearly as bright as day. Davies made out several of his companions of the afternoon and Jake, the son. There were many more, though, whom he did not know, and foremost among them an old man. He was strong, iron-gray and wore a full beard. He looked very much like a blacksmith.

While he was still looking, the old man went boldly forward to the little front porch of the house and knocked at the door. Some one lifted a curtain at the window and peeped out.

"Hello, in there," the old man cried, knocking again and much louder.

"What do you want?" said a voice.

"We want that nigger."

"Well, you can't have him. I've told you people once."

"Bring him out or we'll break down the door," said the old man.

"If you do, it's at your own risk. I'll give you three minutes to get off that porch."

"We want that nigger."

"If you don't get off that porch I'll fire through the door," said the voice, solemnly. "One, two—"

The old man backed cautiously away.

"Come out, Mathews," yelled the crowd. "You've got to give him up. We ain't going back without him."

Slowly the door opened, as if the individual within was very well satisfied as to his power to handle the mob. It revealed the tall form of Sheriff Mathews, armed with his Winchester. He looked around very stolidly and then addressed the old man as one would a friend.

"You can't have him, Morgan," he said, "it's against the law."

"Law or no law," said the old man, "I want that nigger."

"I can't let you have him, Morgan. It's against the law. You oughtn't to be coming around here at this time of night acting so."

"Well, we'll take him, then," said the old man, making a move.

The sheriff leveled his gun on the instant.

"Stand back, there," he shouted, noticing a movement on the part of the crowd. "I'll blow ye into kingdom come, sure as hell."

The crowd halted at this assurance.

The sheriff lowered his weapon as if he thought the danger were over.

"You all ought to be ashamed of yourselves," he said, softly, his voice sinking to a gentle, neighborly reproof, "tryin' to upset the law that way."

"The nigger didn't upset the law, did he?" asked one, derisively.

The sheriff made no answer.

"Give us that scoundrel, Mathews, you'd better do it," said the old man. "It'll save a heap of trouble."

"I'll not argue with you, Morgan. I said you couldn't have him, and you can't. If you want bloodshed, all right. But don't blame me. I'll kill the first man that tries to make a move this way."

He shifted his gun handily and waited. The crowd stood outside his little fence murmuring.

Presently the old man retired and spoke to several leaders.

There was more murmuring, and then he came back to the dead line.

"We don't want to cause trouble, Mathews," he began, explanatively, moving his hand oratorically, "but we think you ought to see that it won't do you any good to stand out. We think that—"

Davies was watching young Jake, the son, whose peculiar attitude attracted his attention. The latter was standing poised at the edge of the crowd, evidently seeking to remain unobserved. His eyes were on the sheriff, who was hearkening to the old man. Suddenly, when the sheriff seemed for a moment mollified and unsuspecting, he made a quick run for the porch. There was an intense movement all along the line, as the life and death of the deed became apparent. Quickly the sheriff drew his gun to his shoulder. He pressed both triggers at the same time, but not before Jake reached him. The latter knocked the gun barrel upward and fell upon his man. Both shots blazed out over the heads of the crowd in red puffs, and then followed a general onslaught. Men leaped the fence by tens, and crowded upon the little cottage. They swarmed on every side of the house, and crowded about the porch and the door, where four men were scuffling with the sheriff. The latter soon gave up, vowing vengeance. Torches were brought and a rope. A wagon drove up and was backed into the yard. Then began the calls for the negro.

The negro had been crouched in his corner in the cellar, trembling for his fate ever since the first attack. He had not dozed or lost consciousness during the intervening hours, but cowered there, wondering and praying. He was terrified lest the sheriff might not get him away in time. He was afraid that every sound meant a new assault. Now, however, he had begun to have the faintest glimmerings of hope when the new murmurs of contention arose. He heard the gallop of the horses' feet, voices of the men parleying, the ominous knock on the door.

At this sound, his body quaked and his teeth chattered. He began to quiver in each separate muscle and run cold. Already he saw the men at him, beating and kicking him.

"Before God, boss, I didn't mean to," he chattered, contemplating the chimera of his brain with startling eyes. "Oh, my God! boss, no, no. Oh, no, no."

He crowded closer to the wall. Another sound greeted his ears. It was the roar of a shotgun. He fell, groveling upon the floor, his nails digging in the earth.

"Oh, my Lawd, boss," he moaned, "oh, my Lawd, boss, don't kill me. I won't do it no mo'. I didn't go to do it. I didn't." His teeth were in the wet earth.

It was but now that the men were calling each other to the search. Five jumped to the outside entrance way of the low cellar, carrying a rope. Three others followed with their torches. They descended into the dark hole and looked cautiously about.

Suddenly, in the farthest corner, they espied him. In his agony, he had worked himself into a crouching position, as if he were about to spring. His hands were still in the earth. His eyes were rolling, his mouth foaming.

"Oh, my Lawd!" he was repeating monotonously, "oh, my Lawd!"

"Here he is. Pull him out, boys," cried several together.

The negro gave one yell of horror. He quite bounded as he did so, coming down with a dead chug on the earthen floor. Reason had forsaken him. He was a groveling, foaming brute. The last gleam of intelligence was that which notified him of the set eyes of his pursuers.

Davies was standing ten feet back when they began to reappear. He noted the heads of the torches, the disheveled appearance of the men, the scuffling and pulling. Then he clapped his hands over his mouth and worked his fingers convulsively, almost unconscious of what he was doing.

"Oh, my God," he whispered, his voice losing power.

The sickening sight was that of negro Jeff, foaming at the mouth, blood-shot in the eyes, his hands working convulsively, being dragged up the cellar steps, feet foremost. They had tied a rope about his waist and feet, and had hauled him out, leaving his head to hang and drag. The black face was distorted beyond all human semblance.

"Oh, my God!" said Davies again, biting his fingers unconsciously.

The crowd gathered about, more horror-stricken than gleeful at their own work. The negro was rudely bound and thrown like a sack of wheat into the wagon bed. Father and son mounted to drive, and the crowd took their horses. Wide-eyed and brain-racked, Davies ran for his own. He was so excited, he scarcely knew what he was doing.

Slowly the gloomy cavalcade took its way up the Sand River Pike. The moon was pouring down a wash of silvery light. The shadowy trees were stirring with a cool night wind. Davies hurried after and joined the silent, tramping throng.

"Are they going to hang him?" he asked.

"That's what they got him for," answered the man nearest him.

Davies dropped again into silence and tried to recover his nerves. The gloomy company seemed a terrible thing. He drew near the wagon and looked at the negro.

The latter seemed out of his senses. He was breathing heavily and groaning. His eyes were fixed and staring, his face and hands bleeding as if they had been scratched or trampled on. He was bundled up like limp wheat.

Davies could not stand it longer. He fell back, sick at heart. It seemed a ghastly, unmerciful way to do. Still, the company moved on and he followed, past fields lit white by the moon, under dark silent groups of trees, through which the moonlight fell in patches, up hilltops and down into valleys, until at last the little stream came into view, sparkling like a molten flood of silver in the night. After a time the road drew close to the water and made for a wagon bridge, which could be seen a little way ahead. The company rode up to this and halted. Davies dismounted with the others. The wagon was driven up to the bridge and father and son got out.

Fully a score of men gathered about, and the negro was lifted from the wagon. Davies thought he could not stand it, and went down by the waterside slightly above the bridge. He could see long beams of iron sticking out over the water, where the bridge was braced.

The men fastened a rope to a beam and then he could see that they were fixing the other end around the negro's neck.

Finally the curious company stood back.

"Have you anything to say?" a voice demanded.

The negro only lolled and groaned, slobbering at the mouth. He was out of his mind.

Then came the concerted action of four men, a lifting of a black mass in the air, and then Davies saw the limp form plunge down and pull up with a creaking sound of rope. In the weak moonlight it seemed as if the body were struggling, but he could not tell. He watched, wide-mouthed and silent, and then the body ceased moving. He heard the company depart, but that did not seem important. Only the black mass swaying in the pale light, over the shiny water of the stream seemed wonderful.

He sat down upon the bank and gazed in silence. He was not afraid. Everything was summery and beautiful. The whole cavalcade disappeared, the moon sank. The light of morning began to show as tender lavender and gray in the east. Still he sat. Then came the roseate hue of day, to which the waters of the stream responded, the white pebbles shining beautifully at the bottom. Still the body hung black and limp, and now a light breeze sprang up and stirred it visibly. At last he arose and made his way back to Pleasant Valley.

Since his duties called him to another day's work here, he idled about, getting the details of what was to be done. He talked with citizens and officials, rode out to the injured girl's home, rode to Baldwin to see the sheriff. There was singular silence and placidity in that corner. The sheriff took his defeat as he did his danger, philosophically.

It was evening again before he remembered that he had not discovered whether the body had been removed. He had not heard why the negro came back or how he was caught. The little cabin was two miles away, but he decided to walk, the night was so springlike. Before he had traveled half way, the moon arose and stretched long shadows of budding trees across his path. It was not long before he came upon the cabin, set well back from the road and surrounded with a few scattered trees. The ground between the door and the road was open, and strewn with the scattered chips of a woodpile. The roof was sagged and the windows patched in places, but, for all that, it had the glow of a home. Through the front door, which stood open, the blaze of a fire shone, its yellow light filling the interior with golden fancies.

Davies stopped at the door and knocked, but received no answer. He looked in on the battered cane chairs and aged furniture with considerable interest.

A door in the rear room opened, and a little negro girl entered, carrying a battered tin lamp, without any chimney. She had not heard his knock, and started perceptibly at the sight of his figure in the doorway. Then she raised her smoking lamp above her head in order to see better and approached.

There was something comical about her unformed figure and loose gingham dress. Her black head was strongly emphasized by little pigtails of hair done up in white twine, which stood out all over her head. Her dark skin was made apparently more so by contrast with her white teeth and the whites of her eyes.

Davies looked at her for a moment and asked, "Is this where Ingalls lives?"

The girl nodded her head. She was exceedingly subdued, and looked as if she had been crying.

"Has the body been brought here?" he asked.

"Yes, suh," she answered, with a soft negro accent.

"When did they bring it home?"

"This moanin'."

"Are you his sister?"

"Yes, suh."

"Well, can you tell me how they caught him?" asked Davies, feeling slightly ashamed to intrude thus. "What did he come back for?"

"To see us," said the girl.

"Well, did he want anything? He didn't come just to see you, did he?"

"Yes, suh," said the girl, "he come to say good-by."

Her voiced wavered.

"Didn't he know he might get caught?" asked Davies.

"Yes, suh, I think he did."

She still stood very quietly holding the poor battered lamp up, and looking down.

"Well, what did he have to say?" asked Davies.

"He said he wanted tuh see motha'. He was a-goin' away."

The girl seemed to regard Davies as an official of some sort, and he knew it.

"Can I have a look at the body?" he asked.

The girl did not answer, but started as if to lead the way.

"When is the funeral?" he asked.

"Tomorrow."

The girl led him through several bare sheds of rooms to the furthermost one of the line. This last seemed a sort of storage shed for odds and ends. It had several windows, but they were bare of glass, and open to the moonlight, save for a few wooden boards nailed across from the outside. Davies had been wondering all the while at the lonely and forsaken air of the place. No one seemed about but this little girl. If they had colored neighbors, none thought it worth while to call.

Now, as he stepped into this cool, dark, exposed outer room, the desolation seemed complete. The body was there in the middle of the bare room, stretched upon an ironing board, which rested on a box and a chair, and covered with a white sheet. All the corners of the room were quite dark, and only in the middle were shining splotches of moonlight.

Davies came forward, but the girl left him, carrying her lamp. She did not seem able to remain. He lifted the sheet, for he could see well enough, and looked at the stiff, black form. The face was extremely distorted, even in death, and he could see where the rope had tightened. A bar of cool moonlight lay across the face and breast. He was still looking, thinking soon to restore the covering, when a sound, half sigh, half groan, reached his ears.

He started as if a ghost had touched him. His muscles tightened. Instantly his heart was hammering like mad in his chest. His first impression was that it came from the dead.

"Oo-o-ohh," came the sound again, this time whimpering, as if someone were crying.

He turned quickly, for now it seemed to come from the corner. Greatly disturbed, he hesitated, and then as his eyes strained he caught the shadow of something. It was in the extreme corner, huddled up, dark, almost indistinguishable—crouching against the cold walls.

"Oh, oh, oh," was repeated, even more plaintively than before.

Davies began to understand. He approached lightly. Then he made out an old black mammy, doubled up and weeping. She was in the very niche of the corner, her head sunk on her knees, her tears falling, her body rocking to and fro.

Davies drew silently back. Before such grief, his intrusion seemed cold and unwarranted. The sensation of tears came to his eyes. He covered the dead, and withdrew.

Out in the moonlight, he struck a pace, but soon stopped and looked back. The whole dreary cabin, with its one golden door, where the light was, seemed a pitiful thing. He swelled with feeling and pathos as he looked. The night, the tragedy, the grief, he saw it all.

"I'll get that in," he exclaimed, feelingly, "I'll get it all in."

Issues for Discussion

1. In James T. Farrell's "The Fastest Runner on Sixty-First Street," Morty acts out two seemingly inconsistent formal "codes of conduct" in order to gain the esteem and adulation he wants. Use the statements of the culture conflict theorists to describe how these codes of conduct emerged, what they involved, and why Morty behaves in such an inconsistent manner.
2. Like Morty, Tony Rabuski needs friends and respect. But Tony's ethnicity and stupidity create additional impediments for him even though he is a white boy in a white man's world. Read the following paragraph and describe the artificial barriers established between and among communities that interfere with their social, moral, and economic development.

   And this became more and more important to Tony. There were those names, "Polack," "dirty Polack," "white Polack." If you could be called a "Polack," you weren't considered white. Well, when he beat them up, was he or wasn't he white? They knew. After the way he clouted these black ones, how could the other kids say that Tony Rabuski wasn't white? That showed them all. That he was a hero. He was a hero as much as Morty Aiken was.

3. Conflict theorists suggest as society becomes more complex there is an increasing likelihood that people will not be able to, or want to, make the adjustments necessary to adapt to the new values. Jeff York, in Robert Penn Warren's "The Patented Gate and the Mean Hamburger," is forced to come to grips with the "progress" offered by city life. Explain how the patented gate symbolizes the totality of Jeff York's existence. What does the hamburger stand symbolize?
4. Recall the interaction between Slick Hardin and Mrs. York. Ultimately, who copes more successfully with city life, Mrs. York or her husband?
5. Theodore Dreiser's "Nigger Jeff" illustrates the existence of competing codes of conduct (both formal and informal) between groups even in

small communities. Identify the competing group interests in the rural community of Pleasant Valley.
6. How did the mob nullify the formal legal system? How did members of the mob justify their behavior?
7. What is the significance of the newspaper reporter's observation, "No one seemed about but this little girl. If they had colored neighbors, none thought it worth while to call"?
8. Was the behavior of the people of Pleasant Valley a result of societal change and its resultant complexities, or did the mob act in a traditional and "acceptable" manner? Explain.
9. From a culture conflict theorist's perspective, what is the significance of Nigger Jeff's returning to his home to bid his mother and sister goodbye?

PART IV

Anomie Theory

The Greek word *anomie,* denoting a lack of law or lawlessness, has been used by sociologists to explain the *process* by which a person consciously decides to engage in criminal behavior. Talcott Parsons defines anomie as "the disturbance of the state of internalized expectations of persons occasioned by the processes of change in the normative components of the institutionalized culture...."[1] Anomie theorists generally agree that criminal behavior is normal and functional. According to Durkheim, "there is no society that is not confronted with the problem of criminality.... There is ... no phenomenon that presents more indisputably all the symptoms of normality since it appears closely connected with the conditions of all collective life."[2] That is, crime does not result from individual pathology (biological determinism or psychotic abnormality); rather, as proposed earlier by the classical theorists, a person freely chooses to engage in deviant behavior. The catalyst for this choice lies in inequities in the social and economic structure. Finally, Durkheim claims that no society can eradicate crime, for attempts to do so would lead to an overly repressive environment. Freedom, and with it innovation and change, would disappear. Consequently, criminality has a *functional* effect in that a balance is struck in which freedom (innovation, progress) coexists with crime.[3]

---

1. *The Social System* (New York: Free Press, 1951), p. 253. Writing in his seminal work *Suicide,* Emile Durkheim (1858–1937) described anomie as a state of *normlessness* in which the individual has no acceptable community or institutional model about how to behave (New York: Free Press, 1951), pp. 247–57. Durkheim introduced the term anomie in his *The Division of Laborer in Society* in 1893, but it was Robert Merton who related the effects of anomie to criminal behavior. See Merton's "Social Structure and Anomie," *"American Sociological Review* 3 (October 1938): 672–83; and *Social Theory and Social Structure* (New York: Free Press, 1957), chaps. 4 and 5.

2. *The Rules of Sociological Method* (New York: Free Press, 1964), p. 66.

3. Ibid.

Anomie theorists stress the importance of the social structure on individual behavior. Durkheim suggests anomie is most likely to emerge during times of great social and economic upheaval (e.g., depressions). Merton, however, states that anomie is also prevalent in times of relative social and economic stability. Thus, feelings of normlessness may be experienced whenever people feel incapable of successfully competing within the rules of the existing environment. The Mertonian criteria for the inception of anomie include (1) a set of common values, (2) acceptance of these values by a large segment of the community, (3) means for achieving certain accepted (even prized or cherished) ends, and (4) an awareness that the ends cannot be legitimately achieved by all members of the community.[4] Moreover, normlessness may be accelerated when the society's mores, folkways, and customs (its "collective conscience") strongly reinforce the virtues of material gain. This seems particularly true in American culture: "[T]he pressure of prestige-bearing success tends to eliminate the effective social constraint over means employed to this end. 'The-end-justifies-the-means' doctrine becomes a guiding tenet for action when the culture structure unduly exalts the end and social organization unduly limits possible recourse to approved means."[5] Crime, then, is the result of "socially induced deviations," in which the goals are theoretically attainable by all, but in reality can be secured only by a limited number. This may help explain why crime is often relatively high in low-income areas. In these communities the ends are least attainable, perhaps because of racism or inadequate educational and employment opportunities.

When anomie exists, the individual may consciously choose to act out one of several different roles. Merton calls these behavior choices "modes of adaptation."[6] The behavior most often chosen is *conformity*; the individual accepts both the goals and means of society. *Innovation* occurs when one accepts society's goals but rejects the means; the person "cheats" in order to achieve the end. *Ritualism* involves the rejection of goals but acceptance of means. Ritualistic individuals "go through the motions," usually with the thought of impressing others that they are "playing by the rules of the game" (e.g., attending meetings or church services out of a sense of extremely motivated duty). *Retreatism* occurs when a person rejects both goals and means. Retreatists are often individuals who have continually failed to gain the ends prescribed by society. These individuals, often referred to as "dropouts," include skid-row inhabitants, drug addicts, and vagrants. *Rebellion* also involves a rejection of

---

4. Merton, *Social Theory and Social Structure*, p. 146.

5. Merton, "Social Structure and Anomie," pp. 672–82.

6. Ibid.

goals and means, but the rebel's reaction to a failure to achieve society's ends is the attempt to establish a new social order. Individual adaptation is shunned in favor of structural (societal) change.[7]

Becoming an accepted member of a group or community involves a process of perceiving and adhering to a myriad of role-playing situations. Behavior patterns are acquired from role models. Siblings, peers, parents, teachers, and television personalities, as well as a host of other individuals, contribute to our perceptions of acceptable behavior. Yet confusion may result when we *mistakenly* adopt a role that is not compatible with a particular situation. Our perception of the moment and our acting out of a particular role may simply be the result of a myopic analysis of the event, although at times the unacceptable behavior may emerge as a *conscious* decision to ignore group or societal norms. For example, an ideal of American culture is the attainment of "the good life." Criteria for the good life are not necessarily measured in the Socratic sense of virtue or internal happiness. Rather, an important standard is the quantity and quality of one's material comforts. We are consumed by Horatio Alger's "rages to riches" dream. Unfortunately, our hopes and expectations are often irreconcilable with the realities. Specifically, there may be no apparent correlation between how hard a person strives for the good life and his or her chances of achievement. Anomie theory is steeped in the notion that the social constraints of playing by the rules lose force, and the likelihood of deviance for self-aggrandizement increases, when an individual recognizes the futility of playing by the rules.

One's motive for goal acceptance and the manner in which the end is achieved is particularly important. Anomie theory is predicated on the notion of free will, or conscious choice. The individual, free from biological or psychological constraints, chooses to accept or reject the goals and means. Yet the individual engages in the struggle only after two important choices have been predetermined by the social structure. First, the decision whether to play the game is for all practical purposes a nonchoice situation. The alternative, dropping out of society, is so impractical to most as to not

---

7. Criticism of anomie theory centers on the modes of adaptation (specifically conformity, ritualism, and rebellion), and on its inability to satisfactorily explain motiveless crime and white-collar crime. No matter how grudgingly one conforms, the behavior response of conformity is by definition within the acceptable limits of the legal codes. The behavioral dynamics associated with ritualism appear to relate more to apathy than law-breaking. Finally, it is presumed that rebellion must involve illegal activity in the establishment of a new "social order." Yet a new social order may be achieved in the United States without the citizenry partaking in the traditional activities associated with a coup d'etat.

Nor can anomie be used to explain the existence of "motiveless" deviance, usually the activity of the pre-adult population, or the prevalence of white-collar crime. For general criticism, see Edwin M. Lemert, *Human Deviance, Social Problems, and Social Control* (2nd ed.; Englewood Cliffs, N.J.: Prentice-Hall, 1972), pp. 26–61; and Jack D. Douglas, "Deviance and Order in a Pluralistic Society," in *Theoretical Criminology*, ed. John C. McKinney and Edward A. Tiryakian (New York: Appleton-Century-Crofts, 1970), pp. 367–401.

be a viable alternative. Second, the individual quickly perceives that the means for attaining the goals are inequitably distributed. Impediments to goal achievement may include birth into a socially disadvantaged segment of society, inherited genetic incapabilities, or diminished productivity due to accident or disease. On recognizing that these or other "undesirable" traits are impediments, the individual must make a commitment about how to respond to the environment. Thus come Merton's classifications of *conformity, innovation, ritualism, retreatism,* or *rebellion.*

Support for anomie theory exists in the seeming correlation between the meteoric rise in crime rates and the incredible technological advances achieved since the industrial revolution. Advances in science and technology seem to be simply outpacing the individual's ability to assimilate and cope with change. Additionally, occupational specialization, which entails less need for "teamwork," further serves to alienate. The sense of community is diminished while the potential for deviant reaction is increased.

In Willa Cather's stories "Paul's Case" and "The Bookkeeper's Wife," Paul and Bixby assess their chances of successfully competing in their social environments. Both individuals could easily attain the status of their peers. Yet their situations are confounded by wanting what would ordinarily be reserved for the "socially prominent," or at least for people who are economically better off. The attainment of a status that is seemingly not reserved for them is the generating force for their fling with criminal behavior.

Mrs. Grim in George Garrett's "Thus the Early Gods" is content with her social situation. However, a "great social upheaval" of sorts is descending upon her, threatening to disrupt her tranquil existence. Unable to accept the invasion by lower-class neighbors, she attempts to resist in order to preserve her life style. With the aid of her equally narrow-minded son, they avoid legal assistance (which probably would be of little help) and choose their only seemingly viable alternative—self-help.

PAUL'S CASE
Willa Cather

It was Paul's afternoon to appear before the faculty of the Pittsburgh High School to account for his various misdemeanors. He had been suspended a week ago, and his father had called at the Principal's office and confessed his perplexity about his son. Paul entered the faculty-room suave and smiling. His clothes were a trifle outgrown, and the tan velvet on the collar of his open overcoat was frayed and worn; but for all that there was something of the dandy about him, and he wore an opal pin in his neatly knotted black four-in-hand and a red carnation in his buttonhole. This latter adornment the faculty somehow felt was not properly significant of the contrite spirit befitting a boy under the ban of suspension.

Paul was tall for his age and very thin, with high, cramped shoulders and a narrow chest. His eyes were remarkable for a certain hysterical brilliancy, and he continually used them in a conscious, theatrical sort of way, peculiarly offensive in a boy. The pupils were abnormally large, as though he were addicted to belladonna, but there was a glassy glitter about them which that drug does not produce.

When questioned by the Principal as to why he was there, Paul stated, politely enough, that he wanted to come back to school. This was a lie, but Paul was quite accustomed to lying; found it, indeed, indispensable for overcoming friction. His teachers were asked to state their respective charges against him, which they did with such a rancor and aggrievedness as evinced that this was not a usual case. Disorder and impertinence were among the offenses named, yet each of his instructors felt that it was scarcely possible to put into words the real cause of the trouble, which lay in a sort of hysterically defiant manner of the boy's; in the contempt which they all knew he felt for them, and which he seemingly made not the least effort to conceal. Once, when he had been making a synopsis of a paragraph at the blackboard, his English teacher had stepped to his side and attempted to guide his hand. Paul had started back with a shudder and thrust his hands violently behind him. The astonished woman could scarcely have been more hurt and embarrassed had he struck at her. The insult was so involuntary and definitely personal as to be unforgettable. In one way and another, he had made all his teachers, men and women alike, conscious of the same feeling of physical aversion. In one class he habitually sat with his hands shading his eyes; in another he always looked out of the window during the recitation; in another he made a running commentary on the lecture, with humorous intent.

His teachers felt this afternoon that his whole attitude was symbolized by his shrug and his flippantly red carnation flower, and they fell upon him without mercy, his English teacher leading the pack. He stood through it smiling, his pale lips parted over his white teeth. (His lips were continually twitching, and he had a habit of raising his eyebrows that was contemptuous and irritating to the last degree.) Older boys than Paul had broken down and shed tears under that ordeal, but his set smile did not once desert him, and his only sign of discomfort was the nervous trembling of the fingers that toyed with the buttons of his overcoat, and an occasional jerking of the other hand which held his hat. Paul was always smiling, always glancing about him, seeming to feel that people might be watching him and trying to detect something. This conscious expression, since it was so far as possible from boyish mirthfulness, was usually attributed to insolence or "smartness."

As the inquisition proceeded, one of his instructors repeated an impertinent remark of the boy's, and the Principal asked him whether he thought that a courteous speech to make to a woman. Paul shrugged his shoulders slightly and his eyebrows twitched.

"I don't know," he replied. "I didn't mean to be polite or impolite, either. I guess it's a sort of way I have, of saying things regardless."

The Principal asked him whether he didn't think that a way it would be well to get rid of. Paul grinned and said he guessed so. When he was told that he could go, he bowed gracefully and went out. His bow was like a repetition of the scandalous red carnation.

His teachers were in despair, and his drawing master voiced the feeling of them all when he declared there was something about the boy which none of them understood. He added: "I don't really believe that smile of his comes altogether from insolence; there's something sort of haunted about it. The boy is not strong, for one thing. There is something wrong about the fellow."

The drawing master had come to realize that, in looking at Paul, one saw only his white teeth and the forced animation of his eyes. One warm afternoon the boy had gone to sleep at his drawing-board, and his master had noted with amazement what a white, blue-veined face it was; drawn and wrinkled like an old man's about the eyes, the lips twitching even in his sleep.

His teachers left the building dissatisfied and unhappy; humiliated to have felt so vindictive towards a mere boy, to have uttered this feeling in cutting terms, and to have set each other on, as it were, in the gruesome game of intemperate reproach. One of them remembered having seen a miserable street cat set at bay by a ring of tormentors.

As for Paul, he ran down the hill whistling the Soldiers' Chorus from *Faust,* looking wildly behind him now and then to see whether some of his teachers were not there to witness his lightheartedness. As it was now late in the afternoon and Paul was on duty that evening as usher at Carnegie Hall, he decided that he would not go home to supper.

When he reached the concert hall the doors were not yet open. It was chilly outside, and he decided to go up into the picture gallery—always deserted at this hour—where there were some of Raffelli's gay studies of Paris streets and an airy blue Venetian scene or two that always exhilarated him. He was delighted to find no one in the gallery but the old guard, who sat in the corner, a newspaper on his knee, a black patch over one eye and the other closed. Paul possessed himself of the place and walked confidently up and down, whistling under his breath. After a while he sat down before a blue Rico and lost himself. When he bethought him to look at his watch, it was after seven o'clock, and he rose with a start and ran downstairs, making a face at Augustus Caesar, peering out from the east room, and an evil gesture at the Venus de Milo as he passed her on the stairway.

When Paul reached the ushers' dressing room half-a-dozen boys were there already, and he began excitedly to tumble into his uniform. It was one of the few that at all approached fitting, and Paul thought it very becoming—though he knew the tight, straight coat accentuated his narrow chest, about which he was exceedingly sensitive. He was always excited while he dressed, twanging all over to the tuning of the strings and the preliminary flourishes of the horns in the music room; but tonight he seemed quite beside himself, and he teased and plagued the boys until, telling him that he was crazy, they put him down on the floor and sat on him.

Somewhat calmed by his suppression, Paul dashed out to the front of the house to seat the early comers. He was a model usher. Gracious and smiling he ran up and down the aisles. Nothing was too much trouble for him; he carried messages and brought programs as though it were his greatest pleasure in life, and all the people in his section thought him a charming boy, feeling that he remembered and admired them. As the house filled, he grew more and more vivacious and animated, and the color came to his cheeks and lips. It was very much as though this were a great reception and Paul were the host. Just as the musicians came out to take their place, his English teacher arrived with checks for the seats which a prominent manufacturer had taken for the season. She betrayed some embarrassment when she handed Paul the tickets, and a *hauteur* which subsequently made her feel very foolish. Paul was startled for a moment and had the feeling of wanting to put her out; what business had she here among all these fine people and gay colors? He looked her over and decided that she was not appropriately dressed and must be a fool to sit downstairs in such togs. The tickets had probably been sent her out of kindness, he reflected, as he put down a seat for her, and she had about as much right to sit there as he had.

When the symphony began Paul sank into one of the rear seats with a long sigh of relief, and lost himself as he had done before the Rico. It was not that symphonies, as such, meant anything in particular to Paul, but the first sigh of the instruments seemed to free some hilarious spirit within him; something that struggled there like the genie in the bottle found by the Arab fisherman. He felt a sudden zest of life; the lights danced before his eyes and the concert hall blazed into unimaginable splendor. When the soprano soloist came on, Paul forgot even the nastiness of his teacher's being there and gave himself up to the peculiar intoxication such personages always had for him. The soloist chanced to be a German woman, by no means in her first youth, and the mother of many children; but she wore a satin gown and a tiara, and she had that indefinable air of achievement, that world-shine upon her, which always blinded Paul to any possible defects.

After a concert was over, Paul was often irritable and wretched until he got to sleep—and tonight he was even more than usually restless. He had the feeling of not being able to let down; of its being impossible to give up this delicious excitement which was the only thing that could be called living at all. During the last number he withdrew and, after hastily changing his clothes in the dressing room, slipped out to the side door where the singer's carriage stood. Here he began pacing rapidly up and down the walk, waiting to see her come out.

Over yonder the Schenley, in its vacant stretch, loomed big and square through the fine rain, the windows of its twelve stories glowing like those of a lighted cardboard house under a Christmas tree. All the actors and singers of any importance stayed there when they were in the city, and a number of the big manufacturers of the place lived there in the winter. Paul had often hung about the hotel, watching the people go in and out, longing to enter and leave schoolmasters and dull care behind him forever.

At last the singer came out, accompanied by the conductor, who helped her into her carriage and closed the door with a cordial *auf wiedersehen*—which set Paul to wondering whether she were not an old sweetheart of his. Paul followed the carriage over to the hotel, walking so rapidly as not to be far from the entrance when the singer alighted and disappeared behind the swinging glass doors which were opened by a Negro in a tall hat and a long coat. In the moment that the door was ajar, it seemed to Paul that he, too, entered. He seemed to feel himself go after her up the steps, into the warm, lighted building, into an exotic, a tropical world of shiny, glistening surfaces and basking ease. He reflected upon the mysterious dishes that were brought into the dining room, the green bottles in buckets of ice, as he had seen them in the supper party pictures of the Sunday supplement. A quick gust of wind brought the rain down with sudden vehemence, and Paul was startled to find that he was still outside in the slush of the gravel driveway; that his boots were letting in the water and his scanty overcoat was clinging wet about him; that the lights in front of the concert hall were out, and that the rain was driving in sheets between him and the orange glow of the windows above him. There it was, what he wanted—tangibly before him, like the fairy world of a Christmas pantomime; as the rain beat in his face, Paul wondered whether he were destined always to shiver in the black night outside, looking up at it.

He turned and walked reluctantly towards the car tracks. The end had to come sometime; his father in his nightclothes at the top of the stairs, explanations that did not explain, hastily improvised fictions that were forever tripping him up, his upstairs room and its horrible yellow wallpaper, the creaking bureau with the greasy plush collar-box, and over his painted wooden bed the pictures of George Washington and John Calvin, and the framed motto, "Feed my Lambs," which had been worked in red worsted by his mother, whom Paul could not remember.

Half an hour later, Paul alighted from the Negley Avenue car and went slowly down one of the side streets off the main thoroughfare. It was a highly respectable street, where all the houses were exactly alike, and where businessmen of moderate means begot and reared large families of children, all of whom went to Sabbath school and learned the shorter catechism, and were interested in arithmetic; all of whom were as exactly alike as their homes, and of a piece with the monotony in which they lived. Paul never went up Cordelia Street without a shudder of loathing. His home was next to the house of the Cumberland minister. He approached it tonight with the nerveless sense of defeat, the hopeless feeling of sinking back forever into ugliness and commonness that he had always had when he came home. The moment he turned into Cordelia Street he felt the waters close above his head. After each of these orgies of living, he experienced all the physical depression which follows a debauch; the loathing of respectable beds, of common food, of a house permeated by kitchen odors; a shuddering repulsion for the flavorless, colorless mass of everyday existence; a morbid desire for cool things and soft lights and fresh flowers.

The nearer he approached the house, the more absolutely unequal Paul felt to the sight of it all; his ugly sleeping chamber; the cold bathroom with the grimy zinc tub, the cracked mirror, the dripping spiggots; his father, at the top of the stairs, his hairy legs sticking out from his nightshirt, his feet thrust into carpet slippers. He was so much later than usual that there would certainly be inquiries and reproaches. Paul stopped short before the door. He felt that he could not be accosted by his father tonight; that he could not toss again on that miserable bed. He would not go in. He would tell his father that he had no carfare, and it was raining so hard that he had gone home with one of the boys and stayed all night.

Meanwhile, he was wet and cold. He went around to the back of the house and tried one of the basement windows, found it open, raised it cautiously, and scrambled down the cellar wall to the floor. There he stood, holding his breath, terrified by the noise he had made; but the floor above him was silent, and there was no creak on the stairs. He found a soapbox, and carried it over to the soft ring of light that streamed from the furnace door, and sat down. He was terribly afraid of rats, so he did not try to sleep, but sat looking distrustfully at the dark, still terrified lest he might have awakened his father. In such reactions, after one of the experiences which made days and nights out of the dreary blanks of the calendar, when his senses were deadened, Paul's head was always singularly clear. Suppose his father had heard him getting in at the window and had come down and shot him for a burglar? Then, again, suppose his father had come down, pistol in hand, and he had cried out in time to save himself, and his father had been horrified to think how nearly he had killed him? Then, again, suppose a day should come when his father would remember that night, and wish there had been no warning cry to stay his hand? With this last supposition Paul entertained himself until daybreak.

The following Sunday was fine; the sodden November chill was broken by the last flash of autumnal summer. In the morning Paul had to go to church and Sabbath school, as always. On seasonable Sunday afternoons the burghers of Cordelia Street usually sat out on their front "stoops," and talked to their neighbors on the next stoop, or called to those across the street in neighborly fashion. The men sat placidly on gay cushions upon the steps that led down to the sidewalk, while the women, in their Sunday "waists," sat in rockers on the cramped porches, pretending to be greatly at their ease. The children played in the streets; there were so many of them that the place resembled the recreation grounds of a kindergarten. The men on the steps—all in their shirt sleeves, their vests unbuttoned— sat with their legs well apart, their stomachs comfortably protruding, and talked of the prices of things, or told anecdotes of the sagacity of their various chiefs and overlords. They occasionally looked over the multitude of squabbling children, listened affectionately to their high-pitched, nasal voices, smiling to see their own proclivities reproduced in their offspring, and interspersed their legends of the iron kings with remarks about their sons' progress at school, their grades in arithmetic, and the amounts they had saved in their toy banks.

On this last Sunday of November, Paul sat all the afternoon on the lowest step of his "stoop," staring into the street, while his sisters, in their rockers, were talking to the minister's daughters next door about how many shirtwaists they had made in the last week, and how many waffles someone had eaten at the last church supper. When the weather was warm, and his father was in a particularly jovial frame of mind, the girls made lemonade, which was always brought out in a red-glass pitcher, ornamented with forget-me-nots in blue enamel. This the girls thought very fine, and the neighbors joked about the suspicious color of the pitcher.

Today Paul's father, on the top step, was talking to a young man who shifted a restless baby from knee to knee. He happened to be the young man who was daily held up to Paul as a model, and after whom it was his father's dearest hope that he would pattern. This young man was of a ruddy complexion, with a compressed, red mouth, and faded, nearsighted eyes, over which he wore thick spectacles, with gold bows that curved about his ears. He was clerk to one of the magnates of a great steel corporation, and was looked upon in Cordelia Street as a young man with a future. There was a story that, some five years ago—he was now barely twenty-six—he had been a trifle "dissipated," but in order to curb his appetites and save the loss of time and strength that a sowing of wild-oats might have entailed, he had taken his chief's advice, oft reiterated to his employees, and at twenty-one had married the first woman whom he could persuade to share his fortunes. She happened to be an angular schoolmistress, much older than he, who also wore thick glasses, and who had now borne him four children, all nearsighted, like herself.

The young man was relating how his chief, now cruising in the Mediterranean, kept in touch with all the details of the business, arranging his office hours on his yacht just as though he were at home, and "knocking off work enough to keep two stenographers busy." His father told, in turn, the plan his corporation was considering, of putting in an electric railway plant at Cairo. Paul snapped his teeth; he had an awful apprehension that they might spoil it all before he got there. Yet he rather liked to hear these legends of the iron kings, that were told and retold on Sundays and holidays; these stories of palaces in Venice, yachts on the Mediterranean, and high play at Monte Carlo appealed to his fancy, and he was interested in the triumphs of cash boys who had become famous, though he had no mind for the cash-boy stage.

After supper was over, and he had helped to dry the dishes, Paul nervously asked his father whether he could go to George's to get some help in his geometry, and still more nervously asked for carfare. This latter request he had to repeat, as his father, on principle, did not like to hear requests for money whether much or little. He asked Paul whether he could not go to some boy who lived nearer, and told him that he ought not to leave his schoolwork until Sunday; but he gave him the dime. He was not a poor man, but he had a worthy ambition to come up in the world. His only reason for allowing Paul to usher was that he thought a boy ought to be earning a little.

Paul bounded upstairs, scrubbed the greasy odor of the dish-water from his hands with the ill-smelling soap he hated, and then shook over his fingers a few drops of violet water from the bottle he kept hidden in his drawer. He left the house with his geometry conspicuously under his arm, and the moment he got out of Cordelia Street and boarded a downtown car, he shook off the lethargy of two deadening days, and began to live again.

The leading juvenile of the permanent stock company which played at one of the downtown theaters was an acquaintance of Paul's, and the boy had been invited to drop in at the Sunday-night rehearsals whenever he could. For more than a year Paul had spent every available moment loitering about Charley Edwards' dressing room. He had won a place among Edwards' following not only because the young actor, who could not afford to employ a dresser, often found him useful, but because he recognized in Paul something akin to what churchmen term "vocation."

It was at the theater and at Carnegie Hall that Paul really lived; the rest was but a sleep and a forgetting. This was Paul's fairy tale, and it had for him all the allurement of a secret love. The moment he inhaled the gassy, painty, dusty odor behind the scenes, he breathed like a prisoner set free, and felt within him the possibility of doing or saying splendid, brilliant things. The moment the cracked orchestra beat out the overture from *Martha*, or jerked at the serenade from *Rigoletto*, all stupid and ugly things slid from him, and his senses were deliciously, yet delicately fired.

Perhaps it was because, in Paul's world, the natural nearly always wore the guise of ugliness, that a certain element of artificiality seemed to him necessary in beauty. Perhaps it was because his experience of life elsewhere was so full of Sabbath-school picnics, petty economies, wholesome advice as to how to succeed in life, and the unescapable odors of cooking, that he found this existence so alluring, these smartly clad men and women so attractive, that he was so moved by these starry apple orchards that bloomed perennially under the limelight.

It would be difficult to put it strongly enough how convincingly the stage entrance of that theater was for Paul the actual portal of Romance. Certainly none of the company ever suspected it, least of all Charley Edwards. It was very like the old stories that used to float about London of fabulously rich Jews, who had subterranean halls, with palms, and fountains, and soft lamps and richly appareled women who never saw the disenchanting light of Londay day. So, in the midst of that smoke-palled city, enamored of figures and grimy toil, Paul had his secret temple, his wishing-carpet, his bit of blue-and-white Mediterranean shore bathed in perpetual sunshine.

Several of Paul's teachers had a theory that his imagination had been perverted by garish fiction; but the truth was, he scarcely ever read at all. The books at home were not such as would either tempt or corrupt a youthful mind, and as for reading the novels that some of his friends urged upon him—well, he got what he wanted much more quickly from music; any sort of music, from an orchestra to a barrel organ. He needed only the spark, the indescribable thrill that made his imagination master of his senses, and he could make plots and pictures enough of his own. It was equally true that he was not stage-struck—not, at any rate, in the usual acceptance of that expression. He had no desire to become an actor, any more than he had to become a musician. He felt no necessity to do any of these things; what he wanted was to see, to be in the atmosphere, float on the wave of it, to be carried out, blue league after blue league, away from everything.

After a night behind the scenes, Paul found the schoolroom more than ever repulsive; the bare floors and naked walls; the prosy men who never wore frock coats, or violets in their buttonholes; the women with their dull gowns, shrill voices, and pitiful seriousness about prepositions that govern the dative. He could not bear to have the other pupils think, for a moment, that he took these people seriously; he must convey to them that he considered it all trivial, and was there only by way of a joke, anyway. He had autograph pictures of all the members of the stock company which he showed his classmates, telling them the most incredible stories of his familiarity with these people, of his acquaintance with the soloists who came to Carnegie Hall, his suppers with them and the flowers he sent them. When these stories lost their effect, and his audience grew listless, he would bid all the boys good-bye, announcing that he was going to travel for a while; going to Naples, to California, to Egypt. Then, next Monday, he would slip back, conscious and nervously smiling; his sister was ill, and he would have to defer his voyage until spring.

Matters went steadily worse with Paul at school. In the itch to let his instructors know how heartily he despised them, and how thoroughly he was appreciated elsewhere, he mentioned once or twice that he had no time to fool with theorems; adding—with a twitch of the eyebrows and a touch of that nervous bravado which so perplexed them—that he was helping the people down at the stock company; they were old friends of his.

The upshot of the matter was that the Principal went to Paul's father, and Paul was taken out of school and put to work. The manager at Carnegie Hall was told to get another usher in his stead; the doorkeeper at the theater was warned not to admit him to the house; and Charley Edwards remorsefully promised the boy's father not to see him again.

The members of the stock company were vastly amused when some of Paul's stories reached them—especially the women. They were hardworking women, most of them supporting indolent husbands or brothers, and they laughed rather bitterly at having stirred the boy to such fervid and florid inventions. They agreed with the faculty and with his father that Paul's was a bad case.

The east-bound train was plowing through a January snowstorm; the dull dawn was beginning to show gray when the engine whistled a mile out of Newark. Paul started up from the seat where he had lain curled in uneasy slumber, rubbing the breath-misted window glass with his hand, and peered out. The snow was whirling in curling eddies above the white bottom lands, and the drifts lay already deep in the fields and along the fences, while here and there the long dead grass and dried weed stalks protruded black above it. Lights shone from the scattered houses, and a gang of laborers who stood beside the track waved their lanterns.

Paul had slept very little, and he felt grimy and uncomfortable. He had made the all-night journey in a day coach because he was afraid if he took a Pullman he might be seen by some Pittsburgh businessman who had noticed him in Denny & Carson's office. When the whistle woke him, he clutched quickly at his breastpocket, glancing about him with an uncertain smile. But the little, clay-bespattered Italians were still sleeping, the slatternly women across the aisle were in open-mouthed oblivion, and even the crumby, crying babies were for the nonce stilled. Paul settled back to struggle with his impatience as best he could.

When he arrived at the Jersey City station, he hurried through his breakfast, manifestly ill at ease and keeping a sharp eye about him. After he reached the Twenty-third Street station, he consulted a cabman, and had himself driven to a men's furnishing establishment which was just opening for the day. He spent upward of two hours there, buying with endless reconsidering and great care. His new street suit he put on in the fitting room; the frock coat and dress clothes he had bundled into the cab with his new shirts. Then he drove to a hatter's and a shoe house. His next errand was at Tiffany's, where he selected silver-mounted brushes and a scarf pin. He would not wait to have his silver marked, he said. Lastly, he stopped at a trunk shop on Broadway, and had his purchases packed into various traveling bags.

It was a little after one o'clock when he drove up to the Waldorf, and, after settling with the cabman, went into the office. He registered from Washington; said his mother and father had been abroad, and that he had come down to await the arrival of their steamer. He told his story plausibly and had no trouble, since he offered to pay for them in advance, in engaging his rooms; a sleeping room, sitting room and bath.

Not once, but a hundred times Paul had planned this entry into New York. He had gone over every detail of it with Charley Edwards, and in his scrapbook at home there were pages of description about New York hotels, cut from the Sunday papers.

When he was shown to his sitting room on the eighth floor, he saw at a glance that everything was as it should be; there was but one detail in his mental picture that the place did not realize, so he rang for the bellboy and sent him down for flowers. He moved about nervously until the boy returned, putting away his new linen and fingering it delightedly as he did so. When the flowers came, he put them hastily into water, and then tumbled into a hot bath. Presently he came out of his white bathroom, resplendent in his new silk underwear, and playing with the tassels of his red robe. The snow was whirling so fiercely outside his windows that he could scarcely see across the street; but within, the air was deliciously soft and fragrant. He put the violets and jonquils on the tabouret beside the couch, and threw himself down with a long sigh, covering himself with a Roman blanket. He was thoroughly tired; he had been in such haste, he had stood up to such a strain, covered so much ground in the last twenty-four hours, that he wanted to think how it had all come about. Lulled by the sound of the wind, the warm air, and the cool fragrance of the flowers, he sank into deep, drowsy retrospection.

It had been wonderfully simple; when they had shut him out of the theater and concert hall, when they had taken away his bone, the whole thing was virtually determined. The rest was a mere matter of opportunity. The only thing that at all surprised him was his own courage—for he realized well enough that he had always been tormented by fear, a sort of apprehensive dread that, of late years, as the meshes of the lies he had told closed about him, had been pulling the muscles of his body tighter and tighter. Until now, he could not remember a time when he had not been dreading something. Even when he was a little boy, it was always there—behind him, or before, or on either side. There had always been the shadowed corner, the dark place into which he dared not look, but from which something seemed always to be watching him—and Paul had done things that were not pretty to watch, he knew.

But now he had a curious sense of relief, as though he had at last thrown down the gauntlet to the thing in the corner.

Yet it was but a day since he had been sulking in the traces; but yesterday afternoon that he had been sent to the bank with Denny & Carson's deposit as usual—but this time he was instructed to leave the book to be balanced. There was above two thousand dollars in checks, and nearly a thousand in the banknotes which he had taken from the book and quietly transferred to his pocket. At the bank he had made out a new deposit slip. His nerves had been steady enough to permit of his returning to the office, where he had finished his work and asked for a full day's holiday tomorrow, Saturday, giving a perfectly reasonable pretext. The bankbook, he knew, would not be returned before Monday or Tuesday, and his father would be out of town for the next week. From the time he slipped the banknotes into his pocket until he boarded the night train for New York, he had not known a moment's hesitation.

How astonishingly easy it had all been; here he was, the thing done; and this time there would be no awakening, no figure at the top of the stairs. He watched the snowflakes whirling by his window until he fell asleep.

When he awoke, it was four o'clock in the afternoon. He bounded up with a start; one of his precious days gone already! He spent nearly an hour in dressing, watching every stage of his toilet carefully in the mirror. Everything was quite perfect; he was exactly the kind of boy he had always wanted to be.

When he went downstairs, Paul took a carriage and drove up Fifth Avenue toward the Park. The snow had somewhat abated; carriages and tradesmen's wagons were hurrying soundlessly to and fro in the winter twilight; boys in woolen mufflers were shoveling off the doorsteps; the avenue stages made fine spots of color against the white street. Here and there on the corners were stands, with whole flower gardens blooming behind glass windows, against which the snowflakes stuck and melted; violets, roses, carnations, lilies of the valley—somehow vastly more lovely and alluring that they blossomed thus unnaturally in the snow. The Park itself was a wonderful stage winter-piece.

When he returned, the pause of the twilight had ceased, and the tune of the streets had changed. The snow was falling faster, lights streamed from the hotels that reared their many stories fearlessly up into the storm, defying the raging Atlantic winds. A long, black stream of carriages poured down the avenue, intersected here and there by other streams, tending horizontally. There were a score of cabs about the entrance of his hotel, and his driver had to wait. Boys in livery were running in and out of the awning stretched across the sidewalk, up and down the red velvet carpet laid from the door to the street. Above, about, within it all, was the rumble and roar, the hurry and toss of thousands of human beings as hot for pleasure as himself, and on every side of him towered the glaring affirmation of the omnipotence of wealth.

The boy set his teeth and drew his shoulders together in a spasm of realization; the plot of all dramas, the text of all romances, the nerve-stuff of all sensations was whirling about him like the snow-flakes. He burnt like a faggot in a tempest.

When Paul came down to dinner, the music of the orchestra floated up the elevator shaft to greet him. As he stepped into the thronged corridor, he sank back into one of the chairs against the wall to get his breath. The lights, the chatter, the perfumes, the bewildering medley of color—he had, for the moment, the feeling of not being able to stand it. But only for a moment; these were his own people, he told himself. He went slowly about the corridors, through the writing rooms, smoking rooms, reception rooms, as though he were exploring the chambers of an enchanted palace, built and peopled for him alone.

When he reached the dining room he sat down at a table near a window. The flowers, the white linen, the many-colored wine glasses, the gay toilets of the women, the low popping of corks, the undulating repetitions of the *Blue Danube* from the orchestra, all flooded Paul's dream with bewildering radiance. When the roseate tinge of his champagne was added—that cold, precious, bubbling stuff that creamed and foamed in his glass—Paul wondered that there were honest men in the world at all. This was what all the world was fighting for, he reflected; this was what all the struggle was about. He doubted the reality of his past. Had he ever known a place called Cordelia Street, a place where fagged-looking businessmen boarded the early car? Mere rivets in a machine they seemed to Paul—sickening men, with combings of children's hair always hanging to their coats, and the smell of cooking in their clothes. Cordelia Street—ah, that belonged to another time and country! Had he not always been thus, had he not sat here night after night, from as far back as he could remember, looking pensively over just such shimmering textures, and slowly twirling the stem of a glass like this one between his thumb and middle finger? He rather thought he had.

He was not in the least abashed or lonely. He had no especial desire to meet or to know any of these people; all he demanded was the right to look on and conjecture, to watch the pageant. The mere stage properties were all he contended for. Nor was he lonely later in the evening, in his loge at the Opera. He was entirely rid of his nervous misgivings, of his forced aggressiveness, of the imperative desire to show himself different from his surroundings. He felt now that his surroundings explained him. Nobody questioned the purple; he had only to wear it passively. He had only to glance down at his dress coat to reassure himself that here it would be impossible for anyone to humiliate him.

He found it hard to leave his beautiful sitting room to go to bed that night, and sat long watching the raging storm from his turret window. When he went to sleep, it was with the lights turned on in his bedroom; partly because of his old timidity, and partly so that, if he should wake in the night, there would be no wretched moment of doubt, no horrible suspicion of yellow wallpaper, or of Washington and Calvin above his bed.

On Sunday morning the city was practically snowbound. Paul breakfasted late, and in the afternoon he fell in with a wild San Francisco boy, a freshman at Yale, who said he had run down for a "little flyer" over Sunday. The young man offered to show Paul the night side of the town, and the two boys went off together after dinner, not returning to the hotel until seven o'clock the next morning. They had started out in the confiding warmth of a champagne friendship, but their parting in the elevator was singularly cool. The freshman pulled himself together to make his train, and Paul went to bed. He awoke at two o'clock in the afternoon, very thirsty and dizzy, and rang for ice water, coffee, and the Pittsburgh papers.

On the part of the hotel management, Paul excited no suspicion. There was this to be said for him, that he wore his spoils with dignity and in no way made himself conspicuous. His chief greediness lay in his ears and eyes, and his excesses were not offensive ones. His dearest pleasures were the gray winter twilight in his sitting room; his quiet enjoyment of his flowers, his clothes, his wide divan, his cigarette and his sense of power. He could not remember a time when he had felt so at peace with himself. The mere release from the necessity of petty lying, lying every day and every day, restored his self-respect. He had never lied for pleasure, even at school; but to make himself noticed and admired, to assert his difference from other Cordelia Street boys; and he felt a good deal more manly, more honest, even, now that he had no need for boastful pretensions, now that he could, as his actor friends used to say, "dress the part." It was characteristic that remorse did not occur to him. His golden days went by without a shadow, and he made each as perfect as he could.

On the eighth day after his arrival in New York, he found the whole affair exploited in the Pittsburgh papers, exploited with a wealth of detail which indicated that local news of a sensational nature was at a low ebb. The firm of Denny & Carson announced that the boy's father had refunded the full amount of his theft, and that they had no intention of prosecuting. The Cumberland minister had been interviewed, and expressed his hope of yet reclaiming the motherless lad, and Paul's Sabbath school teacher declared that she would spare no effort to that end. The rumor had reached Pittsburgh that the boy had been seen in a New York hotel, and his father had gone East to find him and bring him home.

Paul had just come in to dress for dinner; he sank into a chair, weak in the knees, and clasped his head in his hands. It was to be worse than jail, even; the tepid waters of Cordelia Street were to close over him finally and forever. The gray monotony stretched before him in hopeless, unrelieved years; Sabbath school, Young People's Meeting, the yellow-papered room, the damp dish towels; it all rushed back upon him with sickening vividness. He had the old feeling that the orchestra had suddenly stopped, the sinking sensation that the play was over. The sweat broke out on his face, and he sprang to his feet, looked about him with his white, conscious smile, and winked at himself in the mirror. With something of the childish belief in miracles with which he had so often gone to class, all his lessons unlearned, Paul dressed and dashed whistling down the corridor to the elevator.

He had no sooner entered the dining room and caught the measure of the music, than his remembrance was lightened by his old elastic power of claiming the moment, mounting with it, and finding it all sufficient. The glare and glitter about him, the mere scenic accessories had again, and for the last time, their old potency. He would show himself that he was game, he would finish the thing splendidly. He doubted, more than ever, the existence of Cordelia Street, and for the first time he drank his wine recklessly. Was he not, after all, one of these fortunate beings? Was he not still himself, and in his own place? He drummed a nervous accompaniment to the music and looked about him, telling himself over and over that it had paid.

He reflected drowsily, to the swell of the violin and the chill sweetness of his wine, that he might have done it more wisely. He might have caught an outbound steamer and been well out of their clutches before now. But the other side of the world had seemed too far away and too uncertain then; he could not have waited for it; his need had been too sharp. If he had to choose over again, he would do the same thing tomorrow. He looked affectionately about the dining room, now gilded with a soft mist. Ah, it had paid indeed!

Paul was awakened next morning by a painful throbbing in his head and feet. He had thrown himself across the bed without undressing, and had slept with his shoes on. His limbs and hands were lead heavy, and his tongue and throat were parched. There came upon him one of those fateful attacks of clear-headedness that never occurred except when he was physically exhausted and his nerves hung loose. He lay still and closed his eyes and let the tide of realities wash over him.

His father was in New York; "stopping at some joint or other," he told himself. The memory of successive summers on the front stoop fell upon him like a weight of black water. He had not a hundred dollars left; and he knew now, more than ever, that money was everything, the wall that stood between all he loathed and all he wanted. The thing was winding itself up; he had thought of that on his first glorious day in New York, and had even provided a way to snap the thread. It lay on his dressing table now; he had got it out last night when he came blindly up from dinner—but the shiny metal hurt his eyes, and he disliked the look of it, anyway.

He rose and moved about with a painful effort, succumbing now and again to attacks of nausea. It was the old depression exaggerated; all the world had become Cordelia Street. Yet somehow he was not afraid of anything, was absolutely calm; perhaps because he had looked into the dark corner at last, and knew. It was bad enough, what he saw there; but somehow not so bad as his long fear of it had been. He saw everything clearly now. He had a feeling that he had made the best of it, that he had lived the sort of life he was meant to live, and for half an hour he sat staring at the revolver. But he told himself that was not the way, so he went downstairs and took a cab to the ferry.

When Paul arrived at Newark, he got off the train and took another cab, directing the driver to follow the Pennsylvania tracks out of the town. The snow lay heavy on the roadways and had drifted deep in the open fields. Only here and there the dead grass or dried weed stalks projected, singularly black, above it. Once well into the country, Paul dismissed the carriage and walked, floundering along the tracks, his mind a medley of irrelevant things. He seemed to hold in his brain an actual picture of everything he had seen that morning. He remembered every feature of both his drivers, the toothless old woman from whom he had bought the red flowers in his coat, the agent from whom he had got his ticket, and all of his fellow passengers on the ferry. His mind, unable to cope with vital matters near at hand, worked feverishly and deftly at sorting and grouping these images. They made for him a part of the ugliness of the world, of the ache in his head, and the bitter burning on his tongue. He stooped and put a handful of snow into his mouth as he walked, but that, too, seemed hot. When he reached a little hillside, where the tracks ran through a cut some twenty feet below him, he stopped and sat down.

The carnations in his coat were drooping with the cold, he noticed; all their red glory over. It occurred to him that all the flowers he had seen in the show windows that first night must have gone the same way, long before this. It was only one splendid breath they had, in spite of their brave mockery at the winter outside the glass. It was a losing game in the end, it seemed, this revolt against the homilies by which the world is run. Paul took one of the blossoms carefully from his coat and scooped a little hole in the snow, where he covered it up. Then he dozed a while, from his weak condition, seeming insensible to the cold.

The sound of an approaching train woke him, and he started to his feet, remembering only his resolution, and afraid lest he should be too late. He stood watching the approaching locomotive, his teeth chattering, his lips drawn away from them in a frightened smile; once or twice he glanced nervously sidewise, as though he were being watched. When the right moment came, he jumped. As he fell, the folly of his haste occurred to him with merciless clearness, the vastness of what he had left undone. There flashed through his brain, clearer than ever before, the blue of Adriatic water, the yellow of Algerian sands.

He felt something strike his chest—his body was being thrown swiftly through the air, on and on, immeasurably far and fast, while his limbs gently relaxed. Then, because the picture-making mechanism was crushed, the disturbing visions flashed into black, and Paul dropped back into the immense design of things.

THE BOOKKEEPER'S WIFE
Willa Cather

Nobody but the janitor was stirring about the offices of the Remsen Paper Company, and still Percy Bixby sat at his desk, crouched on his high stool and staring out at the tops of the tall buildings flushed with the winter sunset, at the hundreds of windows, so many rectangles of white electric light, flashing against the broad waves of violet that ebbed across the sky. His ledgers were all in their places, his desk was in order, his office coat on its peg, and yet Percy's smooth, thin face wore the look of anxiety and strain which usually meant that he was behind in his work. He was trying to persuade himself to accept a loan from the company without the company's knowledge. As a matter of fact, he had already accepted it. His books were fixed, the money, in a black-leather bill-book, was already inside his waistcoat pocket.

He had still time to change his mind, to rectify the false figures in his ledger, and to tell Stella Brown that they couldn't possibly get married next month. There he always halted in his reasoning, and went back to the beginning.

The Remsen Paper Company was a very wealthy concern, with easy, old-fashioned working methods. They did a long-time credit business with safe customers, who never thought of paying up very close on their large indebtedness. From the payments on these large accounts Percy had taken a hundred dollars here and two hundred there until he made up the thousand he needed. So long as he stayed by the books himself and attended to the mail-orders he couldn't possibly be found out. He could move these little shortages about from account to account indefinitely. He could have all the time he needed to pay back the deficit, and more time than he needed.

Although he was so far along in one course of action, his mind still clung resolutely to the other. He did not believe he was going to do it. He was the least of a sharper in the world. Being scrupulously honest even in the most trifling matters was a pleasure to him. He was the sort of young man that Socialists hate more than they hate capitalists. He loved his desk, he loved his books, which had no handwriting in them but his own. He never thought of resenting the fact that he had written away in those books the good red years between twenty-one and twenty-seven. He would have hated to let any one else put so much as a pen-scratch in them. He liked all the boys about the office; his desk, worn smooth by the sleeves of his alpaca coat; his rulers and inks and pens and calendars. He had a great pride in working economics, and he always got so far ahead when supplies

115

were distributed that he had drawers full of pencils and pens and rubber bands against a rainy day.

Percy liked regularity; to get his work done on time, to have his half-day off every Saturday, to go to the theater Saturday night, to buy a new necktie twice a month, to appear in a new straw hat on the right day in May, and to know what was going on in New York. He read the morning and evening papers coming and going on the elevated, and preferred journals of approximate reliability. He got excited about ballgames and elections and business failures, was not above an interest in murders and divorce scandals, and he checked the news off as neatly as he checked his mail-orders. In short, Percy Bixby was like the model pupil who is satisfied with his lessons and his teachers and his holidays, and who would gladly go to school all his life. He had never wanted anything outside his routine until he wanted Stella Brown to marry him, and that had upset everything.

It wasn't, he told himself for the hundredth time, that she was extravagant. Not a bit of it. She was like all girls. Moreover, she made good money, and why should she marry unless she could better herself? The trouble was that he had lied to her about his salary. There were a lot of fellows rushing Mrs. Brown's five daughters, and they all seemed to have fixed on Stella as first choice and this or that one of the sisters as second. Mrs. Brown thought it proper to drop an occasional hint in the presence of these young men to the effect that she expected Stella to "do well." It went without saying that hair and complexion like Stella's could scarcely be expected to do poorly. Most of the boys who went to the house and took the girls out in a bunch to dances and movies seemed to realize this. They merely wanted a whirl with Stella before they settled down to one of her sisters. It was tacitly understood that she came too high for them. Percy had sensed all this through those slumbering instincts which awake in us all to befriend us in love or in danger.

But there was one of his rivals, he knew, who was a man to be reckoned with. Charley Greengay was a young salesman who wore tailor-made clothes and spotted waistcoats, and had a necktie for every day in the month. His air was that of a young man who is out for things that come high and who is going to get them. Mrs. Brown was ever and again dropping a word before Percy about how the girl that took Charley would have her flat furnished by the best furniture people, and her china-closet stocked with the best ware, and would have nothing to worry about but nicks and scratches. It was because he felt himself pitted against this pulling power of Greengay's that Percy had brazenly lied to Mrs. Brown, and told her that his salary had been raised to fifty a week, and that now he wanted to get married.

When he threw out this challenge to Mother Brown, Percy was getting thirty-five a week, and he knew well enough that there were several thousand young men in New York who would do his work as well as he did for thirty.

These were the factors in Percy's present situation. He went over them again and again as he sat stooping on his tall stool. He had quite lost track of time when he heard the janitor call good night to the watchman. Without thinking what he was doing, he slid into his overcoat, caught his hat, and rushed out to the elevator, which was waiting for the janitor. The moment the car dropped, it occurred to him that the thing was decided without his having made up his mind at all. The familiar floors passed him, ten, nine, eight, seven. By the time he reached the fifth, there was no possibility of going back; the click of the drop-lever seemed to settle that. The money was in his pocket. Now, he told himself as he hurried out into the exciting clamor of the street, he was not going to worry about it any more.

When Percy reached the Browns' flat on 123rd Street that evening he felt just the slightest chill in Stella's greeting. He could make that all right, he told himself, as he kissed her lightly in the dark three-by-four entrance-hall. Percy's courting had been prosecuted mainly in the Bronx or in winged pursuit of a Broadway car. When he entered the crowded sitting-room he greeted Mrs. Brown respectfully and the four girls playfully. They were all piled on one couch, reading the continued story in the evening paper, and they didn't think it necessary to assume more formal attitudes for Percy. They looked up over the smeary pink sheets of paper, and handed him, as Percy said, the same old jolly:

"Hullo, Perc'! Come to see me, ain't you? So flattered!"

"Any sweet goods on you, Perc'? Anything doing in the bong-bong line tonight?"

"Look at his new neckwear! Say, Perc', remember me. That tie would go lovely with my new tailored waist."

"Quit your kiddin', girls!" called Mrs. Brown, who was drying shirt-waists on the dining-room radiator. "And, Percy, mind the rugs when you're steppin' round among them gum-drops."

Percy fired his last shot at the recumbent figures, and followed Stella into the dining-room, where the table and two large easy-chairs formed, in Mrs. Brown's estimation, a proper background for a serious suitor.

"I say, Stell'," he began as he walked about the table with his hands in his pockets, "seems to me we ought to begin buying our stuff." She brightened perceptibly. "Ah," Percy thought, "so that *was* the trouble!" "Tomorrow's Saturday; why can't we make an afternoon of it?" he went on cheerfully. "Shop till we're tired, then go to Houtin's for dinner, and end up at the theater."

As they bent over the lists she had made of things needed, Percy glanced at her face. She was very much out of her sisters' class and out of his, and he kept congratulating himself on his nerve. He was going in for something much too handsome and expensive and distinguished for him, he felt, and it took courage to be a plunger. To begin with, Stella was the sort of girl who had to be well dressed. She had pale primrose hair, with bluish tones in it, very soft and fine, so that it lay smooth however she dressed it, and pale-blue eyes, with blond eyebrows and long, dark lashes. She would have been a little too remote and languid even for the fastidious Percy had it not been for her hard, practical mouth, with lips that always kept their pink even when the rest of her face was pale. Her employers, who at first might be struck by her indifference, understood that anybody with that sort of mouth would get through the work.

After the shopping-lists had been gone over, Percy took up the question of the honeymoon. Stella said she had been thinking of Atlantic City. Percy met her with firmness. Whatever happened, he couldn't leave his books now.

"I want to do my traveling right here on Forty-second Street, with a high-price show every night," he declared. He made out an itinerary, punctuated by theaters and restaurants, which Stella consented to accept as a substitute for Atlantic City.

"They give your fellows a week off when they're married, don't they?" she asked.

"Yes, but I'll want to drop into the office every morning to look after my mail. That's only businesslike."

"I'd like to have you treated as well as the others, though." Stella turned the rings about on her pale hand and looked at her polished fingertips.

"I'll look out for that. What do you say to a little walk, Stell'?" Percy put the question coaxingly. When Stella was pleased with him she went to walk with him, since that was the only way in which Percy could ever see her alone. When she was displeased, she said she was too tired to go out. Tonight she smiled at him incredulously, and went to put on her hat and gray fur piece.

Once they were outside, Percy turned into a shadowy side street that was only partly built up, a dreary waste of derricks and foundation holes, but comparatively solitary. Stella liked Percy's steady, sympathetic silences; she was not a chatterbox herself. She often wondered why she was going to marry Bixby instead of Charley Greengay. She knew that Charley would go further in the world. Indeed, she had often coolly told herself that Percy would never go very far. But, as she admitted with a shrug, she was "weak to Percy." In the capable New York stenographer, who estimated values coldly and got the most for the least outlay, there was something left that belonged to another kind of woman—something that liked the very things in Percy that were not good business assets. However much she dwelt upon the effectiveness of Greengay's dash and color and assurance, her mind always came back to Percy's neat little head, his clean-cut face, and warm, clear, gray eyes, and she liked them better than Charley's fullness and blurred floridness. Having reckoned up their respective chances with no doubtful result, she opposed a mild obstinacy to her own good sense. "I guess I'll take Percy, *anyway*," she said simply, and that was all the good her clever business brain did her.

Percy spent a night of torment, lying tense on his bed in the dark, and figuring out how long it would take him to pay back the money he was advancing himself. Any fool could do it in five years, he reasoned, but he was going to do it in three. The trouble was that his expensive courtship had taken every penny of his salary. With competitors like Charley Greengay, you had to spend money or drop out. Certain birds, he reflected ruefully, are supplied with more attractive plumage when they are courting, but nature hadn't been so thoughtful for men. When Percy reached the office in the morning he climbed on his tall stool and leaned his arms on his ledger. He was so glad to feel it there that he was faint and weak-kneed.

Oliver Remsen, Junior, had brought new blood into the Remsen Paper Company. He married shortly after Percy Bixby did, and in the five succeeding years he had considerably enlarged the company's business and profits. He had been particularly successful in encouraging efficiency and loyalty in the employees. From the time he came into the office he had stood for shorter hours, longer holidays, and generous consideration of men's necessities. He came out of college on the wave of economic reform, and he continued to read and think a good deal about how the machinery of labor is operated. He knew more about the men who worked for him than their mere office records.

Young Remsen was troubled about Percy Bixby because he took no summer vacations—always asked for the two weeks' extra pay instead. Other men in the office had skipped a vacation now and then, but Percy had stuck to his desk for five years, had tottered to his stool through attacks of grippe and tonsillitis. He seemed to have grown fast to his ledger, and it was to this that Oliver objected. He liked his men to stay men, to look like men and live like men. He remembered how alert and wide-awake Bixby had seemed to him when he himself first came into the office. He had picked Bixby out as the most intelligent and interested of his father's employees, and since then had often wondered why he never seemed to see chances to forge ahead. Promotions, of course, went to the men who went after them. When Percy's baby died, he went to the funeral and asked Percy to call on him if he needed money. Once when he chanced to sit down by Bixby on the elevated and found him reading Bryce's *American Commonwealth*, he asked him to make use of his own large office library. Percy thanked him, but he never came for any books. Oliver wondered whether his bookkeeper really tried to avoid him.

One evening Oliver met the Bixbys in the lobby of a theater. He introduced Mrs. Remsen to them, and held them for some moments in conversation. When they got into their motor, Mrs. Remsen said:

"Is that little man afraid of you, Oliver? He looked like a scared rabbit."

Oliver snapped the door, and said with a shade of irritation:

"I don't know what's the matter with him. He's the fellow I've told you about who never takes a vacation. I half believe it's his wife. She looks pitiless enough for anything."

"She's very pretty of her kind." mused Mrs. Remsen, "but rather chilling. One can see that she has ideas about elegance."

"Rather unfortunate ones for a bookkeeper's wife. I surmise that Percy felt she was overdressed, and that made him awkward with me. I've always suspected that fellow of good taste."

After that, when Remsen passed the counting-room and saw Percy screwed up over his ledger, he often remembered Mrs. Bixby, with her cold, pale eyes and long lashes, and her expression that was something between indifference and discontent. She rose behind Percy's bent shoulders like an apparition.

One spring afternoon Remsen was closeted in his private office with his lawyer until a late hour. As he came down the long hall in the dusk he glanced through the glass partition into the counting-room, and saw Percy Bixby huddled up on his tall stool, though it was too dark to work. Indeed, Bixby's ledger was closed, and he sat with his two arms resting on the brown cover. He did not move a muscle when young Remsen entered.

"You are late, Bixby, and so am I," Oliver began genially as he crossed to the front of the room and looked out at the lighted window of other tall buildings. "The fact is, I've been doing something that men have a foolish way of putting off. I've been making my will."

"Yes, sir." Percy brought it out with a deep breath.

"Glad to be through with it," Oliver went on. "Mr. Melton will bring the paper back tomorrow, and I'd like to ask you to be one of the witnesses."

"I'd be very proud, Mr. Remsen."

"Thank you, Bixby. Good night." Remsen took up his hat just as Percy slid down from his stool.

"Mr. Remsen, I'm told you're going to have the books gone over."

"Why, yes, Bixby. Don't let that trouble you. I'm taking in a new partner, you know, an old college friend. Just because he is a friend, I insist upon all the usual formalities. But it is a formality, and I'll guarantee the expert won't make a scratch on your books. Good night. You'd better be coming, too." Remsen had reached the door when he heard "Mr. Remsen!" in a desperate voice behind him. He turned, and saw Bixby, standing uncertainly at one end of the desk, his hand still on his ledger, his uneven shoulders drooping forward and his head hanging as if he were seasick. Remsen came back and stood at the other end of the long desk. It was too dark to see Bixby's face clearly.

"What is it, Bixby?"

"Mr. Remsen, five years ago, just before I was married, I falsified the books a thousand dollars, and I used the money." Percy leaned forward against his desk, which took him just across the chest.

"What's that, Bixby?" Young Remsen spoke in a tone of polite surprise. He felt painfully embarrassed.

"Yes, sir. I thought I'd get it all paid back before this. I've put back three hundred, but the books are still seven hundred out of true. I've played the shortages about from account to account these five years, but an expert would find 'em in twenty-four hours."

"I don't just understand how—" Oliver stopped and shook his head.

"I held it out of the Western remittances, Mr. Remsen. They were coming in heavy just then. I was up against it. I hadn't saved anything to marry on, and my wife thought I was getting more money than I was. Since we've been married, I've never had the nerve to tell her. I could have paid it all back if it hadn't been for the unforeseen expenses."

Remsen sighed.

"Being married is largely unforeseen expenses, Percy. There's only one way to fix this up: I'll give you seven hundred dollars in cash tomorrow, and you can give me your personal note, with the understanding that I hold ten dollars a week out of your pay-check until it is paid. I think you ought to tell your wife exactly how you are fixed, though. You can't expect her to help you much when she doesn't know."

That night Mrs. Bixby was sitting in their flat, waiting for her husband. She was dressed for a bridge party, and often looked with impatience from her paper to the Mission clock, as big as a coffin and with nothing but two weights dangling in its hollow framework. Percy had been loath to buy the clock when they got their furniture, and he had hated it ever since. Stella had changed very little since she came into the flat a bride. Then she wore her hair in a Floradora pompadour; now she wore it hooded close about her head like a scarf, in a rather smeary manner, like an Impressionist's brush-work. She heard her husband come in and close the door softly. While he was taking off his hat in the narrow tunnel of a hall, she called to him:

"I hope you've had something to eat downtown. You'll have to dress right away." Percy came in and sat down. She looked up from the evening paper she was reading. "You've no time to sit down. We must start in fifteen minutes."

He shaded his eyes from the glaring overhead light.

"I'm afraid I can't go anywhere tonight. I'm all in."

Mrs. Bixby rattled her paper, and turned from the theatrical page to the fashions.

"You'll feel better after you dress. We won't stay late."

Her even persistence usually conquered her husband. She never forgot anything she had once decided to do. Her manner of following it up grew more chilly, but never weaker. Tonight there was no spring in Percy. He closed his eyes and replied without moving:

"I can't go. You had better telephone the Burks we aren't coming. I have to tell you something disagreeable."

Stella rose.

"I certainly am not going to disappoint the Burks and stay at home to talk about anything disagreeable."

"You're not very sympathetic, Stella."

She turned away.

"If I were, you'd soon settle down into a pretty dull proposition. We'd have no social life now if I didn't keep at you."

Percy roused himself a little.

"Social life? Well, we'll have to trim that pretty close for a while. I'm in debt to the company. We've been living beyond our means ever since we were married."

"We can't live on less than we do," Stella said quietly. "No use in taking that up again."

Percy sat up, clutching the arms of his chair.

"We'll have to take it up. I'm seven hundred dollars short, and the books are to be audited tomorrow. I told young Remsen and he's going to take my note and hold the money out of my pay-checks. He could send me to jail, of course."

Stella turned and looked down at him with a gleam of interest.

"Oh, you've been playing solitaire with the books, have you? And he's found you out! I hope I'll never see that man again. Sugar face!" She said this with intense acrimony. Her forehead flushed delicately, and her eyes were full of hate. Young Remsen was not her idea of a "business man."

Stella went into the other room. When she came back she wore her evening coat and carried long gloves and a black scarf. This she began to arrange over her hair before the mirror above the false fireplace. Percy lay inert in the Morris chair and watched her. Yes, he understood; it was very difficult for a woman with hair like that to be shabby and to go without things. Her hair made her conspicuous, and it had to be lived up to. It had been the deciding factor in her fate.

Stella caught the lace over one ear with a large gold hair-pin. She repeated this until she got a good effect. Then turning to Percy, she began to draw on her gloves.

"I'm not worrying any, because I'm going back into business," she said firmly. "I meant to, anyway, if you didn't get a raise the first of the year. I have the offer of a good position, and we can live in an apartment hotel."

Percy was on his feet in an instant.

"I won't have you grinding in any office. That's flat."

Stella's lower lip quivered in a commiserating smile. "Oh, I won't lose my health. Charley Greengay's a partner in his concern now, and he wants a private secretary."

Percy drew back.

"You can't work for Greengay. He's got too bad a reputation. You've more pride than that, Stella."

The thin sweep of color he knew so well went over Stella's face.

"His business reputation seems to be all right," she commented, working the kid on with her left hand.

"What if it is?" Percy broke out. "He's the cheapest kind of a skate. He gets into scrapes with the girls in his own office. The last one got into the newspapers, and he had to pay the girl a wad."

"He don't get into scrapes with his books, anyway, and he seems to be able to stand getting into the papers. I excuse Charley. His wife's a pill."

"I suppose you think he'd have been all right if he'd married you," said Percy, bitterly.

"Yes, I do." Stella buttoned her glove with an air of finishing something, and then looked at Percy without animosity. "Charley and I both have sporty tastes, and we like excitement. You might as well live in Newark if you're going to sit at home in the evening. You oughtn't to have married a business woman; you need somebody domestic. There's nothing in this sort of life for either of us."

"That means, I suppose, that you're going around with Greengay and his crowd?"

"Yes, that's my sort of crowd, and you never did fit into it. You're too intellectual. I've always been proud of you, Percy. You're better style than Charley, but that gets tiresome. You will never burn much red fire in New York, now, will you?"

Percy did not reply. He sat looking at the minute-hand of the eviscerated Mission clock. His wife almost never took the trouble to argue with him.

"You're old style, Percy," she went on. "Of course everybody marries and wishes they hadn't, but nowadays people get over it. Some women go ahead on the quiet, but I'm giving it to you straight. I'm going to work for Greengay. I like his line of business, and I meet people well. Now I'm going to the Burks'."

Percy dropped his hands limply between his knees.

"I suppose," he brought out, "the real trouble is that you've decided my earning power is not very great."

"That's part of it, and part of it is you're old-fashioned." Stella paused at the door and looked back. "What made you rush me, anyway, Percy?" she asked indulgently. "What did you go and pretend to be a spender and get tied up with me for?"

"I guess everybody wants to be a spender when he's in love," Percy replied.

Stella shook her head mournfully.

"No, you're a spender or you're not. Greengay has been broke three times, fired, down and out, black-listed. But he's always come back, and he always will. You will never be fired, but you'll always be poor." She turned and looked back again before she went out.

Six months later Bixby came to young Oliver Remsen one afternoon and said he would like to have twenty dollars a week held out of his pay until his debt was cleared off.

Oliver looked up at his sallow employee and asked him how he could spare as much as that.

"My expenses are lighter," Bixby replied. "My wife has gone into business with a ready-to-wear firm. She is not living with me any more."

Oliver looked annoyed, and asked him if nothing could be done to readjust his domestic affairs. Bixby said no; they would probably remain as they were.

"But where are you living, Bixby? How have you arranged things?" the young man asked impatiently.

"I'm very comfortable. I live in a boarding-house and have my own furniture. There are several fellows there who are fixed the same way. Their wives went back into business, and they drifted apart."

With a baffled expression Remsen stared at the uneven shoulders under the skin-fitting alpaca desk coat as his bookkeeper went out. He had meant to do something for Percy, but somehow, he reflected, one never did do anything for a fellow who had been stung as hard as that.

THUS THE EARLY GODS
George Garrett

"Decent people just don't act like that," her mother-in-law said.

Jane's mother-in-law was Mrs. Grim. How aptly named! Jane was amused by the thought until she reminded herself that it was her name too.

Jane's husband mumbled assent and held up his highball glass and looked through it to change the sky from blue to amber. Lately everything was being so changed.

Jane herself wasn't paying much attention to Mrs. Grim's desultory monologue. She sat with the other two on the front porch and looked on beyond the path that crawled like a lazy snake from the cottage through the dunes to the beach, beyond the glare and dance of light on the white sand of the beach and beyond the flourish of the breaking waves, perfectly ironed creases that became immaculate explosions into the dizzying blue of the sky, cloudless and pure today. There was a line of pelicans, a slightly lopsided V with one arm stretched out longer than the other, and they flew by with a brown sturdy grace like a crew of oarsmen in a racing shell. They followed the leader at the point. He (she guessed it would *have* to be a male) would spread his wings to soar, and all soared likewise, rising and hovering with delicate balance on invisible currents of air, maintaining always the shape and direction of the formation though, like a single, trained, instantaneous muscular action, like part of a dance. When he pumped his wide wings with a smooth strong motion, the others followed in quick succession. She liked to see them fishing and alone: the twisty, angled high dive followed by a small flash of white, and then up bobbed the pelican to float contented a while before flying again. She had seen them up close too, perched like silly newel posts on the pilings near the Fish Market, long-beaked, drab-feathered, clowns. And she had been disappointed. They seemed grotesquely comic. But now as formations of them passed by the front porch, at home in their native element of air, they seemed to be made of it, to partake of all the wild, wide-flung, dazzling substance and mystery and marvel of the sky. They were creatures of skill and grace and beauty, and she wished she could paint them.

But, of course, her paints were still packed tight in the wooden box underneath the double bed. She wouldn't dream of bringing them out.

"But they're so beautiful!" she exclaimed.

"Who?" the gray-haired woman, firmly in the rocking chair beside her, asked. "Who? Those Quiglys?"

"No, no," Jane said, laughing. "I was thinking about the pelicans."

Her mother-in-law snorted.

"I was speaking of the Quiglys."

Harper, Jane's husband, merely chuckled and sipped his drink.

Mrs. Grim had been talking about the Quigly family steadily ever since they had arrived and opened the beach cottage a few days (how many has it been already?) before. She noticed right away that they had been using her outside shower. ("Lord knows what kind of a staggering water bill I'll have!") She observed that they let their children run wild and free and naked as four little jaybirds all over the dunes and on the beach. And she complained that all of them, the gaunt, grinning scarecrow of a father included, used her path to the beach as if they had a perfect right to, instead of going the longer way around to the public approach. It was clear, too, at the outset that they had no pride.

The Grims hadn't been in the cottage five minutes before the man was standing at the back door, beating on it with bony knuckles, grinning and asking if he could borrow a quarter pound of butter and an electric iron, not explaining why, or, indeed, even making some kind of mannerable small talk about the casual incongruity of the two requests. He didn't introduce himself. He didn't bother to ask who they might be. He just asked for butter and the iron and then stood there waiting until he was given what he wanted.

Mrs. Grim had been fuming about the Quiglys ever since.

"Oh, Mother," Jane had said, mildly amused at first. "What's wrong with them? I mean really. They seem pleasant enough."

Her mother-in-law had stiffened.

"You're not from these parts," she had answered flatly. "So you wouldn't be expected to know or make *distinctions*. They're trash, honey, that's all. Trash, pure and simple."

The element that added insult to injury for Mrs. Grim was the occupation of Joe Quigly, whom she insisted on calling The Man, never by name. It turned out that he was a bulldozer operator. Farther south, more than a mile down the beach, he was daily engaged in levelling the pristine dunes for something or other. A new subdivision of crackerbox houses maybe. Perhaps even a motel. She wouldn't condescend to inquire.

"It really shouldn't bother you," Jane had said. "There's so much space down there, and there's a whole mile between here and there."

"When we first built this place, my late husband and I," Mrs. Grim had told her, "there wasn't another cottage for miles. It was so peaceful. Now houses are popping up everywhere like the heat rash. Like pimples. They're tearing the dunes down, and new people—not the kind of people you'd care to have around if you had any say so about the matter—are coming here by the hordes to live. They're ruining the place. They're like a lot of weeds choking us out.

"You'd have to know how everything was in the beginning to appreciate what I mean," she added.

Of course, she never failed to remind Jane that she was an outsider, from the north, and wouldn't be expected to offer her opinions on subjects she couldn't possibly know anything about, among them the Quiglys. Jane never failed to resent this either.

At first, their very first night in the cottage, Harper, too, had been amused.

"Oh, you'll come to love her when you know her and understand her better," he said. "Everyone does. It's just that she was born out of her time or, anyway, that she had to live on beyond it. She's a lady living in a time when that word doesn't mean anything. And all she sees around her is change, change, change. Change and decay. The good, happy, comfortable world she grew up in turned inside out, turned into something else after the Depression and the War. She's just a minor, eccentric victim of the great social revolution. A bewildered mastodon wandering around in the postglacial age."

But by the next night he was past that kind of fancy speech-making.

"Quit getting in a stew about nothing," he said. "Don't pay it no never mind."

Which was both strange grammar and an unfamiliar accent coming from him. Jane's husband was a lawyer now in Philadelphia. It had taken him a day and a night to pick up the accent and the idiom of a speech he couldn't have used at all since he was a child, *if* he had used it then. It had taken another full day for him to lose the half irony that made his new guise acceptable. It had taken another day and a very bad night (But she was so *nervous* visiting here for the first time. Didn't he even understand *that?*) for him to start in drinking. And now he wasn't shaving any more or brushing his teeth or changing his clothes or bothering to go down to the beach. And now he was always taking his mother's side.

They *did* look something alike. (Strangely. For wasn't it always the daughter who was supposed to end up looking more and more like the mother?) Sitting together side by side on the front porch, she with her empty hands folded, he with his clasping the almost empty glass, short, square-bodied, long-torsoed, they were clearly cut from the same pattern. Sometimes Harper's lips turned tight and down in precisely the same expression of unspoken disapproval. Sometimes, now, his small, quick, pale blue eyes reminded her of Mrs. Grim's. And Jane, slender ("Honey, you'll have to eat plenty while you're down here and put some meat on those bones. Harp, boy, you ought to be ashamed to let you wife get so frail and wispy."), milk-skinned and long-limbed, was beginning to feel made out of another substance, a member of another race.

At this moment, inspired by the sight of the flying pelicans, images to her at once of rigor and beauty and harmony and freedom, she felt like arguing.

"Now that you mention it, the Quigly children *are* beautiful."

Mrs. Grim grunted at that.

"Well if you think naked savages are beautiful, you might say so. Each one to her own taste, as the old lady said."

"As a matter of fact, I *have* seen photographs of naked savages which I thought were beautiful, the savages that is," Jane persisted.

Harper stood up, sighed, and stretched.

"Tell you what," he said. "You want to see some savages around here? You just drop over to Black Bottom about ten o'clock on a Saturday night."

"That would cure her of notions," Mrs. Grim said, chuckling. She said the word *notions* as if it signified some kind of physical disease, barely mentionable in polite company. "That surely would cure her."

"You'd get yourself a bellyful of beautiful savages," Harper said.

"Where are you going?" Jane said.

"To pour myself another little drink. *If* you don't mind."

"Suit yourself," she said. "It's your vacation."

"Did you say *vocation?*"

"I did not."

"Much obliged."

Harper's mother rocked busily and steadily, looking straight ahead. Jane turned again to watch the fine line of the waves rising, hovering, exploding on the sand in snowy profusion. She heard Harper stumble over something in the kitchen and curse. Well, there was nothing to be done about it.

A whoop and a holler! A shrill pandemonium of treble cries and then a burst of sun-bronzed flesh as four blonde naked Quigly children shot around the corner of the porch, scattered like a flushed covey of quail down the path, and vanished in the dunes. Mrs. Grim was half out of her rocking chair, rigid, her face etched in lines of anger. Harper leaned on the door frame shaking his head.

"They won't never learn," he said.

"I tried to speak to the mother (*if* she is the mother) yesterday. And do you know she was *drunk?* Stone drunk in the middle of the day. I mean staggering around inside of that trailer blind drunk. No wonder those poor little children have to run around wild without a soul to look after them."

"They seem to be getting along all right, considering," Jane said.

"It's a wonder to me they don't all drown in the ocean," Mrs. Grim said. "I'd feel kind of sorry for The Man, if he wasn't so common and worthless himself. They tell me when he gets home from work the two of them start drinking together and just keep on until they pass out cold. The children just have to fend for themselves."

"Who told you that?"

"A perfectly legitimate soruce. Someone who ought to know," Mrs. Grim said indignantly.

"She didn't mean it to sound that way, Mother." Harper said. "She was just wondering."

Not even Jane now. Just *she*.

"I *did* mean it to sound that way," Jane said. "Gossip makes me sick."

"Well!" Mrs. Grim said.

"What in hell got into *you*?" Harper said.

"I don't know. I'm sorry. I just don't know."

Jane brushed past him running back toward the bedroom, fighting the impulse to tears. She flung herself on the bed and pulled a pillow over her head. It was a silly, childish gesture. He wasn't going to come running behind her and try to comfort her. He and his mother would talk about it in low voices, and after a while he'd come back to the bedroom and talk to her. He wouldn't offer any sympathy. And she was furious with herself that what she wanted was his sympathy.

She was confused about all of it she realized. It wasn't just the usual battle, the immemorial tug of war between mother-in-law and daughter-in-law. It was that all right, intensified by the inescapable fact that Harper was an only child. But it was other things as well. She was seeing her husband for the first time in his native environment, without the well-mannered, gentle, acquired protective coloration he wore in her world, a world of strangers to him. (What camouflage was there for her here?) He was different. He seemed to sense it too, to succumb in helpless fury to old pressures and forces. She felt that as long as they stayed here they were lost to each other. The man she had married and lived with was a ghost. The one in her bed at night now was not a very attractive stranger. In that sense Mrs. Grim had become in her eyes the evil enchantress of a child's fairy tale. But then, after all, the whole business was so childish!

Then there were the Quiglys, the Battleground. They lived, the whole tribe of them, in a small trailer behind the cottage and across a dirt road, just at the edge of a palmetto jungle. It was a sagging, worn-out trailer, set up on cinder blocks. And the yard, if you could call the littered and trampled space between the trailer and the road a yard, was a perfect mess. In the center of that space there was the cross-eyed wreck of an old Buick convertible. It never moved. Sun baked it and the sudden summer showers soaked it. Every day Joe Quigly came home from work and washed and sponged it down, apparently to protect the paint and chrome from the salt air that corroded everything under the sun before long. After he'd finished, he'd climb in the driver's seat and just sit there. It looked (from the distance of the bedroom window where she always watched him) as if he pretended to be driving it. Maybe he had wrecked it and it wouldn't run any more. Maybe he had bought it as is from a junk yard and it didn't even have an engine. Maybe he simply didn't have the money for gas. (Which would be an odd thing for a bulldozer operator. She had heard they made lots of money. Unless . . . unless, maybe, alas, Mrs. Grim was quite right, and both Joe Quigly and his poor, frazzle-haired slattern of a wife, who usually appeared once a day anyway wrapped in an oversize pink dressing gown and wearing sneakers, blinking in the hard sunlight and stumbling over to the topless garbage can by the road to dispose of a bundle of—empty bottles?—*were alcoholics.*) In any case, Joe Quigly seemed to love that automobile and to be very possessive about it. If he found his children playing in it when he came trudging up the dirt road home, he ran and chased them out and away with kicks and blows and curses. They didn't seem to mind. They laughed and ran away and left him his car.

The strange thing to Jane was that neither did she. She should have cared. A man who mistreats his children! Of course he didn't really mistreat them. He had a tantrum and they had to flee, but it didn't seem to mean anything to them or, seriously, to him. It seemed to be a kind of game. It made her uneasy to think that she might have tolerated such a blow or kick or curse coming from him in just that spirit, though she was sure that if Harper ever struck her she would be badly hurt. Quigly was a curious one. Long, lean, shaggy-haired, his face high-boned, deeply tanned and lined, he moved around with a clumsy grace like an animal trying to walk on its hind legs. He grinned a snaggle- and yellow-tooth grin at her if they happened to pass, and he ran a hand through his thick, unruly blonde hair. He was a kind of caricature of the country bumpkin. But—and this was what touched and troubled her—there was something else, indefinable, about him that was utterly alien, yet intriguing. It was as if the clothes, the flesh and bones, the face he wore were all composite parts of a disguise, donned by choice and for some reason. Somehow he communicated a sense of elemental shiftlessness, of sly, supple and insinuative and irresponsible endurance. Thus the early gods, she thought, must have taken on their guise of mortal flesh and moved among us.

She had tried unsuccessfully to express this complex thing that she sensed to Harper after she'd seen Joe Quigly standing at the back door waiting for his quarter pound of butter and the electric iron. Harper had laughed at her.

"You artists! Him? He's a typical cracker boy. That's the way they all are. Godlike, my ass! Not worth a damn. Crooked as a bunch of snakes."

Since the bad night and the others following it when Harper tumbled into his side of the bed, dead drunk, and snored as soon as his face touched the pillow, she had discovered that she was increasingly fascinated by the myth she had made up for Joe Quigly. Oh, not in the ordinary way, to be sure. Not *that* way. But as one might be attracted by some wonderful new beast on display at the zoo. There was nothing to it, she assured herself, beyond that simple feeling of curiosity and delight.

Then yesterday something had happened. With Harper drinking and Mrs. Grim deep in a historical novel and Jane restless and bored, she had gone for a long, lonely walk down the beach. She passed the last of the houses and the few bathers splashing in the surf, and she walked on, following the straight and narrow ribbon of soft sand that seemed to stretch, like some ultimate desert, to infinity. The sun felt warm and good. After a while, alone and happy, she sat down at the foot of a high dune to enjoy it, soon lay back and closed her eyes, dozing in the light. It seemed to penetrate her and fill her veins, and she imagined all her blood, streams, rivers, networks, and canals, as becoming a choir of pure molten gold. As she lay there in a complete blank pleasure, she heard at first dimly, then near and loud, a roaring sound, and she sat up just in time to avoid being buried alive by a falling mountain of sand. Choking and spluttering, she struggled to her feet with vague gestures like a drowning person and tried to brush away the sand which covered her. She looked around and then up above her. On top of the dune, poised perilously at the very edge of it, was the flat blade of the bulldozer, and standing above and behind the blade, tall against the whirling sky, straddle-legged, with the afternoon sun glaring behind him, was Joe Quigly, his wild hair tousled by the sea breeze, his head tossed back laughing. Jane was furious. Though she was fully and modestly dressed in shorts and a T-shirt, she felt as if he'd been spying on her naked. And then to be covered up, nearly killed in fact, was no joke. Joe Quigly obviously felt differently about it, and, even if he guessed how she must feel, he didn't care. He was content to laugh at her, and she had to laugh too. She stood there looking up at him and laughing, and she shyly raised her hand to wave at him. He waved back, vanished, backed the bulldozer away from the edge and went to work again.

Neither of them had said a word. Yet she was as pleased as if he'd tossed her a bouquet of flowers.

She kept that story to herself, not daring to mention it to Harper now. He was sure to take a different view of it.

Jane heard the bedroom door close behind her. She turned her head and saw Harper standing over her.

"I don't know what gets into you sometimes."

"I don't either," she said. "I'm sorry."

"You ought to be. That was pretty rude."

"I know it and I really am sorry."

He dropped down on his hands and knees on the floor and crawled under the bed. She heard him fumbling among the luggage they had stored there.

"What are you doing?"

"Looking for your box of paints," he said.

"What on earth for?"

"I got to paint me a sign."

"With those? That's too expensive."

"I'd be glad to use some other paint," he said. "But it happens we ain't got none. We've told these folks for the last time. Now I'm putting up a 'Keep Off' sign."

"That's silly, Harper. You've been drinking and that's a silly idea."

He backed out and raised his head to the level of the bed.

"You don't understand. Not at all," he said. "There happens to be a *legal* problem involved. If they keep on using the path and we don't put up a sign, then it becomes a common pathway. We don't want that, do we?"

"I guess not."

"Want to help me?" he said. "You can letter a whole lot better than I can."

"No," she said. "Just help yourself. The paints are right there somewhere."

"Where are you going?"

"Just for a walk," she said, shutting the door behind her.

She took the public approach to the beach and avoided the path to save herself from having to pass under the gray scrutiny of Mrs. Grim. She set off south at a good pace, feeling the warm sand between her toes. The tide was coming in now. Jane liked high tide best, though it was hard to explain why, even to herself. Somehow when the tide was high you felt you knew, were familiar with the things the water covered and concealed. At low tide shallow slough were mysteries. If you waded you were apt to step on something hidden there, some submarine creature, a quick, brittle, scuttling crab, a jellyfish. (She remembered with a shiver a story of someone stepping on a corpse in the surf.) High tide, though, seemed to be a blessing, the blue waves breaking over and finally covering the beach. The natural impulse of water. It seemed like a fine idea for water to want to cover the land. Perhaps that's how old Noah looked at it, she thought.

She almost tripped over a dead pelican and started back a step in surprise. It lay on the sand, a crumpled mass of wet feathers, a beak slack as a drunk's jaw, as an idiot's, bloody peepholes for eyes (the little birds had already plucked them like grapes), and crawling with black flies and small bugs. She was stabbed with a chill omen. She had to hold her nose as she stepped by.

After the last houses and the last bather—a great fat bald-headed man in a two-piece bathing suit bobbing and splashing like a happy hippo—she felt liberated at last. The sun glared on the empty sand ahead of her. She imagined herself as a pilgrim lost in a far land. It was almost blinding it was so bright, and the breeze had died down so that she could feel the heat of the sun. She started to run. She ran along the beach at the foot of the dunes, ran breathless until she heard the bulldozer working nearby above her.

She was panting and dripping with sweat, for it had been a long run. With nervous, clumsy fingers she took off her clothes. She looked back once to where the last houses were like small toys and saw not a soul now on the beach. She threw her clothes aside and didn't care, was suddenly drunk with the sea and the sun and the sky and her lonely freedom. She lay back and closed her eyes and let the sun bathe her. Her brain was blank and heat-struck, and her flesh crawled with rivulets of sweat. Would he come to the edge of the dune and stand tall and see her now? Would he laugh then, or be struck blind? Would he bury her alive under mountains of sand? It was a stange sweet dream.

She must have been dozing literally, for when she came to herself, the sun had gone behind the dunes and she was in shadow. The breeze had sprung up cool. She was goose-pimpled. The sand was uncomfortable and she felt cold and ashamed. She covered herself quickly with her hands and arms and looked around. Still no one on the beach. No one, thank God, had seen here there. No one, she was sure. What in the world had possessed her to do something like that? Crouching over, she slipped into her clothing and noticed, dismayed, that in her distraction, in her fierce haste, she had ripped off half the buttons of her shorts. She must have been insane.

When she was dressed again and had brushed the sand off her arms and legs, she was ready to start the long walk back. It was then that she heard the laughter, soft and mocking, heard as if at a great distance of time and space, like the light laughter of a ghost, like the memory of laughter. She looked up just in time to see four small blond faces, haloed by light, the Quigly children peering over the edge of the dune, disappear into the camouflage of even blonder, blown sea wheat. Stiff and ashamed, she walked briskly away, following now in reverse the path her bare feet had made in the sand.

When she had to pass the dead pelican again, lapped at, tumbled and turned by the incoming tide, she was afraid she was going to be sick.

It was nearly dark when she came up the back way to the cottage. He was in the red shell of a car, hands gripping the steering wheel, mouth wide open, driving in some furious daydream, and he didn't see her pass by. Her feet were hurting and she limped a little, but he had nothing, not even pity, to offer her. Just at the edge of the path, facing the trailer was a sign, crudely lettered with great smears of her good paint (a half-empty tube lay by the path), multicolored, the squandered paint dripping away from the letters as if they had been written in blood:

> KEEP OFF THIS HERE PATH!
>
> This means you

And beneath this was drawn a skull and crossbones.

Jane opened the back door and went into the kitchen. She poured herself a drink of Harper's whiskey and tossed it off.

"Is that you?" he called.

"Yes" she said. "It's me. I mean it is I."

She walked through the house to the front porch. Harper was sitting in his mother's rocker with a double-barrel shotgun in his lap. He was vigorously cleaning it with an oily rag. Jane leaned against the door frame behind him in weariness and slack despair and watched him work. He jerked his head around and grinned at her.

"Did you see my sign? Did you see the sign I put up?"

"Yes," she said. "I saw it."

"I found Daddy's old shotgun in the closet," he went on. "Next time I'm going to shoot. They've been warned aplenty. The next time one of them sets a foot on this land, I'm going to get me some tailfeathers."

Just then Mrs. Grim came bustling through the living room. She brushed past Jane as if she didn't see her, and her eyes, her small, pale blue eyes, were bright with triumph and pleasure. She put a box at the feet of her son.

"Honey boy," she cried. "I found the shells for the gun. I knew they were here somewhere and I found them."

Issues for Discussion

1. Anomie theorists suggest criminal behavior is a reaction to the existing rules of the game that the individual perceives as being insurmountable, at least to the extent that he or she personally is prevented from adequately competing in the struggle of life. Read the following quotation from Willa Cather's "Paul's Case" and explain the actor's criminality in terms of anomie theory.

   Half an hour later, Paul alighted from the Negley Avenue car and went slowly down one of the side streets off the main thoroughfare. It was a highly respectable street, where all the houses were exactly alike, and where businessmen of moderate means begot and reared large families of children, all of whom went to Sabbath school and learned the shorter catechism, and were interested in arithmetic; all of whom were as exactly alike as their homes, and of a piece with the monotony in which they lived. Paul never went up Cordelia Street without a shudder of loathing. His home was next to the house of the Cumberland minister. He approached it tonight with the nerveless sense of defeat, the hopeless feeling of sinking back forever into ugliness and commonness that he had always had when he came home. The moment he turned into Cordelia Street he felt the waters close above his head. After each of these orgies of living, he experienced all the physical depression which follows a debauch; the loathing of respectable beds, of common food, of a house permeated by kitchen odors; a shuddering repulsion for the flavorless, colorless mass of everyday existence; a morbid desire for cool things and soft lights and fresh flowers.

2. Willa Cather's portrayal of Percy Bixby in "The Bookkeeper's Wife" is similar in many respects to her casting of Paul in "Paul's Case." Discuss these similarities, and relate them to their involvement in criminal behavior.
3. Paul's adversary is the spirit or environment that molds the people of

Cordelia Street. Percy's cause for ruin is Charley Greengay. Explain how Cordelia Street and Charley Greengay are catalysts for anomie in Paul and Percy.
4. What significance would the anomie theorist extract from the following statement by Percy's wife, Stella?

"No, you're a spender or you're not. Greengay has been broke three times, fired, down and out, black-listed. But he's always come back, and he always will. You will never be fired, but you'll always be poor."

5. The leading characters in George Garrett's "Thus the Early Gods," Mrs. Grim and Harper, are confronted with a social upheaval much different from Paul and Percy's. Society, and the ill wind that seemingly accompanies it, is creeping closer and closer to the heretofore cloistered existence of Mrs. Grim and Harper. The Quigly family is to Mrs. Grim what Cordelia Street was to Paul. Read the following comment made by Harper to his wife, Jane, and explain how Harper's comments suggest that his mother is undergoing a sense of normlessness.

"Oh, you'll come to love her when you know her and understand her better," he said. "Everyone does. It's just that she was born out of her time or, anyway, that she had to live on beyond it. She's a lady living in a time when that word doesn't mean anything. And all she sees around her is change, change, change. Change and decay. The good, happy, comfortable world she grew up in turned inside out, turned into something else after the Depression and the War. She's just a minor, eccentric victim of the great social revolution. A bewildered mastodon wandering around in the postglacial age."

6. What is the symbolic significance of the sign that Harper paints and places on the pathway?
7. Merton's five modes of adaption are conformity, innovation, ritualism, retreatism, and rebellion. Does the behavior of Paul, Percy, Mrs. Grim, Harper, or Jane represent "adaption" to the social milieu within the meaning of these criteria? Explain.

PART V _____

Psychiatric Theories

The Freudian School

The suspicion that deviant behavior reflects a sick, emotionally disturbed, or psychotic individual predates the modern era.[1] Evidence even exists illustrating a form of "psychiatry" practiced by cavemen called *trephining* in which a hole is scraped in the patient's skull in order to let the evil-causing demons escape their bondage. Hippocrates (460-377 BC), known as the "father of medicine," recommended a seemingly less radical approach when he advised hysterical women to get married and become pregnant in order to cure their ailments.[2] More rational help for disturbed persons was forthcoming in the nineteenth and twentieth centuries.[3] Sigmund Freud (1856-1939) and two of his more famous students, Alfred Adler (1870-1937) and Carl Jung (1875-1960), used *psychoanalysis* as a tool for helping their patients.[4] Freud postulated that people are controlled

---

1. See F. H. Garrison, *An Introduction to the History of Medicine* (3rd ed.; Philadelphia: Saunders, 1913).

2. Nolan P. C. Lewis, *A Short History of Psychiatric Achievement* (New York: Norton, 1941), p. 35.

3. The discussion in this chapter is limited to what are called "functional" disorders rather than behavior attributed to "organic" dysfunctions. Organic disorders involve impairments due to injury or disease. See Thomas S. Szasz, *The Myth of Mental Illness: Foundations of a Theory of Personal Conduct* (New York: Hoeber-Harper, 1961).

4. For a summary of the "psychoanalytic" schools, see Ruth S. Monroe, *Schools of Psychoanalytic Thought* (New York: Dryden, 1955); and Charles Bremner, *An Elementary Textbook of Psychoanalysis* (New York: Doubleday, 1974). Psychoanalytic explanations are eloquently critiqued in David Feldman, "Psychoanalysis and Crime," in *Man: Society in Crisis*, ed. Bernard Rosenberg et al. (New York: Macmillan, 1964), pp. 50–58.

by their psyche, which is made up of three parts: id, ego, and superego. The *id* controls one's innate drives, including sex, aggression, and all other urges, desires, and instincts. The id's impulses do not generally conform to the standards of the typical community. Unconventional drives must be suppressed, which results in a sense of frustration for the individual.

Shortly after birth, the conscious part of the personality, the *ego*, develops. The ego may be viewed as an agent interceding on behalf of the id. The ego controls the instincts of the id, directing the individual to act in conformity with acquired norms, mores, folkways, and customs.

Finally, the *superego* emerges from the ego. The superego is one's conscience, specifically, a person's sense of morality. The superego is responsible for "punishing" the individual for failure to conform to society's expectations. Simply, the superego suppresses the instinctual drives of the id. Comparing the functions of the ego and superego, Mulvihill and Tumin state that "the ego is the part of the psyche that 'listens' to the wishes of the id and the approval or objection of the superego and decides what sort of behavior will result."[5]

When the id, ego, and superego are working in harmony, the individual is considered to be stable, or "normal." Conflict may arise among the three components, however. An overpowering superego may cause an excess of guilt feelings about instinctual needs. In these cases the individual may unconsciously attempt to atone for "sins" by engaging in criminal behavior, hoping to be apprehended and punished. The punishment will serve to relieve the person of guilt feelings. Or, if the superego is not sufficiently active to control the id, the resultant instinctual behavior will probably conflict with society's norms.[6]

By way of clarification, Freudians perceive criminal behavior as purposive—there is an ulterior or hidden motive for the behavior. A person engages in asocial activities to relieve repressed needs.[7] Guilt feelings are caused by a dominant superego. Unconsciously, the person desires punishment for the conflict generated between the id and the superego. Pathological behavior represents the individual's attempt to minimize the anxiety experienced when instinctual forces threaten to overwhelm him. Guilt, however, is not relieved by committing the criminal act, but rather by accepting state-sanctioned punishment for the deviant behavior: punishment minimizes temporarily the effects of the superego.

---

5. Donald J. Mulvihill and Melvin M. Tumin, *Crimes of Violence. A Staff Report to the National Commission on the Causes and Prevention of Violence*, vol. 12 (Washington, D.C.: U.S. Government Printing Office, 1969), p. 460.

6. Ibid., pp. 460–61.

7. See David Abrahamsen, *The Psychology of Crime* (New York: Columbia University Press, 1960).

The Behaviorists

Behavior learning theorists, or behaviorists, disregard much of Freudian thought. One leader of behaviorism, B. F. Skinner,[8] notes that no scientific data establish that the unconscious controls behavior. Rather, behaviorists believe individual behavior is controlled by environmental experiences.[9] That is, perception, motivational forces, and ultimate behavior patterns are shaped by life experiences; and action (behavior) is a response to a specific stimulus (i.e., stimulus–organism–response). Moreover, since behavior is *learned*, behavior modification techniques may be employed to alter perceptions and behavior.[10]

As is true of the Freudian school, behaviorists believe all behavior (criminal and noncriminal) is purposive. The means employed to gratify one's needs may involve criminal activity, but there is, at least to the actor, an internal justification or rationalization for the behavior.

Insanity Tests

Aside from sterilization and castration, sometimes performed to prevent procreation by the "feebleminded"[11] or sexual "psychopaths,"[12] applications of our current knowledge about the disturbed mind have dealt mainly with the issue of whether or not a particular defendant is "not guilty by reason of insanity." Criminal liability depends on the state's ability to prove that the actor had sufficient *mens rea* (criminal intent), *actus reus* (criminal act), and causation (the link between intent and the criminal act resulting in the illegal behavior). The insanity defense declares that the actor was mentally incapable of forming the required criminal intent at the time of the crime. Standard insanity models today include the "right and wrong"

---

8. The earliest systematic research with behavior modification is attributed to the work of Ivan Petrovich Pavlov (1849–1936). Pavlov's most famous experiments involve the conditioning of dogs to salivate when a bell is rung.

9. See Max Bruck, "Behavior Modification Theory and Practice: A Critical Review," *Social Work* 13 (April 1968): 43.

10. Behavior modification may be directed at the actor. Or, behavior may be altered by changing the social, political or economic environment in which the actor resides. See Saleem Shah, "Treatment of Offenders: Some Behavioral Concepts, Principles, and Approaches," *Federal Probation* 30 (June 1966): 37.

11. See *Buck v. Bell*, 274 U.S. 200 (1927) in which the sterilization of Carrie Buck was upheld by the U.S. Supreme Court. Justice Holmes' majority opinion contains the now famous quotation "Three generations of imbeciles are enough" (cf. p. 207).

12. No generally acceptable definition of "psychopath" exists. In a search of the literature Husley Carson found 202 terms and 55 traits indicating "psychopathic" behavior. "The Psychopath and the Psychopathic," *Journal of Criminal Psychopathology* 4 (1943): 522–27.

test,[13] the "irresistible impulse" test,[14] and the "product test."[15] Using the right and wrong test the defendant suggests that he was not able to distinguish between acceptable and proscribed behavior. To meet the criteria for the irresistible impulse test the defendant must assert that he could not prevent himself from acting in the deviant manner, although he knew he was violating the law. Finally, following the *Durham* rule (product test) the defense must show that the defendant's act was the result (i.e., product) of a mental disease or defect.[16]

The key to understanding the behavior of the deviant actors in Flannery O'Connor's "A Good Man Is Hard to Find" and Edgar Allan Poe's "The Tell-Tale Heart" and "The Cask of Amontillado" lies in identifying the *motive* for the behavior. O'Connor's character, The Misfit, justifies his behavior in terms of environmental influences. Yet his "explanation" also hints that he is the product of an uncontrolled id. Poe's characters seem to be reacting more to petty injustices by their victims. In both stories the actors are able to justify to themselves their extreme behavior. But, again, one must read the stories closely in order to establish whether the Freudian explanation of behavior is more plausible than that offered by the behaviorists. In both Poe stories, the purposive nature of the behavior is clearly apparent.

---

13. The right and wrong test emerged out of the *M'Naughten's Case* (8 Eng. Rep. 718) in which M'Naughten attempted to assassinate England's prime minister, Sir Robert Peel, but instead killed his secretary, Edward Drummond.

14. In this test the defendant will be found innocent by reason of insanity if he can convince the jury that he would have committed the act even if "a policeman were at his elbow." Most American jurisdictions have rejected this strict rule in favor of the *M'Naughten* rule.

15. See *Durham v. United States,* 214 F. 2d 862 (1954).

16. The product test has been modified by the Model Penal Code's insanity defense: "A person is not responsible for the criminal conduct if at the time of such conduct as a result of mental disease or defect he lacks substantial capacity either to appreciate the criminality of his conduct or to conform his conduct to the requirements of the law." See *Model Penal Code. Proposed Official Draft* (1962), sect. 4.01.

A GOOD MAN IS HARD TO FIND
Flannery O'Conner

The grandmother didn't want to go to Florida. She wanted to visit some of her connections in east Tennessee and she was seizing at every chance to change Bailey's mind. Bailey was the son she lived with, her only boy. He was sitting on the edge of his chair at the table, bent over the orange sports section of the *Journal*. "Now look here, Bailey," she said, "see here, read this," and she stood with one hand on her thin hip and the other rattling the newspaper at his bald head. "Here this fellow that calls himself The Misfit is aloose from the Federal Pen and headed toward Florida and you read here what it says he did to these people. Just you read it. I wouldn't take my children in any direction with a criminal like that aloose in it. I couldn't answer to my conscience if I did."

Bailey didn't look up from his reading so she wheeled around then and faced the children's mother; a young woman in slacks, whose face was as broad and innocent as a cabbage and was tied around with a green headkerchief that had two points on the top like rabbit's ears. She was sitting on the sofa, feeding the baby his apricots out of a jar. "The children have been to Florida before," the old lady said. "You all ought to take them somewhere else for a change so they would see different parts of the world and be broad. They never have been to east Tennessee."

The children's mother didn't seem to hear her, but the eight-year-old boy, John Wesley, a stocky child with glasses, said, "If you don't want to go to Florida, why dontcha stay at home?" He and the little girl, June Star, were reading the funny papers on the floor.

"She wouldn't stay at home to be queen for a day," June Star said without raising her yellow head.

"Yes, and what would you do if this fellow, The Misfit, caught you?" the grandmother asked.

"I'd smack his face," John Wesley said.

"She wouldn't stay at home for a million bucks," June Star said. "Afraid she'd miss something. She has to go everywhere we go."

"All right, Miss," the grandmother said. "Just remember that the next time you want me to curl your hair."

June Star said her hair was naturally curly.

The next morning the grandmother was the first one in the car, ready to go. She had her big black valise that looked like the head of a hippopotamus in one corner, and underneath it she was hiding a basket with Pitty Sing, the cat, in it. She didn't intend for the cat to be left alone in the house for three days because he would miss her too much and she was afraid he might brush against one of the gas burners and accidentally asphyxiate himself. Her son, Bailey, didn't like to arrive at a motel with a cat.

She sat in the middle of the back seat with John Wesley and June Star on either side of her. Bailey and the children's mother and the baby sat in the front and they left Atlanta at eight forty-five with the mileage on the car at 55890. The grandmother wrote this down because she thought it would be interesting to say how many miles they had been when they got back. It took them twenty minutes to reach the outskirts of the city.

The old lady settled herself comfortably, removing her white cotton gloves and putting them up with her purse on the shelf in front of the back window. The children's mother still had on slacks and still had her head tied up in a green kerchief, but the grandmother had on a navy blue straw sailor hat with a bunch of white violets on the brim and a navy blue dress with a small white dot in the print. Her collar and cuffs were white organdy trimmed with lace and at her neckline she had pinned a purple spray of cloth violets containing a sachet. In case of an accident, anyone seeing her dead on the highway would know at once that she was a lady.

She said she thought it was going to be a good day for driving, neither too hot nor too cold, and she cautioned Bailey that the speed limit was fifty-five miles an hour and that the patrolmen hid themselves behind billboards and small clumps of trees and sped out after you before you had a chance to slow down. She pointed out interesting details of the scenery: Stone Mountain; the blue granite that in some places came up to both sides of the highway; the brilliant red clay banks slightly streaked with purple; and the various crops that made rows of green lace-work on the ground. The trees were full of silver-white sunlights and the meanest of them sparkled. The children were reading comic magazines and their mother had gone back to sleep.

"Let's go through Georgia fast so we won't have to look at it much," John Wesley said.

"If I were a little boy," said the grandmother, "I wouldn't talk about my native state that way. Tennessee has the mountains and Georgia has the hills."

"Tennessee is just a hillbilly dumping ground," John Wesley said, "and Georgia is a lousy state too."

"You said it," June Star said.

"In my time," said the grandmother, folding her thin veined fingers, "children were more respectful of their native states and their parents and everything else. People did right then. Oh look at the cute little pickaninny!" she said and pointed to a Negro child standing in the door of a shack. "Wouldn't that make a picture, now?" she asked and they all turned and looked at the little Negro out of the back window. He waved.

"He didn't have any britches on," June Star said.

"He probably didn't have any," the grandmother explained. "Little niggers in the country don't have things like we do. If I could paint, I'd paint that picture," she said.

The children exchanged comic books.

The grandmother offered to hold the baby and the children's mother passed him over the front seat to her. She set him on her knee and bounced him and told him about the things they were passing. She rolled her eyes and screwed up her mouth and stuck her leathery thin face into his smooth bland one. Occasionally he gave her a faraway smile. They passed a large cotton field with five or six graves fenced in the middle of it, like a small island. "Look at the graveyard!" the grandmother said, pointing it out. "That was the old family burying ground. That belonged to the plantation."

"Where's the plantation?" John Wesley asked.

"Gone With the Wind," said the grandmother. "Ha. Ha."

When the children finished all the comic books they had brought, they opened the lunch and ate it. The grandmother ate a peanut butter sandwich and an olive and would not let the children throw the box and the paper napkins out the window. When there was nothing else to do they played a game by choosing a cloud and making the other two guess what shape it suggested. John Wesley took one the shape of a cow and June Star guessed a cow and John Wesley said, no, an automobile, and June Star said he didn't play fair, and they began to slap each other over the grandmother.

The grandmother said she would tell them a story if they would keep quiet. When she told a story, she rolled her eyes and waved her head and was very dramatic. She said once when she was a maiden lady she had been courted by a Mr. Edgar Atkins Teagarden from Jasper, Georgia. She said he was a very good-looking man and a gentleman and that he brought her a watermelon every Saturday afternoon with his initials cut in it, E.A.T. Well, one Saturday, she said, Mr. Teagarden brought the watermelon and there was nobody at home and he left it on the front porch and returned in his buggy to Jasper, but she never got the watermelon, she said, because a nigger boy ate it when he saw the initials, E.A.T.! This story tickled John Wesley's funny bone and he giggled and giggled but June Star didn't think it was any good. She said she wouldn't marry a man that just brought her a watermelon on Saturday. The grandmother said she would have done well to marry Mr. Teagarden because he was a gentleman and had bought Coca-Cola stock when it first came out and that he had died only a few years ago, a very wealthy man.

They stopped at The Tower for barbecued sandwiches. The Tower was a part-stucco and part-wood filling station and dance hall set in a clearing outside of Timothy. A fat man named Red Sammy Butts ran it and there were signs stuck here and there on the building and for miles up and down the highway saying, TRY RED SAMMY'S FAMOUS BARBECUE. NONE LIKE FAMOUS RED SAMMY'S! RED SAM! THE FAT BOY WITH THE HAPPY LAUGH. A VETERAN! RED SAMMY'S YOUR MAN!

Red Sammy was lying on the bare ground outside The Tower with his head under a truck while a gray monkey about a foot high, chained to a small chinaberry tree, chattered nearby. The monkey sprang back into the tree and got on the highest limb as soon as he saw the children jump out of the car and run toward him.

Inside, The Tower was a long dark room with a counter at one end and tables at the other and dancing space in the middle. They all sat down at a broad table next to the nickelodeon and Red Sam's wife, a tall burnt-brown woman with hair and eyes lighter than her skin, came and took their order. The children's mother put a dime in the machine and played "The Tennessee Waltz," and the grandmother said that tune always made her want to dance. She asked Bailey if he would like to dance but he only glared at her. He didn't have a naturally sunny disposition like she did and trips made him nervous. The grandmother's brown eyes were very bright. She swayed her head from side to side and pretended she was dancing in her chair. June Star said play something she could tap to so the children's mother put in another dime and played a fast number and June Star stepped out onto the dance floor and did her tap routine.

"Ain't she cute?" Red Sam's wife said, leaning over the counter. "Would you like to come be my little girl?"

"No, I certainly wouldn't," June Star said. "I wouldn't live in a broken-down place like this for a million bucks!" and she ran back to the table.

"Ain't she cute?" the woman repeated, stretching her mouth politely.

"Aren't you ashamed?" hissed the grandmother.

Red Sam came in and told his wife to quit lounging on the counter and hurry up with these people's order. His khaki trousers reached just to his hip bones and his stomach hung over them like a sack of meal swaying under his shirt. He came over and sat down at a table nearby and let out a combination sigh and yodel. "You can't win," he said. "You can't win," and he wiped his sweating red face off with a gray handkerchief. "These days you don't know who to trust," he said. "Ain't that the truth?"

"People are certainly not nice like they used to be," said the grandmother.

"Two fellers come in here last week," Red Sammy said, "driving a Chrysler. It was a old beat-up car but it was a good one and these boys looked all right to me. Said they worked at the mill and you know I let them fellers charge the gas they bought? Now why did I do that?"

"Because you're a good man!" the grandmother said at once.

"Yes'm, I suppose so," Red Sam said as if he were struck with this answer.

His wife brought the orders, carrying the five plates all at once without a tray, two in each hand and one balanced on her arm. "It isn't a soul in this green world of God's that you can trust," she said. "And I don't count nobody out of that, not nobody," she repeated, looking at Red Sammy.

"Did you read about that criminal, The Misfit, that's escaped?" asked the grandmother.

"I wouldn't be a bit surprised if he didn't attack this place right here," said the woman. "If he hears about it being here, I wouldn't be none surprised to see him. If he hears it's two cent in the cash register, I wouldn't be a tall surprised if he . . ."

"That'll do," Red Sam said. "Go bring these people their Co'Colas," and the woman went off to get the rest of the order.

"A good man is hard to find," Red Sammy said. "Everything is getting terrible. I remember the day you could go off and leave your screen door unlatched. Not no more."

He and the grandmother discussed better times. The old lady said that in her opinion Europe was entirely to blame for the way things were now. She said the way Europe acted you would think we were made of money and Red Sam said it was no use talking about it, she was exactly right. The children ran outside into the white sunlight and looked at the monkey in the lacy chinaberry tree. He was busy catching fleas on himself and biting each one carefully between his teeth as if it were a delicacy.

They drove off again into the hot afternoon. The grandmother took cat naps and woke up every few minutes with her own snoring. Outside of Toombsboro she woke up and recalled an old plantation that she had visited in this neighborhood once when she was a young lady. She said the house had six white columns across the front and that there was an avenue of oaks leading up to it and two little wooden trellis arbors on either side in front where you sat down with your suitor after a stroll in the garden. She recalled exactly which road to turn off to get to it. She knew that Bailey would not be willing to lose any time looking at an old house, but the more she talked about it, the more she wanted to see it once again and find out if the little twin arbors were still standing. "There was a secret panel in this house," she said craftily, not telling the truth but wishing that she were, "and the story went that all the family silver was hidden in it when Sherman came through but it was never found. . . ."

"Hey!" John Wesley said. "Let's go see it! We'll find it! We'll poke all the woodwork and find it! Who lives there? Where do you turn off at? Hey Pop, can't we turn off there?"

"We never have seen a house with a secret panel!" June Star shrieked. "Let's go to the house with the secret panel! Hey, Pop, can't we go see the house with the secret panel!"

"It's not far from here, I know," the grandmother said. "It wouldn't take over twenty minutes."

Bailey was looking straight ahead. His jaw was as rigid as a horseshoe. "No," he said.

The children began to yell and scream that they wanted to see the house with the secret panel. John Wesley kicked the back of the front seat and June Star hung over her mother's shoulder and whined desperately into her ear that they never had any fun even on their vacation, that they could never do what THEY wanted to do. The baby began to scream and John Wesley kicked the back of the seat so hard that his father could feel the blows in his kidney.

"All right!" he shouted and drew the car to a stop at the side of the road. "Will you all shut up? Will you all just shut up for one second? If you don't shut up, we won't go anywhere."

"It would be very educational for them," the grandmother murmured.

"All right," Bailey said, "but get this. This is the only time we're going to stop for anything like this. This is the one and only time."

"The dirt road that you have to turn down is about a mile back," the grandmother directed. "I marked it when we passed."

"A dirt road," Bailey groaned.

After they had turned around and were headed toward the dirt road, the grandmother recalled other points about the house, the beautiful glass over the front doorway and the candle lamp in the hall. John Wesley said that the secret panel was probably in the fireplace.

"You can't go inside this house," Bailey said. "You don't know who lives there."

"While you all talk to the people in front, I'll run around behind and get in a window," John Wesley suggested.

"We'll all stay in the car," his mother said.

They turned onto the dirt road and the car raced roughly along in a swirl of pink dust. The grandmother recalled the times when there were no paved roads and thirty miles was a day's journey. The dirt road was hilly and there were sudden washes in it and sharp curves on dangerous embankments. All at once they would be on a hill, looking down over the blue tops of trees for miles around, then the next minute, they would be in a red depression with the dust-coated trees looking down on them.

"This place had better turn up in a minute," Bailey said, "or I'm going to turn around."

The road looked as if no one had traveled on it in months.

"It's not much farther," the grandmother said and just as she said it, a horrible thought came to her. The thought was so embarrassing that she turned red in the face and her eyes dilated and her feet jumped up, upsetting her valise in the corner. The instant the valise moved, the newspaper top she had over the basket under it rose with a snarl and Pitty Sing, the cat, sprang onto Bailey's shoulder.

The children were thrown to the floor and their mother, clutching the baby, was thrown out the door onto the ground; the old lady was thrown into the front seat. The car turned over once and landed right side up in a gulch on the side of the road. Bailey remained in the driver's seat with the cat—gray-striped with a broad white face and an orange nose—clinging to his neck like a caterpillar.

As soon as the children saw they could move their arms and legs they scrambled out of the car, shouting, "We've had an ACCIDENT!" The grandmother was curled up under the dashboard, hoping she was injured so that Bailey's wrath would not come down on her all at once. The horrible thought she had had before the accident was that the house she had remembered so vividly was not in Georgia but in Tennessee.

Bailey removed the cat from his neck with both hands and flung it out the window against the side of a pine tree. Then he got out of the car and started looking for the children's mother: She was sitting against the side of the red gutted ditch, holding the screaming baby, but she only had a cut down her face and a broken shoulder. "We've had an ACCIDENT!" the children screamed in a frenzy of delight.

"But nobody's killed," June Star said with disappointment as the grandmother limped out of the car, her hat still pinned to her head but the broken front brim standing up at a jaunty angle and the violet spray hanging off the side. They all sat down in the ditch, except the children, to recover from the shock. They were all shaking.

"Maybe a car will come along," said the children's mother hoarsely.

"I believe I have injured an organ," said the grandmother, pressing her side, but no one answered her. Bailey's teeth were clattering. He had on a yellow sport shirt with bright blue parrots designed in it and his face was as yellow as the shirt. The grandmother decided that she would not mention that the house was in Tennessee.

The road was about ten feet above and they could see only the tops of the trees on the other side of it. Behind the ditch they were sitting in there were more woods, tall and dark and deep. In a few minutes they saw a car some distance away on top of a hill, coming slowly as if the occupants were watching them. The grandmother stood up and waved both arms dramatically to attract their attention. The car continued to come on slowly, disappeared around a bend and appeared again, moving even slower, on top of the hill they had gone over. It was a big black battered hearselike automobile. There were three men in it.

It came to a stop just over them and for some minutes, the driver looked down with a steady expressionless gaze to where they were sitting, and didn't speak. Then he turned his head and muttered something to the other two and they got out. One was a fat boy in black trousers and a red sweat shirt with a silver stallion embossed on the front of it. He moved around on the right side of them and stood staring, his mouth partly open in a kind of loose grin. The other had on khaki pants and a blue striped coat and a gray hat pulled down very low, hiding most of his face. He came around slowly on the left side. Neither spoke.

The driver got out of the car and stood by the side of it, looking down at them. He was an older man than the other two. His hair was just beginning to gray and he wore silver-rimmed spectacles that gave him a scholarly look. He had a long creased face and didn't have on any shirt or undershirt. He had on blue jeans that were too tight for him and was holding a black hat and a gun. The two boys also had guns.

"We've had an ACCIDENT!" the children screamed.

The grandmother had the peculiar feeling that the bespectacled man was someone she knew. His face was as familiar to her as if she had known him all her life but she could not recall who he was. He moved away from the car and began to come down the embankment, placing his feet carefully so that he wouldn't slip. He had on tan and white shoes and no socks, and his ankles were red and thin. "Good afternoon," he said. "I see you all had you a little spill."

"We turned over twice!" said the grandmother.

"Oncet," he corrected. "We seen it happen. Try their car and see will it run, Hiram," he said quietly to the boy with the gray hat.

"What you got that gun for?" John Wesley asked. "Whatcha gonna do with that gun?"

"Lady," the man said to the children's mother, "would you mind calling them children to sit down by you? Children make me nervous. I want all you all to sit down right together there where you're at."

"What are you telling us what to do for?" June Star asked.

Behind them the line of woods gaped like a dark open mouth. "Come here," said their mother.

"Look here now," Bailey began suddenly, "we're in a predicament! We're in. . . ."

The grandmother shrieked. She scrambled to her feet and stood staring. "You're The Misfit!" she said. "I recognized you at once!"

"Yes'm," the man said, smiling slightly as if he were pleased in spite of himself to be known, "but it would have been better for all of you, lady, if you hadn't of reckernized me."

Bailey turned his head sharply and said something to his mother that shocked even the children. The old lady began to cry and The Misfit reddened.

"Lady," he said, "don't you get upset. Sometimes a man says things he don't mean. I don't reckon he meant to talk to you thataway."

"You wouldn't shoot a lady, would you?" the grandmother said and removed a clean handkerchief from her cuff and began to slap at her eyes with it.

The Misfit pointed the toe of his shoe into the ground and made a little hole and then covered it up again. "I would hate to have to," he said.

"Listen," the grandmother almost screamed, "I know you're a good man. You don't look a bit like you have common blood. I know you must come from nice people!"

"Yes mam," he said, "finest people in the world." When he smiled he showed a row of strong white teeth. "God never made a finer woman than my mother and my daddy's heart was pure gold," he said. The boy with the red sweat shirt had come around behind them and was standing with his gun at his hip. The Misfit squatted down on the ground. "Watch them children, Bobby Lee," he said. "You know they make me nervous." He looked at the six of them huddled together in front of him and he seemed to be embarrassed as if he couldn't think of anything to say. "Ain't a cloud in the sky," he remarked, looking up at it. "Don't see no sun but don't see no cloud neither."

"Yes, it's a beautiful day," said the grandmother. "Listen," she said, "you shouldn't call yourself The Misfit because I know you're a good man at heart. I can just look at you and tell."

"Hush!" Bailey yelled. "Hush! Everybody shut up and let me handle this!" He was squatting in the position of a runner about to sprint forward but he didn't move.

"I pre-chate that, lady," The Misfit said and drew a little circle in the ground with the butt of his gun.

"It'll take a half a hour to fix this here car," Hiram called, looking over the raised hood of it.

"Well, first you and Bobby Lee get him and that little boy to step over yonder with you," The Misfit said, pointing to Bailey and John Wesley. "The boys want to ast you something," he said to Bailey. "Would you mind stepping back in them woods there with them?"

"Listen," Bailey began, "we're in a terrible predicament! Nobody realizes what this is," and his voice cracked. His eyes were as blue and intense as the parrots in his shirt and he remained perfectly still.

The grandmother reached up to adjust her hat brim as if she were going to the woods with him but it came off in her hand. She stood staring at it and after a second she let it fall on the ground. Hiram pulled Bailey up by the arm as if he were assisting an old man. John Wesley caught hold of his father's hand and Bobby Lee followed. They went off toward the woods and just as they reached the dark edge, Bailey turned and supporting himself against a gray naked pine trunk, he shouted, "I'll be back in a minute, Mamma, wait on me!"

"Come back this instant!" his mother shrilled but they all disappeared into the woods.

"Bailey Boy!" the grandmother called in a tragic voice but she found she was looking at The Misfit squatting on the ground in front of her. "I just know you're a good man," she said desperately. "You're not a bit common!"

"Nome, I ain't a good man," The Misfit said after a second as if he had considered her statement carefully, "but I ain't the worst in the world neither. My daddy said I was different breed of dog from my brothers and sisters. 'You know,' Daddy said, 'it's some that can live their whole life out without asking about it and it's others has to know why it is, and this boy is one of the latters. He's going to be into everything!' " He put on his black hat and looked up suddenly and then away deep into the woods as if he were embarrassed again. "I'm sorry I don't have on a shirt before you ladies," he said, hunching his shoulders slightly. "We buried our clothes that we had on when we escaped and we're just making do until we can get better. We borrowed these from some folks we met," he explained.

"That's perfectly all right," the grandmother said. "Maybe Bailey has an extra shirt in his suitcase."

"I'll look and see terrectly," The Misfit said.

"Where are they taking him?" the children's mother screamed.

"Daddy was a card himself," The Misfit said. "You couldn't put anything over on him. He never got in trouble with the Authorities though. Just had the knack of handling them."

"You could be honest too if you'd only try," said the grandmother. "Think how wonderful it would be to settle down and live a comfortable life and not have to think about somebody chasing you all the time."

The Misfit kept scratching in the ground with the butt of his gun as if he were thinking about it. "Yes'm, somebody is always after you," he murmured.

The grandmother noticed how thin his shoulder blades were just behind his hat because she was standing up, looking down on him. "Do you ever pray?" she asked.

He shook his head. All she saw was the black hat wiggle between his shoulder blades. "Nome," he said.

There was a pistol shot from the woods, followed closely by another. Then silence. The old lady's head jerked around. She could hear the wind move through the tree tops like a long satisfied insuck of breath. "Bailey Boy!" she called.

"I was a gospel singer for a while," The Misfit said. "I been most everything. Been in the arm service, both land and sea, at home and abroad, been twice married, been an undertaker, been with the railroads, plowed Mother Earth, been in a tornado, seen a man burnt alive oncet," and he looked up at the children's mother and the little girl who were sitting close together, their faces white and their eyes glassy; "I even seen a woman flogged," he said.

"Pray, pray," the grandmother began, "pray, pray. . . ."

"I never was a bad boy that I remember of," The Misfit said in an almost dreamy voice, "but somewheres along the line I done something wrong and got sent to the penitentiary. I was buried alive," and he looked up and held her attention to him by a steady stare.

"That's when you should have started to pray," she said. "What did you do to get sent to the penitentiary that first time?"

"Turn to the right it was a wall," The Misfit said, looking up again at the cloudless sky. "Turn to the left, it was a wall. Look up it was a ceiling, look down it was a floor. I forget what I done, lady. I set there and set there, trying to remember what it was I done and I ain't recalled it to this day. Oncet in a while, I would think it was coming to me, but it never come."

"Maybe they put you in by mistake," the old lady said vaguely.

"Nome," he said. "It wasn't no mistake. They had the papers on me."

"You must have stolen something," she said.

The Misfit sneered slightly. "Nobody had nothing I wanted," he said. "It was a head-doctor at the penitentiary said what I had done was kill my daddy but I known that for a lie. My daddy died in nineteen ought nineteen of the epidemic flu and I never had a thing to do with it. He was buried in the Mount Hopewell Baptist churchyard and you can go there and see for yourself."

"If you would pray," the old lady said, "Jesus would help you."

"That's right," The Misfit said.

"Well then, why don't you pray?" she asked trembling with delight suddenly.

"I don't want no hep," he said. "I'm doing all right by myself."

Bobby Lee and Hiram came ambling back from the woods. Bobby Lee was dragging a yellow shirt with bright blue parrots in it.

"Throw me that shirt, Bobby Lee," The Misfit said. The shirt came flying at him and landed on his shoulder and he put it on. The grandmother couldn't name what the shirt reminded her of. "No, lady," The Misfit said while he was buttoning it up, "I found out the crime don't matter. You can do one thing or you can do another, kill a man or take a tire off his car, because sooner or later you're going to forget what it was you done and just be punished for it."

The children's mother had begun to make heaving noises as if she couldn't get her breath. "Lady," he asked, "would you and that little girl like to step off yonder with Bobby Lee and Hiram and join your husband?"

"Yes, thank you," the mother said faintly. Her left arm dangled helplessly and she was holding the baby, who had gone to sleep, in the other. "Hep that lady up, Hiram," The Misfit said as she struggled to climb out of the ditch, "and Bobby Lee, you hold onto that little girl's hand."

"I don't want to hold hands with him," June Star said. "He reminds me of a pig."

The fat boy blushed and laughed and caught her by the arm and pulled her off into the woods after Hiram and her mother.

Alone with The Misfit, the grandmother found that she had lost her voice. There was not a cloud in the sky nor any sun. There was nothing around her but woods. She wanted to tell him that he must pray. She opened and closed her mouth several times before anything came out. Finally she found herself saying, "Jesus, Jesus," meaning, Jesus will help you, but the way she was saying it, it sounded as if she might be cursing.

"Yes'm," The Misfit said as if he agreed. "Jesus thown everything off balance. It was the same case with Him as with me except He hadn't committed any crime and they could prove I had committed one because they had the papers on me. Of course," he said, "they never shown me my papers. That's why I sign myself now. I said long ago, you get you a signature and sign everything you do and keep a copy of it. Then you'll know what you done and you can hold up the crime to the punishment and see do they match and in the end you'll have something to prove you ain't been treated right. I call myself The Misfit," he said, "because I can't make what all I done wrong fit what all I gone through in punishment."

There was a piercing scream from the woods, followed closely by a pistol report. "Does it seem right to you, lady, that one is punished a heap and another ain't punished at all?"

"Jesus!" the old lady cried. "You've got good blood! I know you wouldn't shoot a lady! I know you come from nice people! Pray! Jesus, you ought not to shoot a lady. I'll give you all the money I've got!"

"Lady," The Misfit said, looking beyond her far into the woods, "there never was a body that give the undertaker a tip."

There were two more pistol reports and the grandmother raised her head like a parched old turkey hen crying for water and called, "Bailey Boy, Bailey Boy!" as if her heart would break.

"Jesus was the only One that ever raised the dead," The Misfit continued, "and He shouldn't have done it. He thown everything off balance. If He did what He said, then it's nothing for you to do but thow away everything and follow Him, and if He didn't then it's nothing for you to do but enjoy the few minutes you got left the best way you can—by killing somebody or burning down his house or doing some other meanness to him. No pleasure but meanness," he said and his voice had become almost a snarl.

"Maybe He didn't raise the dead," the old lady mumbled, not knowing what she was saying and feeling so dizzy that she sank down in the ditch with her legs twisted under her.

"I wasn't there so I can't say He didn't," The Misfit said, "I wisht I had of been there," he said, hitting the ground with his fist. "It ain't right I wasn't there because if I had of been there I would of known. Listen lady," he said in a high voice, "if I had of been there I would of known and I wouldn't be like I am now." His voice seemed about to crack and the grandmother's head cleared for an instant. She saw the man's face twisted close to her own as if he were going to cry and she murmured, "Why, you're one of my babies. You're one of my own children!" She reached out and touched him on he shoulder. The Misfit sprang back as if a snake had bitten him and shot her three times through the chest. Then he put his gun down on the ground and took off his glasses and began to clean them.

Hiram and Bobby Lee returned from the woods and stood over the ditch, looking down at the grandmother who half sat and half lay in a puddle of blood with her legs crossed under her like a child's and her face smiling up at the cloudless sky.

Without his glasses, The Misfit's eyes were red-rimmed and pale and defenseless-looking. "Take her off and thow her where you thown the others," he said, picking up the cat that was rubbing itself against his leg.

"She was a talker, wasn't she?" Bobby Lee said, sliding down the ditch with a yodel.

"She would of been a good woman," The Misfit said, "if it had been somebody there to shoot her every minute of her life."

"Some fun!" Bobby Lee said.

"Shut up, Bobby Lee," The Misfit said. "It's no real pleasure in life."

THE TELL-TALE HEART
Edgar Allan Poe

True—nervous—very, very dreadfully nervous I had been and am! but why *will* you say that I am mad? The disease had sharpened my senses—not destroyed—not dulled them. Above all was the sense of hearing acute. I heard all things in the heaven and in the earth. I heard many things in hell. How, then, am I mad? Hearken! and observe how healthily—how calmly I can tell you the whole story.

It is impossible to say how first the idea entered my brain; but once conceived, it haunted me day and night. Object there was none. Passion there was none. I loved the old man. He had never wronged me. He had never given me insult. For his gold I had no desire. I think it was his eye! yes, it was this! He had the eye of a vulture—a pale blue eye, with a film over it. Whenever it fell upon me, my blood ran cold; and so by degrees—very gradually—I made up my mind to take the life of the old man, and thus rid myself of the eye forever.

Now this is the point. You fancy me mad. Madmen know nothing. But you should have seen *me*. You should have seen how wisely I proceeded—with what caution—with what foresight—with what dissimulation I went to work!

I was never kinder to the old man than during the whole week before I killed him. And every night, about midnight, I turned the latch of his door and opened it—oh, so gently! And then, when I had made an opening sufficient for my head, I put in a dark lantern, all closed, closed, so that no light shone out, and then I thrust in my head. Oh, you would have laughed to see how cunningly I thrust it in! I moved it slowly—very very slowly, so that I might not disturb the old man's sleep. It took me an hour to place my whole head within the opening so far that I could see him lay upon his bed. Ha!—would a madman have been so wise as this? And then, when my head was well in the room, I undid the lantern cautiously—oh, so cautiously—cautiously (for the hinges creaked)—I undid it just so much that a single thin ray fell upon the vulture eye. And this I did for seven long nights—every night just at midnight—but I found the eye always closed; and so it was impossible to do the work; for it was not the old man who vexed me, but his Evil Eye. And every morning, when the day broke, I went boldly into the chamber and spoke courageously to him, calling him by name in a hearty tone, and inquiring how he had passed the night. So you see he would have been a very profound old man, indeed, to suspect that every night, just at twelve, I looked in upon him while he slept.

Upon the eighth night I was more than usually cautious in opening the door. A watch's minute hand moves more quickly than did mine. Never before that night had I *felt* the extent of my own powers—of my sagacity. I could scarcely contain my feelings of triumph. To think that there I was opening the door, little by little, and he not even to dream of my secret deeds or thoughts. I farily chuckled at the idea; and perhaps he heard me; for he moved on the bed suddenly, as if startled. Now you may think that I drew back—but no. His room was as black as pitch with the thick darkness (for the shutters were close fastened, through fear of robbers), and so I knew that he could not see the opening of the door, and I kept pushing it on steadily, steadily.

I had my head in, and was about to open the lantern, when my thumb slipped upon the tin fastening, and the old man sprang up in the bed, crying out—"Who's there?"

I kept quite still and said nothing. For a whole hour I did not move a muscle, and in the meantime I did not hear him lie down. He was still sitting up in the bed listening;—just as I have done, night after night, hearkening to the death watches in the wall.

Presently I heard a slight groan and I knew it was the groan of mortal terror. It was not a groan of pain or of grief—oh no!—it was the low stifled sound that arises from the bottom of the soul when overcharged with awe. I knew the sound well. Many a night, just at midnight, when all the world slept, it has welled up from my own bosom, deepening, with its dreadful echo, the terrors that distracted me. I say I knew it well. I knew what the old man felt, and pitied him, although I chuckled at heart. I knew that he had been lying awake ever since the first slight noise, when he had turned in the bed. His fears had been ever since growing upon him. He had been trying to fancy them causeless, but could not. He had been saying to himself—"It is nothing but the wind in the chimney—it is only a mouse crossing the floor," or "it is merely a cricket which has made a single chirp." Yes, he has been trying to comfort himself with these suppositions; but he had found all in vain. *All in vain:* because Death, in approaching him, had stalked with his black shadow before him, and enveloped the victim. And it was the mournful influence of the unperceived shadow that caused him to feel—although he neither saw nor heard—to *feel* the presence of my head within the room.

When I had waited a long time, very patiently, without hearing him lie down, I resolved to open a little—a very, very little crevice in the lantern. So I opened it—you cannot imagine how stealthily, stealthily—until, at length, a single dim ray, like the thread of the spider, shot from out the crevice and fell full upon the vulture eye.

It was open—wide, wide open—and I grew furious as I gazed upon it. I saw it with perfect distinctness—all a dull blue, with a hideous veil over it that chilled the very marrow in my bones; but I could see nothing else of the old man's face or person: for I had directed the ray as if by instinct, precisely upon the damned spot.

And now have I not told you that what you mistake for madness is but over-acuteness of the senses?—now, I say, there came to my ears a low, dull, quick sound, such as a watch makes when enveloped in cotton. I knew *that* sound well too. It was the beating of the old man's heart. It increased my fury, as the beating of a drum stimulates the soldier into courage.

But even yet I refrained and kept still. I scarcely breathed. I held the lantern motionless. I tried how steadily I could maintain the ray upon the eye. Meantime the hellish tattoo of the heart increased. It grew quicker and quicker, and louder, I say, louder and louder every instant. The old man's terror *must* have been extreme! It grew louder, I say, louder every moment!—do you mark me well? I have told you that I am nervous: so I am. And now at the dead hour of the night, amid the dreadful silence of that old house, so strange a noise as this excited me to uncontrollable terror. Yet, for some minutes longer I refrained and stood still. But the beating grew louder, louder! I thought the heart must burst. And now a new anxiety seized me—the sound would be heard by a neighbor! The old man's hour had come! With a loud yell, I threw open the lantern and leaped into the room. He shrieked once—once only. In an instant I dragged him to the floor, and pulled the heavy bed over him, I then smiled gaily, to find the deed so far done. But, for many minutes, the heart beat on with a muffled sound. This, however, did not vex me; it would not be heard through the wall. At length it ceased. The old man was dead. I removed the bed and examined the corpse. Yes, he was stone, stone dead. I placed my hand upon the heart and held it there many minutes. There was no pulsation. He was stone dead. His eye would trouble me no more.

If still you think me mad, you will think so no longer when I describe the wise precautions I took for the concealment of the body. The night waned, and I worked hastily, but in silence. First of all I dismembered the corpse. I cut off the head and the arms and the legs.

I then took up three planks from the flooring of the chamber, and deposited all between the scantlings. I then replaced the boards so cleverly, so cunningly, that no human eye—not even *his*—could have detected anything wrong. There was nothing to wash out—no stain of any kind—no blood-spot whatever. I had been too wary for that. A tub had caught all—ha! ha!

When I made an end of these labors, it was four o'clock—still dark as midnight. As the bell sounded the hour, there came a knocking at the street door. I went down to open it with a light heart,—for what had I now to fear? There entered three men, who introduced themselves, with perfect suavity, as officers of the police. A shriek had been heard by a neighbor during the night: suspicion of foul play had been aroused; information had been lodged at the police office, and they (the officers) had been deputed to search the premises.

I smiled,—for *what* had I to fear? I bade the gentlemen welcome. The shriek, I said, was my own in a dream. The old man, I mentioned, was absent in the country. I took my visitors all over the house. I bade them search—search *well*. I led them, at length, to *his* chamber. I showed them his treasures, secure, undisturbed. In the enthusiasm of my confidence, I brought chairs into the room, and desired them *here* to rest from their fatigues, while I myself, in the wild audacity of my perfect triumph, placed my own seat upon the very spot beneath which reposed the corpse of the victim.

The officers were satisfied. My *manner* had convinced them. I was singularly at ease. They sat, and while I answered cheerily, they chatted of familiar things. But, ere long, I felt myself getting pale and wished them gone. My head ached, and I fancied a ringing in my ears: but still they sat and still chatted. The ringing became more distinct:—it continued and became more distinct: I talked more freely to get rid of the feeling: but it continued and gained definitiveness—until at length, I found that the noise was *not* within my ears.

No doubt I now grew *very* pale;—but I talked more fluently, and with a heightened voice. Yet the sound increased—and what could I do? It was *a low, dull, quick sound—much such a sound as a watch makes when enveloped in cotton*. I gasped for breath—and yet the officers heard it not. I talked more quickly—more vehemently; but the noise steadily increased. I arose and argued about trifles, in a high key and with violent gesticulations, but the noise steadily increased. Why *would* they not be gone? I paced the floor to and fro with heavy strides, as if excited to fury by the observation of the men—but the noise steadily increased. Oh God! what *could* I do? I foamed—I raved—I swore. I swung the chair upon which I had been sitting, and grated it upon the boards, but the noise arose over all and continually increased. It grew louder—louder—*louder!* And still the men chatted pleasantly, and smiled. Was it possible they heard not? Almighty God!—no, no! They heard!—they suspected!—they *knew!*—they were making a *mockery* of my horror!—this I thought, and this I think. But anything was better than this agony! Any thing was more tolerable than this derision! I could bear those hypocritical smiles no longer! I felt that I must scream or die!—and now—again!—hark! louder! louder! *louder!*—

"Villains!" I shrieked, "dissemble no more! I admit the deed!—tear up the planks!—here, here!—it is the beating of his hideous heart!"

THE CASK OF AMONTILLADO
Edgar Allan Poe

The thousand injuries of Fortunato I had borne as I best could; but when he ventured upon insult, I vowed revenge. You, who so well know the nature of my soul, will not suppose, however, that I gave utterance to a threat. At length I would be avenged; this was a point definitively settled—but the very definitiveness with which it was resolved, precluded the idea of risk. I must not only punish, but punish with impunity. A wrong is unredressed when retribution overtakes its redresser. It is equally unredressed when the avenger fails to make himself felt as such to him who has done the wrong.

It must be understood, that neither by word nor deed had I given Fortunato cause to doubt my good-will. I continued, as was my wont, to smile in his face, and he did not perceive that my smile *now* was at the thought of his immolation.

He had a weak point—this Fortunato—although in other regards he was a man to be respected and even feared. He prided himself on his connoisseurship in wine. Few Italians have the true virtuoso spirit. For the most part their enthusiasm is adopted to suit the time and opportunity—to practice imposture upon the British and Austrian *millionnaires*. In painting and gemmary Fortunato, like his countrymen, was a quack—but in the matter of old wines he was sincere. In this respect I did not differ from him materially: I was skillful in the Italian vintages myself, and bought largely whenever I could.

It was about dusk, one evening during the supreme madness of the carnival season, that I encountered my friend. He accosted me with excessive warmth, for he had been drinking much. The man wore motley. He had on a tight-fitting parti-striped dress, and his head was surmounted by the conical cap and bells. I was so pleased to see him, that I thought I should never have done wringing his hand.

I said to him: "My dear Fortunato, you are luckily met. How remarkably well you are looking today! But I have received a pipe of what passes for Amontillado, and I have my doubts."

"How?" said he. "Amontillado? A pipe? Impossible! And in the middle of the carnival!"

"I have my doubts," I replied; "and I was silly enough to pay the full Amontillado price without consulting you in the matter. You were not to be found, and I was fearful of losing a bargain."

"Amontillado!"

"I have my doubts."

"Amontillado!"

"And I must satisfy them."
"Amontillado!"
"As you are engaged, I am on my way to Luchesi. If any one has a critical turn, it is he. He will tell me—"
"Luchesi cannot tell Amontillado from Sherry."
"And yet some fools will have it that his taste is a match for your own."
"Come, let us go."
"Whither?"
"To your vaults."
"My friend, no; I will not impose upon your good nature. I perceive you have an engagement. Luchesi—"
"I have no engagement;—come."
"My friend, no. It is not the engagement, but the severe cold with which I perceive you are afflicted. The vaults are insufferably damp. They are encrusted with niter."
"Let us go, nevertheless. The cold is merely nothing. Amontillado! You have been imposed upon. And as for Luchesi, he cannot distinguish Sherry from Amontillado."

Thus speaking, Fortunato possessed himself of my arm. Putting on a mask of black silk, and drawing a *roquelaire* closely about my person, I suffered him to hurry me to my palazzo.

There were no attendants at home; they had absconded to make merry in honor of the time. I had told them that I should not return until the morning, and had given them explicit orders not to stir from the house. These orders were sufficient, I well knew, to insure their immediate disappearance, one and all, as soon as my back was turned.

I took from their sconces two flambeaux, and giving one to Fortunato, bowed him through several suites of rooms to the archway that led into the vaults. I passed down a long and winding staircase, requesting him to be cautious as he followed. We came at length to the foot of the descent, and stood together on the damp ground of the catacombs of the Montresors.

The gait of my friend was unsteady, and the bells upon his cap jingled as he strode.

"The pipe?" said he.

"It is farther on," said I; "but observe the white webwork which gleams from these cavern walls."

He turned toward me, and looked into my eyes with two filmy orbs that distilled the rheum of intoxication.

"Niter?" he asked, at length.

"Niter," I replied. "How long have you had that cough?"

"Ugh! ugh! ugh!—ugh! ugh! ugh!—ugh! ugh! ugh!—ugh! ugh! ugh!—ugh! ugh! ugh!"

My poor friend found it impossible to reply for many minutes.

"It is nothing," he said, at last.

"Come," I said, with decision, "we will go back; your health is precious. You are rich, respected, admired, beloved; you are happy, as once I was. You are a man to be missed. For me it is no matter. We will go back; you will be ill, and I cannot be responsible. Besides, there is Luchesi—"

"Enough," he said; "the cough is a mere nothing; it will not kill me. I shall not die of a cough."

"True—true," I replied; "and, indeed, I had no intention of alarming you unnecessarily; but you should use all proper caution. A draught of this Medoc will defend us from the damps."

Here I knocked off the neck of a bottle which I drew from a long row of its fellows that lay upon the mould.

"Drink," I said, presenting him the wine.

He raised it to his lips with a leer. He paused and nodded to me familiarly, while his bells jingled.

"I drink," he said, "to the buried that repose around us."

"And I to your long life."

He again took my arm, and we proceeded.

"These vaults," he said, "are expensive."

"The Montresors," I replied, "were a great and numerous family."

"I forget your arms."

"A huge human foot d'or, in a field azure; the foot crushes a serpent rampant whose fangs are imbedded in the heel."

"And the motto?"

"*Nemo me impune lacessit.*"

"Good!" he said.

The wine sparkled in his eyes and the bells jingled. My own fancy grew warm with the Medoc. We had passed through walls of piled bones, with casks and puncheons intermingling, into the inmost recesses of the catacombs. I paused again, and this time I made bold to seize Fortunato by an arm above the elbow.

"The niter!" I said; "see, it increases. It hangs like moss upon the vaults. We are below the river's bed. The drops of moisture trickle among the bones. Come, we will go back ere it is too late. Your cough—"

"It is nothing," he said; "let us go on. But first, another draught of the Medoc."

I broke and reached him a flagon of De Grâve. He emptied it at a breath. His eyes flashed with a fierce light. He laughed and threw the bottle upward with a gesticulation I did not understand.

I looked at him in surprise. He repeated the movement—a grotesque one.

"You do not comprehend?" he said.

"Not I," I replied.
"Then you are not of the brotherhood."
"How?"
"You are not of the masons."
"Yes, yes," I said; "yes, yes."
"You? Impossible! A mason?"
"A mason," I replied.
"A sign," he said.
"It is this," I answered, producing a trowel from beneath the folds of my *roquelaire*.
"You jest," he exclaimed, recoiling a few paces. "But let us proceed to the Amontillado."

"Be it so," I said, replacing the tool beneath the cloak, and again offering him my arm. He leaned upon it heavily. We continued our route in search of the Amontillado. We passed through a range of low arches, decending again, arrived at a deep crypt, in which the foulness of the air caused our flambeaux rather to glow than flame.

At the most remote end of the crypt there appeared another less spacious. Its walls had been lined with human remains, piled to the vault overhead, in the fashion of the great catacombs of Paris. Three sides of this interior crypt were still ornamented in this manner. From the fourth the bones had been thrown down, and lay promiscuously upon the earth, forming at one point a mound of some size. Within the wall thus exposed by the displacing of the bones, we perceived a still interior recess, in depth about four feet, in width three, in height six or seven. It seemed to have been constructed for no especial use within itself, but formed merely the interval between two of the colossal supports of the roof of the catacombs, and was backed by one of their circumscribing walls of solid granite.

It was in vain that Fortunato, uplifting his dull torch, endeavored to pry into the depth of the recess. Its termination the feeble light did not enable us to see.

"Proceed," I said; "herein is the Amontillado. As for Luchesi—"

"He is an ignoramus," interrupted my friend, as he stepped unsteadily forward, while I followed immediately at his heels. In an instant he had reached the extremity of the niche, and finding his progress arrested by the rock, stood stupidly bewildered. A moment more and I had fettered him to the granite. In its surface were two iron staples, distant from each other about two feet, horizontally. From one of these depended a short chain, from the other a padlock. Throwing the links about his waist, it was but the work of a few seconds to secure it. He was too much astounded to resist. Withdrawing the key I stepped back from the recess.

"Pass your hand," I said, "over the wall; you cannot help feeling the niter. Indeed it is *very* damp. Once more let me *implore* you to return. No? Then I must positively leave you. But I must first render you all the little attentions in my power."

"The Amontillado!" ejaculated my friend, not yet recovered from his astonishment.

"True," I replied, "the Amontillado."

As I said these words I busied myself among the pile of bones of which I have before spoken. Throwing them aside, I soon uncovered a quantity of building stone and mortar. With these materials and with the aid of my trowel, I began vigorously to wall up the entrance of the niche.

I had scarcely laid the first tier of the masonry when I discovered that the intoxication of Fortunato had in a great measure worn off. The earliest indication I had of this was a low moaning cry from the depth of the recess. It was *not* the cry of a drunken man. There was then a long and obstinate silence. I laid the second tier, and the third, and the fourth; and then I heard the furious vibrations of the chain. The noise lasted for several minutes, during which, that I might hearken to it with the more satisfaction, I ceased my labors and sat down upon the bones. When at last the clanking subsided, I resumed the trowel, and finished without interruption the fifth, the sixth, and the seventh tier. The wall was now nearly upon a level with my breast. I again paused, and holding the flambeaux over the mason-work, threw a few feeble rays upon the figure within.

A succession of loud and shrill screams, bursting suddenly from the throat of the chained form, seemed to thrust me violently back. For a brief moment I hesitated—I trembled. Unsheathing my rapier, I began to grope with it about the recess; but the thought of an instant reassured me. I placed my hand upon the solid fabric of the catacombs, and felt satisfied. I reapproached the wall. I replied to the yells of him who clamored. I re-echoed—I aided—I surpassed them in volume and in strength. I did this, and the clamorer grew still.

It was now midnight, and my task was drawing to a close. I had completed the eighth, the ninth, and the tenth tier. I had finished a portion of the last and the eleventh; there remained but a single stone to be fitted and plastered in. I struggled with its weight; I placed it partially in its destined position. But now there came from out the niche a low laugh that erected the hairs upon my head. It was succeeded by a sad voice, which I had difficulty in recognizing as that of the noble Fortunato. The voice said—

"Ha! ha! ha!—he! he!—a very good joke indeed—an excellent jest. We will have many a rich laugh about it at the palazzo—he! he! he!—over our wine—he! he! he!"

"The Amontillado!" I said.

"He! he! he!—he! he! he!—yes, the Amontillado. But is it not getting late? Will not they be awaiting us at the palazzo, the Lady Fortunato and the rest? Let us be gone."

"Yes," I said, "let us be gone."

"*For the love of God, Montresor!*"

"Yes," I said, "for the love of God!"

But to these words I hearkened in vain for a reply. I grew impatient. I called aloud:

"Fortunato!"

No answer. I called again:

"Fortunato!"

No answer still. I thrust a torch through the remaining aperture and let it fall within. There came forth in return only a jingling of the bells. My heart grew sick—on account of the dampness of the catacombs. I hastened to make an end of my labor. I forced the last stone into its position; I plastered it up. Against the new masonry I re-erected the old rampart of bones. For the half of a century no mortal has disturbed them. *In pace requiescat!*

Issues for Discussion

1. Use Freud's explanation of behavior through the dynamics of the id, ego, and superego to explain the behavior of The Misfit in Flannery O'Connor's "A Good Man Is Hard to Find."
2. Analyze the following quotations and explain why one suggests The Misfit is the product of a dominant id, and the other the product of an overactive superego.

"Throw me that shirt, Bobby Lee," The Misfit said. The shirt came flying at him and landed on his shoulder and he put it on. The grandmother couldn't name what that shirt reminded her of. "No, lady," The Misfit said while he was buttoning it up, "I found out the crime don't matter. You can do one thing or you can do another, kill a man or take a tire off his car, because sooner or later you're going to forget what it was you done and just be punished for it."

"Jesus was the only One that ever raised the dead," The Misfit continued, "and He shouldn't have done it. He thrown everything off balance. If He did what He said, then it's nothing for you to do but throw away everything and follow Him, and if He didn't then it's nothing for you to do but enjoy the few minutes you got left the best way you can—by killing somebody or burning down his house or doing some other meanness to him. No pleasure but meanness," he said and his voice had become almost a snarl.

3. What evidence would behavior modification theorists cite to suggest that the Misfit was merely a product of his environment?
4. There is evidence in the two stories by Edgar Allan Poe that the murderer believes his acts are justified, even necessary. Freudian psychologists and behaviorists would call such behavior "purposive." Yet purposive behavior to the Freudian means that the actor unconsciously wants to be apprehended and punished. The behaviorist suggests that purposive conduct involves behavior the actor feels is justified, or capable of rationalization. Read the following quotations

from "The Tell-Tale Heart" and "The Cask of Amontillado" and indicate which behavior would be considered purposive to Freudian theorists and to behaviorists.

No doubt I now grew *very* pale;—but I talked more fluently, and with a heightened voice. Yet the sound increased—and what could I do? It was *a low, dull, quick sound—much such a sound as a watch makes when enveloped in cotton*. I gasped for breath—and yet the officers heard it not. I talked more quickly—more vehemently; but the noise steadily increased. I arose and argued about trifles, in a high key and with violent gesticulations, but the noise steadily increased. Why *would* they not be gone? I paced the floor to and fro with heavy strides, as if excited to fury by the observation of the men—but the noise steadily increased. Oh God! what *could* I do? I foamed—I raved—I swore. I swung the chair upon which I had been sitting, and grated it upon the boards, but the noise arose over all and continually increased. It grew louder—louder—*louder*! And still the men chatted pleasantly, and smiled. Was it possible they heard not? Almighty God!—no, no! They heard!—they suspected!—they *knew*!—they were making a *mockery* of my horror!—this I thought, and this I think. But any thing was better than this agony! Any thing was more tolerable than this derision! I could bear those hypocritical smiles no longer! I felt that I must scream or die!—and now—again!—hark! louder! louder! *louder*!—

"Villains!" I shrieked, "dissemble no more! I admit the deed!—tear up the planks!—here, here!—it is the beating of his hideous heart!"

No answer still. I thrust a torch through the remaining aperture and let it fall within. There came forth in return only a jingling of the bells. My heart grew sick—on account of the dampness of the catacombs. I hastened to make an end of my labor. I forced the last stone into its position; I plastered it up. Against the new masonry I re-erected the old rampart of bones. For the half of a century no mortal has disturbed them. *In pace requiescat*!

5. Read the following quote from "The Cask of Amontillado," spoken by the murderer, Montresor. Explain whether his behavior is provoked by his unconscious or is a conscious response to his environment.

The thousand injuries of Fortunato I had borne as I best could; but when he ventured upon insult, I vowed revenge. You, who so well know the nature of my soul, will not suppose, however, that I gave utterance to a threat. *At length* I would be avenged; this was a point definitively settled—but the very definitiveness with which it was resolved, precluded the idea of risk. I must not only punish, but punish with impunity. A wrong is unredressed when retribution overtakes its redresser. It is equally unredressed when the avenger fails to make himself felt as such to him who has done the wrong.

6. Assume you are an attorney called upon to defend The Misfit, the madman (in "The Tell-Tale Heart"), and Montresor. In each case explain whether you would use the *M'Naughten, Durham,* or "product test" as defenses for the murderers.

PART VI

Labeling Theory

Labeling theorists contend that positivist statements relating criminal behavior to individual pathology are misleading. Rather, one gains insights on the process of "becoming deviant" by studying the legal environment, especially the dynamics of decision making.[1] According to Howard S. Becker, "Deviance is *not* a quality of the act a person commits, but rather a consequence of the application by others of rules and sanctions to an 'offender.' The deviant is one to whom that label has successfully been applied; deviant behavior is behavior that people so label."[2] Moreover, acquiring the label "deviant" seems largely fortuitous, or bad luck: the offender happens to be in the wrong place at the wrong time, and is apprehended. The "bad luck" hypothesis is especially applicable to the so-called willing victim (victimless) crimes such as adultery, fornication, homosexual copulation, statutory rape, gambling, and drug and alcohol abuse. Says Kai Erickson:

> Some men who drink heavily are called alcoholics and others are not, some men who behave oddly are committed to hospitals and others are not . . . and the difference between those who earn a deviant title in society and those who go their own way in peace is largely determined by the way in which the community filters out and codes the many details of behavior which come to its attention.[3]

1. For a good overview of labeling theory, see Edwin M. Schur, *Labeling Deviant Behavior* (New York: Harper & Row, 1971). For other notable works in this area, see Frank Tannenbaum, *Crime and the Community* (New York: Columbia University Press, 1938); Kai Erickson, "Notes on Sociology of Deviance," *Social Problems* 9 (Spring 1962); Austin Turk, *Criminality and the Legal Order* (Chicago: Rand McNally, 1976); William Chambliss, *Criminal Law in Action* (Santa Barbara, Calif.: Hamilton, 1975); Walter Reihlen, *The Crime Problem* (New York: Meredith, 1967).

2. *Outsiders: Studies in the Sociology of Deviance* (New York: Free Press, 1963), p. 9.

3. Erickson, "Notes on Deviance," p. 308.

In addition, labeling largely depends on the *prestige* and *visibility* of the offenders. The same behavior may be engaged in by different persons or groups, but the political status each possesses (and "status" too is a labeling tactic) determines whether the negative label will be applied.[4] Charles McCaghy illustrates the "politics" of the labeling process:

> Basic to any conflict perspective is the assumption that whichever groups can exert the greatest influence on the legislative and the enforcement processes are most assured that their interests will be protected. What is illegal depends upon the outcome of struggles between concerned parties. Who is treated as criminal depends upon the bureaucratic interpretation of both law and behavior.[5]

The primary factor in the labeling process is the source of the policeman's labeling power—the legal environment, including its institutions and laws. The more intricate and overwhelming the legal milieu is, the more likely a person is to become involved in its machinery. The legal apparatus of most modern societies is immense. The United States, for example, has two distinct legal systems. The Constitution outlines the legal model for the federal system, while the local (state) governments are left to establish their own structure. In both systems, judges, juries, attorneys, rules of procedures, legal administrators, and court support personnel are extensively used. The immensity of the system can be fully appreciated only when one discovers the quantity of laws used to control behavior. At present there are over 2500 *federal* laws; in addition, each state formulates its own restrictions. And indivivuals may be tried by both federal and state courts even though only one crime has been committed.

The number of laws added to the statute books far exceeds those that are deleted. Potential enforcement of archaic laws exists until their formal repeal. Examples of currently enforceable legal dinosaurs include (1) In Minnesota it is illegal to hang male and female undergarments on the same clothesline. (2) Wives in Kentucky must have their husbands' permission to move furniture around their homes. (3) A Florida law requires one to keep one's clothes on while bathing in the family bathtub. (4) Every animal out on the streets after dark in Berea, Ohio, must wear a taillight. (5) Crocodiles may not be tied to hydrants in Michigan. (6) Tickling a female in Norton, Virginia, is illegal. (7) In Natchez, Mississippi, elephants are not permitted to drink beer. (8) It is illegal in Indiana to take a bath in the winter.

---

4. For an excellent illustration of the labeling process, see William J. Chambliss, "The Saints and the Roughnecks," in Chambliss, *Criminal Law in Action*, pp. 71–80.

5. *Deviant Behavior: Crime, Conflict, and Interest Groups* (New York: Macmillan, 1976), p. 89.

INTRODUCTION

Legal maxims like "presumption of innocence," "justice is blind," and "innocent until proven guilty beyond a reasonable doubt" are reminders of the buffer placed between the citizen and the state. Other adages remind us of our legal responsibilities: "All men are presumed to know the law" and "ignorance of the law is no excuse." Regardless of how many laws exist, we are held accountable to all of them. Considering the vast number of laws, the potential impact of these "liability adages" is devastating.

The labeling theorist, however, is only tangentially concerned with how many laws an individual may be subject to. The prevailing interest involves the dynamics of lawmaking coupled with the discretionary enforcement of those laws. From this perspective, the adage that "we are a nation of laws, not men" is highly suspect. Only by understanding the psychological, economic, and political motivation of the *lawmaker* and *law enforcer* may one realize that deviance is the result of selective typing. Thus, it is no accident that courts have become meeting halls for the politically and socially impotent, while the white-collar criminal often enjoys a life of legal anonymity.[6]

The servant of the law formulator is the peace officer. The policeman is indispensable because his decision to arrest amounts to a formal ascription of the deviant label. But his decision is also the product of internal motivation. An inability to identify with different and seemingly threatening life styles may assure the lawmaker that the labeling process will find its intended target.

Discretionary justice and, incidentally, selective labeling, only begin with the arrest. The desk sergeant or precinct captain may put pressure on the officer to terminate the proceedings. The prosecuting attorney may drop the case. The judge might "suggest" that certain violations no longer be brought before him. Or the jury may fail to convict. Finally, the discretionary process continues in the sentencing, bail, and parole proceedings. In short, the labeling theorist perceives the entire process as selective in nature. And the target of the process becomes the social and political "undesirable" in society.

An interesting by-product of the labeling theory involves "the self-

---

6. Critics of labeling theory state that it is not a theory because it does not "explain" deviance. Rather, labeling theory defines in vague terms only the reactions to deviance and the process of selective ascription while leaving unanswered any theory of crime causation. Perhaps the saliant redeeming value of labeling theory involves the concept of the "self-fulfilling prophecy": the act of labeling someone as deviant produces the tendency for him to behave in a manner consistent with the label. Some empirical psychological studies support the self-fulfilling prophecy theory, but the results remain inconclusive. See Jack P. Gibbs, "Conceptions of Deviant Behavior: The Old and the New," *Pacific Sociological Review* 9 (Spring 1966): 9–14; and Bernard A. Thorsell and Lloyd D. Klemki, "The Labeling Process: Reinforcement and Deterrent?" *Law and Society Review*, February 1972, pp. 393–403.

fulfilling prophecy," or what Lemert calls "secondary deviation."[7] Simply stated, people tend to act out role labels assigned to them.

> The effects of criminal stigmatization may not only transform the identity of the offender in the eyes of others, but also reshape to some degree the offender's own self-image, and may impel him into various behavior patterns that will further confirm his negative public identity, increasing the probability of further criminal processing and harsher penalties. The imprisoned drug addict released on parole, for example, may find jobs difficult to secure and may be denied access to the very kinds of legitimate conventional opportunities that he needs to demonstrate his "fitness" to reenter society and effectively remove the label of "dope fiend." Skepticism, suspicion, and withdrawal of trust are likely to prevail long after the offender has "paid his debt to society."[8]

The process has its greatest effect when the label is attached at an impressionable stage of life (e.g., early adolescence). According to Frank Tannenbaum,

> From the community's point of view, the individual who used to do bad and mischievous things has now become a bad and unredeemable human being. From the individual's point of view there has taken place a similar change. He has gone slowly from a sense of grievance and injustice, of being undully mistreated and punished, to a recognition that the definition of him as a human being is different from that of other boys in his neighborhood, his school, street, community. This recognition on his part becomes a process of self-identification and integration with the group which shares his activities. It becomes, in part, a process of rationalization; in part, a simple response to a specialized type of stimulus. The young delinquent becomes bad because he is defined as bad and because he is not believed if he is good. There is a persistent demand for consistency in character.[9]

---

7. Edwin M. Lemert, *Human Deviance, Social Problems, and Social Control* (New Jersey: Prentice-Hall, 1972).

8. *Crime, Power, and Morality* (Scranton, Pa.: Chandler, 1971), p. 50.

9. Tannenbaum, *Crime and Community*, pp. 17–18. Moreover, once the label has been attached, it is extremely difficult to have it, or its effects, eradicated. One study of researchers who feigned mental illness and had themselves committed to an asylum found it was nearly impossible to overcome the label of schizophrenia. See D. L. Rosenham, "On Being Sane in Insane Places," *Science* 179 (January 1973): 250.

INTRODUCTION

In Bret Harte's "The Outcasts of Poker Flat," a classic example of the *politics* of labeling occurs. The "good folk" of Poker Flat decide the town needs a moral facelift. A committee is formed to ascertain whose absence would improve the town's character. The impromptu formation of the committee and its lawmaking and law-enforcing powers render insights about the deficiences of many legal systems.

Sondra Spatt Olsen's "Hoods I Have Known" and John Berryman's "The Imaginary Jew" illustrate *effects* of the labeling process. Olsen's "hoods" try to act out the role associated with this label, although their behavior consistently falls short of any serious legal involvement. Yet the attachment of the sinister name has profound implications in the classroom, which will probably carry over after their "education" ends. In contrast, Berryman's "imaginary" Jew is quite real. The young man willingly accepts a label accurately depicting what he really is, but quickly tries to forsake it after learning the connotations and consequences of being Jewish. The effects of the self-fulfilling prophecy manifest themselves in the process.

THE OUTCASTS OF POKER FLAT
Bret Harte

As Mr. John Oakhurst, gambler, stepped into the main street of Poker Flat on the morning of the 23rd of November, 1850, he was conscious of a change in its moral atmosphere since the preceding night. Two or three men, conversing earnestly together, ceased as he approached, and exchanged significant glances. There was a Sabbath lull in the air, which, in a settlement unused to Sabbath influences, looked ominous.

Mr. Oakhurst's calm, handsome face betrayed small concern in these indications. Whether he was conscious of any predisposing cause, was another question. "I reckon they're after somebody," he reflected; "likely it's me." He returned to his pocket the handkerchief with which he had been whipping away the red dust of Poker Flat from his neat boots, and quietly discharged his mind of any further conjecture.

In point of fact, Poker Flat was "after somebody." It had lately suffered the loss of several thousand dollars, two valuable horses, and a prominent citizen. It was experiencing a spasm of virtuous reaction, quite as lawless and ungovernable as any of the acts that had provoked it. A secret committee had determined to rid the town of all improper persons. This was done permanently in regard of two men who were then hanging from the boughs of a sycamore in the gulch, and temporarily in the banishment of certain other objectionable characters. I regret to say that some of these were ladies. It is but due to the sex, however, to state that their impropriety was professional, and it was only in such easily established standards of evil that Poker Flat ventured to sit in judgment.

Mr. Oakhurst was right in supposing that he was included in this category. A few of the committee had urged hanging him as a possible example, and a sure method of reimbursing themselves from his pockets of the sums he had won from them. "It's agin justice," said Jim Wheeler, "to let this yer young man from Roaring Camp—an entire stranger—carry away our money." But a crude sentiment of equity residing in the breasts of those who had been fortunate enough to win from Mr. Oakhurst overruled this narrower local prejudice.

Mr. Oakhurst received his sentence with philosophic calmness, none the less coolly that he was aware of the hesitation of his judges. He was too much of a gambler not to accept fate. With him life was at best an uncertain game, and he recognized the usual percentage in favor of the dealer.

A body of armed men accompanied the deported wickedness of Poker Flat to the outskirts of the settlement. Besides Mr. Oakhurst, who was known to be a coolly desperate man, and for whose intimidation the armed escort was intended, the expatriated party consisted of a young woman familiarly known as "The Duchess"; another who had won the title of "Mother Shipton"; and "Uncle Billy," a suspected sluice-robber and confirmed drunkard. The cavalcade provoked no comments from the spectators, nor was any word uttered by the escort. Only when the gulch which marked the uttermost limit of Poker Flat was reached, the leader spoke briefly and to the point. The exiles were forbidden to return at the peril of their lives.

As the escort disappeared, their pent-up feelings found vent in a few hysterical tears from the Duchess, some bad language from Mother Shipton, and a Parthian volley of expletives from Uncle Billy. The philosophic Oakhurst alone remained silent. He listened calmly to Mother Shipton's desire to cut somebody's heart out, to the repeated statements of the Duchess that she would die in the road, and to the alarming oaths that seemed to be bumped out of Uncle Billy as he rode forward. With the easy good humor characteristic of his class, he insisted upon exchanging his own riding-horse, "Five-Spot," for the sorry mule which the Duchess rode. But even this act did not draw the party into any closer sympathy. The young woman readjusted her somewhat draggled plumes with a feeble, faded coquetry; Mother Shipton eyed the possessor of "Five-Spot" with malevolence, and Uncle Billy included the whole party in one sweeping anathema.

The road to Sandy Bar—a camp that, not having as yet experienced the regenerating influences of Poker Flat, consequently seemed to offer some invitation to the emigrants—lay over a steep mountain range. It was distant a day's severe travel. In that advanced season the party soon passed out of the moist temperate regions of the foothills into the dry, cold, bracing air of the Sierras. The trail was narrow and difficult. At noon the Duchess, rolling out of her saddle upon the ground, declared her intention of going no farther, and the party halted.

The spot was singularly wild and impressive. A wooded amphitheatre, surrounded on three sides by precipitous cliffs of naked granite, sloped gently toward the crest of another precipice that overlooked the valley. It was, undoubtedly, the most suitable spot for a camp, had camping been advisable. But Mr. Oakhurst knew that scarcely half the journey to Sandy Bar was accomplished, and the party were not equipped or provisioned for delay. This fact he pointed out to his companions curtly, with a philosophic commentary on the folly of "throwing up their hand before the game was played out." But they were furnished with liquor, which in this emergency stood them in place of food, fuel, rest, and prescience. In spite of his remonstrances, it was not long before they were more or less under its influence. Uncle Billy passed rapidly from a bellicose state into one of stupor, the Duchess became maudlin, and Mother Shipton snored. Mr.

Oakhurst alone remained erect, leaning against a rock, calmly surveying them.

Mr. Oakhurst did not drink. It interfered with a profession which required coolness, impassiveness, and presence of mind, and, in his own language, he "couldn't afford it." As he gazed at his recumbent fellow exiles, the loneliness begotten of his pariah trade, his habits of life, his very vices, for the first time seriously oppressed him. He bestirred himself in dusting his black clothes, washing his hands and face, and other acts characteristic of his studiously neat habits, and for a moment forgot his annoyance. The thought of deserting his weaker and more pitiable companions never perhaps occurred to him. Yet he could not help feeling the want of that excitement which, singularly enough, was most conducive to that calm equanimity for which he was notorious. He looked at the gloomy walls that rose a thousand feet sheer above the circling pines around him, at the sky ominously clouded, at the valley below, already deepening into shadow; and, doing so, suddenly he heard his own name called.

A horseman slowly ascended the trail. In the fresh, open face of the newcomer Mr. Oakhurst recognized Tom Simson, otherwise known as "The Innocent," of Sandy Bar. He had met him some months before over a "little game," and had, with perfect equanimity, won the entire fortune—amounting to some forty dollars—of that guileless youth. After the game was finished, Mr. Oakhurst drew the youthful speculator behind the door and thus addressed him: "Tommy, you're a good little man, but you can't gamble worth a cent. Don't try it ever again." He then handed him his money back, pushed him gently from the room, and so made a devoted slave of Tom Simson.

There was a remembrance of this in his boyish and enthusiastic greeting of Mr. Oakhurst. He had started, he said, to go to Poker Flat to seek his fortune. "Alone?" No, not exactly alone; in fact (a giggle), he had run away with Piney Woods. Didn't Mr. Oakhurst remember Piney? She that used to wait on the table at the Temperance House? They had been engaged a long time, but old Jake Woods had objected, and so they had run away, and were going to Poker Flat to be married, and here they were. And they were tired out, and how lucky it was they had found a place to camp, and company. All this the Innocent delivered rapidly, while Piney, a stout, comely damsel of fifteen, emerged from behind the pine-tree, where she had been blushing unseen, and rode to the side of her lover.

Mr. Oakhurst seldom troubled himself with sentiment, still less with propriety; but he had a vague idea that the situation was not fortunate. He retained, however, his presence of mind sufficiently to kick Uncle Billy, who was about to say something, and Uncle Billy was sober enough to recognize in Mr. Oakhurst's kick a superior power that would not bear trifling. He then endeavored to dissuade Tom Simson from delaying further, but in vain. He even pointed out the fact that there was no provision, nor means of making camp. But, unluckily, the Innocent met this objection by assuring the party that he was provided with an extra mule loaded with provisions, and by the discovery of a rude attempt at a log house near the trail. "Piney can stay with Mrs. Oakhurst," said the Innocent, pointing to the Duchess, "and I can shift for myself."

Nothing but Mr. Oakhurst's admonishing foot saved Uncle Billy from bursting into a roar of laughter. As it was, he felt compelled to retire up the cañon until he could recover his gravity. There he confided the joke to the tall pine-trees, with many slaps of his leg, contortions of his face, and the usual profanity. But when he returned to the party, he found them seated by a fire—for the air had grown strangely chill and the sky overcast—in apparently amicable conversation. Piney was actually talking in an impulsive girlish fashion to the Duchess, who was listening with an interest and animation she had not shown for many days. The Innocent was holding forth, apparently with equal effect, to Mr. Oakhurst and Mother Shipton, who was actually relaxing into amiability. "Is this yar a d—d picnic?" said Uncle Billy, with inward scorn, as he surveyed the sylvan group, the glancing firelight, and the tethered animals in the foreground. Suddenly an idea mingled with the alcoholic fumes that disturbed his brain. It was apparently of a jocular nature, for he felt impelled to slap his leg again and cram his fist into his mouth.

As the shadows crept slowly up the mountain, a slight breeze rocked the tops of the pine-trees and moaned through their long and gloomy aisles. The ruined cabin, patched and covered with pine boughs, was set apart for the ladies. As the lovers parted, they unaffectedly exchanged a kiss, so honest and sincere that it might have been heard above the swaying pines. The frail Duchess and the malevolent Mother Shipton were probably too stunned to remark upon this last evidence of simplicity, and so turned without a word to the hut. The fire was replenished, the men lay down before the door, and in a few minutes were asleep.

Mr. Oakhurst was a light sleeper. Toward morning he awoke benumbed and cold. As he stirred the dying fire, the wind, which was now blowing strongly, brought to his cheek that which caused the blood to leave it,— snow!

He started to his feet with the intention of awakening the sleepers, for there was no time to lose. But turning to where Uncle Billy had been lying, he found him gone. A suspicion leaped to his brain, and a curse to his lips. He ran to the spot where the mules had been tethered—they were no longer there. The tracks were already rapidly disappearing in the snow.

The momentary excitement brought Mr. Oakhurst back to the fire with his usual calm. He did not waken the sleepers. The Innocent slumbered peacefully, with a smile on his good-humored, freckled face; the virgin Piney slept beside her frailer sisters as sweetly as though attended by celestial guardians; and Mr. Oakhurst, drawing his blanket over his shoulders, stroked his mustaches and waited for the dawn. It came slowly in a whirling mist of snowflakes that dazzled and confused the eye. What could be seen of the landscape appeared magically changed. He looked over the valley, and summed up the present and future in two words, "Snowed in!"

A careful inventory of the provisions, which, fortunately for the party, had been stored within the hut, and so escaped the felonious fingers of Uncle Billy, disclosed the fact that with care and prudence they might last ten days longer. "That is," said Mr. Oakhurst *sotto voce* to the Innocent, "if you're willing to board us. If you ain't—and perhaps you'd better not—you can wait till Uncle Billy gets back with provisions." For some occult reason, Mr. Oakhurst could not bring himself to disclose Uncle Billy's rascality, and so offered the hypothesis that he had wandered from the camp and had accidentally stampeded the animals. He dropped a warning to the Duchess and Mother Shipton, who of course knew the facts of their associate's defection. "They'll find out the truth about us *all* when they find out anything," he added significantly, "and there's no good frightening them now."

Tom Simson not only put all his worldly store at the disposal of Mr. Oakhurst, but seemed to enjoy the prospect of their enforced seclusion. "We'll have a good camp for a week, and then the snow'll melt, and we'll all go back together." The cheerful gaiety of the young man and Mr. Oakhurst's calm infected the others. The Innocent, with the aid of pine boughs, extemporized a thatch for the roofless cabin, and the Duchess directed Piney in the rearrangement of the interior with a taste and tact that opened the blue eyes of that provincial maiden to their fullest extent. "I reckon now you're used to fine things at Poker Flat," said Piney. The Duchess turned away sharply to conceal something that reddened her cheeks through their professional tint, and Mother Shipton requested Piney not to "chatter." But when Mr. Oakhurst returned from a weary search for the trail, he heard the sound of happy laughter echoed from the rocks. He stopped in some alarm, and his thoughts first naturally reverted to the whiskey, which he had prudently cached. "And yet it don't somehow sound like whiskey," said the gambler. It was not until he caught sight of the blazing fire through the still blinding storm, and the group around it, that he settled to the conviction that it was "square fun."

Whether Mr. Oakhurst had cached his cards with the whiskey as something debarred the free access of the community, I cannot say. It was certain that, in Mother Shipton's words, he "didn't say 'cards' once" during that evening. Haply the time was beguiled by an accordion, produced somewhat ostentatiously by Tom Simson from his pack. Notwithstanding some difficulties attending the manipulation of this instrument, Piney Woods managed to pluck several reluctant melodies from its keys, to an accompaniment by the Innocent on a pair of bone castanets. But the crowning festivity of the evening was reached in a rude camp-meeting hymn, which the lovers, joining hands, sang with great earnestness and vociferation. I fear that a certain defiant tone and Covenanter's swing to its chorus, rather than any devotional quality, caused it speedily to infect the others, who at last joined in the refrain:—

> "I'm proud to live in the service of the Lord
> And I'm bound to die in His army."

The pines rocked, the storm eddied and whirled above the miserable group, and the flames of their altar leaped heavenward, as if in token of the vow.

At midnight the storm abated, the rolling clouds parted, and the stars glittered keenly above the sleeping camp. Mr. Oakhurst, whose professional habits had enabled him to live on the smallest possible amount of sleep, in dividing the watch with Tom Simson somehow managed to take upon himself the greater part of that duty. He excused himself to the Innocent by saying that he had "often been a week without sleep." "Doing what?" asked Tom. "Poker!" replied Oakhurst sententiously. "When a man gets a streak of luck,—nigger-luck,—he don't get tired. The luck gives in first. Luck," continued the gambler reflectively, "is a mighty queer thing. All you know about it for certain is that it's bound to change. And it's finding out when it's going to change that makes you. We've had a streak of bad luck since we left Poker Flat,—you come along, and slap you get into it, too. If you can hold your cards right along you're all right. For," added the gambler, with cheerful irrelevance—

> "I'm proud to live in the service of the Lord
> And I'm bound to die in His army."

The third day came, and the sun, looking through the white-curtained valley, saw the outcasts divide their slowly decreasing store of provisions for the morning meal. It was one of the peculiarities of that mountain climate that its rays diffused a kindly warmth over the wintry landscape, as if in regretful commiseration of the past. But it revealed drift on drift of snow piled high around the hut,—a hopeless, uncharted, trackless sea of white lying below the rocky shores to which the castaways still clung. Through the marvelously clear air the smoke of the pastoral village of Poker Flat rose miles away. Mother Shipton saw it, and from a remote pinnacle of her rocky fastness hurled in that direction a final malediction. It was her last vituperative attempt, and perhaps for that reason was invested with a certain degree of sublimity. It did her good, she privately informed the Duchess. "Just you go out there and cuss, and see." She then set herself to the task of amusing "the child," as she and the Duchess were pleased to call Piney. Piney was no chicken, but it was a soothing and original theory of the pair thus to account for the fact that she didn't swear and wasn't improper.

When night crept up again through the gorges, the reedy notes of the accordion rose and fell in fitful spasms and long-drawn gasps by the flickering campfire. But music failed to fill entirely the aching void left by insufficient food, and a new diversion was proposed by Piney,—story-telling. Neither Mr. Oakhurst nor his female companions caring to relate their personal experiences, this plan would have failed too, but for the Innocent. Some months before he had chanced upon a stray copy of Mr. Pope's ingenious translation of the Iliad. He now proposed to narrate the principal incidents of that poem—having thoroughly mastered the argument and fairly forgotten the words—in the current vernacular of Sandy Bar. And so for the rest of that night the Homeric demigods again walked the earth. Trojan bully and wily Greek wrestled in the winds, and the great pines in the cañon seemed to bow to the wrath of the son of Peleus. Mr. Oakhurst listened with quiet satisfaction. Most especially was he interested in the fate of "Ash-heels," as the Innocent persisted in denominating the "swift-footed Achilles."

So, with small food and much of Homer and the accordion, a week passed over the heads of the outcasts. The sun again forsook them, and again from leaden skies the snowflakes were sifted over the land. Day by day closer around them drew the snowy circle, until at last they looked from their prison over drifted walls of dazzling white, that towered twenty feet above their heads. It became more and more difficult to replenish their fires, even from the fallen trees beside them, now half hidden in the drifts. And yet no one complained. The lovers turned from the dreary prospect and looked into each other's eyes, and were happy. Mr. Oakhurst settled himself coolly to the losing game before him. The Duchess, more cheerful than she had been, assumed the care of Piney. Only Mother Shipton—once the strongest of the party—seemed to sicken and fade. At midnight on the tenth day she called Oakhurst to her side. "I'm going," she said, in a voice of querulous weakness, "but don't say anything about it. Don't waken the kids. Take the bundle from under my head and open it." Mr. Oakhurst did so. It contained Mother Shipton's rations for the last week, untouched. "Give 'em to the child," she said, pointing to the sleeping Piney. "You've starved yourself," said the gambler. "That's what they call it," said the woman querulously, as she lay down again, and, turning her face to the wall, passed quietly away.

The accordion and the bones were put aside that day, and Homer was forgotten. When the body of Mother Shipton had been committed to the snow, Mr. Oakhurst took the Innocent aside, and showed him a pair of snowshoes, which he had fashioned from the old pack-saddle. "There's one chance in a hundred to save her yet," he said, pointing to Piney; "but it's there," he added, pointing toward Poker Flat. "If you can reach there in two days she's safe." "And you?" asked Tom Simson. "I'll stay here," was the curt reply.

The lovers parted with a long embrace. "You are not going, too?" said the Duchess, as she saw Mr. Oakhurst apparently waiting to accompany him. "As far as the cañon," he replied. He turned suddenly and kissed the Duchess, leaving her pallid face aflame, and her trembling limbs rigid with amazement.

Night came, but not Mr. Oakhurst. It brought the storm again and the whirling snow. Then the Duchess, feeding the fire, found that someone had quietly piled beside the hut enough fuel to last a few days longer. The tears rose to her eyes, but she hid them from Piney.

The women slept but little. In the morning, looking into each other's faces, they read their fate. Neither spoke, but Piney, accepting the position of the stronger, drew near and placed her arm around the Duchess's waist. They kept this attitude for the rest of the day. That night the storm reached its greatest fury, and rending asunder the protecting pines, invaded the very hut.

Toward morning they found themselves unable to feed the fire, which gradually died away. As the embers slowly blackened, the Duchess crept closer to Piney, and broke the silence of many hours: "Piney, can you pray?" "No, dear," said Piney simply. The Duchess, without knowing exactly why, felt relieved, and putting her head upon Piney's shoulder, spoke no more. And so reclining, the younger and purer pillowing the head of her soiled sister upon her virgin breast, they fell asleep.

The wind lulled as if it feared to waken them. Feathery drifts of snow, shaken from the long pine boughs, flew like white-winged birds, and settled about them as they slept. The moon through the rifted clouds looked down upon what had been the camp. But all human stain, all trace of earthly travail, was hidden beneath the spotless mantle mercifully flung from above.

They slept all that day and the next, nor did they waken when voices and footsteps broke the silence of the camp. And when pitying fingers brushed the snow from their wan faces, you could scarcely have told, from the equal peace that dwelt upon them, which was she that had sinned. Even the law of Poker Flat recognized this, and turned away, leaving them still locked in each other's arms.

But at the head of the gulch, on one of the largest pinetrees, they found the deuce of clubs pinned to the bark with a bowie-knife. It bore the following, written in pencil in a firm hand:

Beneath this tree
lies the body
of
JOHN OAKHURST,
who struck a streak of bad luck
on the 23d of November, 1850,
and
handed in his checks
on the 7th December, 1850

And pulseless and cold, with a Derringer by his side and a bullet in his heart, though still calm as in life, beneath the snow lay he who was at once the strongest and yet the weakest of the outcasts of Poker Flat.

HOODS I HAVE KNOWN
Sondra Spatt Olsen

Whenever I reminisce about old beaux, I begin with poor Larry Dinhofer, who sat behind me in the eighth grade and asked me to the P.S. 333 prom because I asked him to my graduation party. From gratitude for the first invitation, Larry's mother bought me a monstrous bottle of Sweet Primrose toilet water, which I have kept to this day. The primroses or whatever they were have become so fermented through the years that I now use it for rubbing alcohol and think "Dinhofer" whenever I have an ache in my back. But strictly speaking, although memorable, Larry was not my first but only my first respectable beau. Before Larry I had an unrespectable romance, long suppressed, a seventh-grade affair with the dirty, untrustworthy Danny Tooey, who was a hood.

Perhaps I should explain about hoods. Hoods in Brooklyn are boys who go to school only by the grace of the truant officer, "hood" being short for "hoodlum." "Juvenile delinquent" is a much longer word and not half as piquant. Our seventh-grade hoods were comparatively unaggressive. They never did much but loaf at the back of the class and throw spitballs at each other, sometimes at the teacher. They wore dungarees or chartreuse pants with pistol pockets in imitation of the Avenue E Boys, who were model hoods and real court cases. Our hoods, although harmless, grew aggressive-looking sideburns and great masses of curly black or blond hair. All of them shaved. Danny Tooey was the biggest, tallest, hairiest of the lot and the one who had been left back most often. He was fifteen.

When Danny was first left back into our class, we ignored each other. Our social milieux, even in school, were different. I sat in the front of the room, covered my books, raised my hand in answer to all questions and agreed with the teacher on all points. I had already set my eye on the General Excellence Award at graduation. Danny, as I have already pointed out, never did anything in school except pledge allegiance to the flag, proving that hoods were untrustworthy but not unpatriotic.

Danny did not cover books; he destroyed them. Miss Malcolm thought well-bound books in hoody hands a waste, so Danny scattered the leaves of his worn-out volumes like nuts in May, sometimes maliciously, more often from the sort of pure disinterest playboys show when they run their Jaguars off cliffs in the movies. No one had ever called upon Danny to read from these books, you see. It was *l'acte gratuit*.

When I fell into disgrace, Danny was the first hood whose friendship I won. I was in with the leader of the gang, so to speak. I had been the Winged Messenger of the seventh grade and scurried around corridors clutching notes from Miss Malcolm with the expression postmen have when they meet up with the sleet or snow or fog people have been telling them about. I took my messenger position seriously, even though the notes, whenever I paused to open them, revealed nothing more serious than a date for tea or a lift to the beauty parlor. One day Miss Malcolm decided to affix a postscript to a note that she'd dispatched with me and came around a corner unexpectedly, giving both of us a shock.

"Since you have proved yourself a criminal, I'm going to treat you that way," she announced pontifically before the class, and made me clean out my desk and remove my books and self to the back of the room.

As a criminal, I found myself in a peculiar position. It had only been a note asking for more toilet supplies for the teachers' rest room, and hardly worth the drastic punishment, I felt. It was a mundane confidence I'd broken, though Miss Malcolm had mysteriously underlined "toilet supplies" for some reason I could not fathom. Nevertheless, I was disgraced, not only with the teacher but with all my friends. From that day on Miss Malcolm would not call on me in class, even though I was the only one who knew the three most important Atlantic fishing ports and waved my arm wildly like a drowning Atlantic fisherman. She instructed the class to ignore me too. My friends from the front of the room, oh, perfidy, had been waiting all these years, I found, praying that I would fall from grace. They simply would not turn their heads or accept my notes.

Instead of being crushed by my fate I was confident and not at all apologetic. After all, I was the star pupil. And what would Miss Malcolm do without me when we reached the difficult Middle Atlantic States? As for my friends, "those schmoey kids" as I called them, my contempt for them was boundless. I vowed if I ever achieved my pure state again I'd make them suffer.

Miss Malcolm seated Danny and me in a double seat, thinking, dear woman, that close contact with a hood was the worst punishment anyone could inflict on a clean, well-brought-up little girl. She expected me to cry and beg to be let back, at least to the class middle. That was because Miss Malcolm herself was afraid of that hairy creature who slouched into class with disquieting tread and rumbled unintelligible answers deep in his throat. "Urghs" was Danny's favorite comment, and it frightened Miss Malcolm.

When I arrived at the last seat, last row, Danny didn't know quite what to think. I was obviously a pseudo hood and not destined to stay very long. Danny didn't rumble anything at me but regarded me mildly, even amusedly, that first afternoon. "You staying here, little girl?" he asked sarcastically as I piled my books in the desk. His tone implied that I didn't look dangerous enough to merit such a position. I don't think Danny fully realized the moral turpitude of note-reading.

No, I didn't think I was going to stay with Danny long either, at first. But days went by, and Miss Malcolm's gaze never glided past the dividing line—Raymond de Fato, who occasionally threw a spitball but wore a tie. I began to grow more and more uncomfortable. The classroom was long and crowded. Because of scufflings and murmurings around me I couldn't hear anything that was going on past Raymond; Raymond wouldn't tell me, and even if I did hear no one would call on me. But I could not go to Miss Malcolm begging to be let back. I was proud.

I began to bring *Jane Eyre* to school and spent the whole day reading ferociously. But even that splendid book couldn't make up for the fact that I was missing the Middle Atlantic States. Nor did snubbing Miss Malcolm every day in front of the coatroom bring the desired satisfaction. I couldn't complain at home because my mother thought I should beg for mercy. She said I was "a stubborn fool" and "just like your father." I was an outcast and everybody knew it.

I would have been completely miserable if Danny hadn't decided to take me into his group.

Danny began making the first overtures by looking on with me as I read *Jane Eyre*. Of course I was surprised. Until then it had been mere peaceful coexistence. I didn't even know Danny could read. He'd just sat for days looking at me sardonically from under his tousle of black curls. Occasionally he had cocked an eyebrow at me and his entire broad and grimy brow had moved.

"Dat looks like a good book," he said to me one day, looking interested, and I immediately lent him my four-color pencil to doodle with. From then on we were friends. Even the good girls in my class didn't read Brontë because they couldn't understand words like "choler" and "lineaments." Such praise from a hood made me glow with pleasure.

Our friendship was sealed next day, when we had an examination. Danny gave me his rabbit foot for keeps. It was for luck, he explained, and you could write the answers on a little piece of paper in the claw.

"Are you sure you don't want it?" I remember asking diffidently. "You probably need it more than I do."

"Oh, I can copy off you—dat's all right," he said.

I really didn't want that rabbit foot. A crib sheet was a little too far out on the road to dishonesty for a former star pupil, and I knew my New England products backward and forward anyway. Still, I accepted the foot for luck and as a token. I still remember the softness of it, and the little sharpnesses that were the nails.

The next thing Danny did was introduce me to the boys. This was difficult, but he managed to get them to ask me to lend them pencils. They were the shyest hoods imaginable. There were really ten of us in the back, but I only got to know five: Danny, Harry la Marca, Alan Brodnik, Ronny Abry and Jo-Jo Begoyne.

These were the Destry Road Boys. Because of his age, ability and the fact that he had been approached by the Avenue E Boys for possible merger, Danny was definitely the leader. He ruled with an iron hand. Once Harry and Jo-Jo had a fight in the back of the room, and they might have ripped each other to pieces if Danny hadn't broken it up. They moved silently, slowly, crouching a little by the door to the gym. "You never seen a shiv fight before?" Danny asked when he saw my wonder afterward, and he showed me the knives, six inches long.

"Dose guys are gonna get into real trouble one day—dey're only tirteen—dey don't have any sense," he said. During the fight Miss Malcolm had gone on with the class in the front of the room as though nothing was happening. After twenty years of dealing with crime Miss Malcolm had found her method—the silent or you-don't-exist treatment.

The boys got a great deal of pleasure out of telling me about shiv fights and how the Avenue E Boys got away with robbing a candy store. The Destry Road Boys had never gotten away with anything because they had never pulled anything, except turning in false alarms, which any five-year-old can do. They were a small-time bunch and they knew it. Our neighborhood, Newton Park, was just too quiet and genteel to start any trouble, and there wasn't any point going over to Avenue E to find some because Danny wouldn't let them. "You want to get your heads knocked off?" he asked. Danny was the most cautious, perhaps because he was the only gang leader I've ever known. He'd been around and he knew that it was safest to do nothing and if anybody asked you anything to just mumble along.

I found that I too could expound to the boys on topics they hadn't heard before, usually last month's lessons. I think I may have been more interesting than Miss Malcolm, because when I told them about Cortes in Mexico and killing the great chief Montezuma, their eyes gleamed and they clasped imaginary sword handles. Alan Brodnik expressed a desire to make a poniard or a rapier in shop that week. "Swords, dat's all you guys need," Danny said in disgust, but I could see that he was interested too.

"Why didn't dey make a deal wit Montezuma and get a percentage?" he asked me once when I got involved with the more intricate dealings. "A percentage is better. Dopey Spaniards." I could see that Danny had everything all figured out.

I had been sitting in the back of the room for a week and a half when I began to notice a perceptible change in Danny. He began to wear white polo shirts instead of his old, saggy yellow one and smelled faintly of Ivory soap. His face was clean and his hair was somehow higher, pulled together into a compact pompadour. Danny even turned his club jacket inside out so that the plain black showed instead of the worn fuchsia silk with its huge black "Destry Boys" lettering. "'Stoo flashy," Danny said, and that afternoon, after lunch, all the boys had their jackets turned around too.

Soon, whenever Danny and I read together because of Danny's pageless volumes, his fingers curled around my white-clean covers were white-clean too. The fingers also turned the pages exactly right, which proved that Danny could actually read as fast as I did. I began to think that Danny wasn't really a hood, or was just pretending, or that being a hood wasn't so bad at all if only the teacher would notice you. If we listened very carefully, Danny and I, we could hear Miss Malcolm's voice reading *Evangeline* far off, and once, when we got to the part that goes

> *Black were her eyes as the berry that grows on the thorn by the wayside—*
> *Black; yet how softly they gleamed beneath the brown shade of her tresses!*
> *Sweet was her breath as the breath of kine that feed in the meadows . . .*

Danny bent over and whispered. "She looks like you."

Since I was definitely blond and blue-eyed, and since Danny had never whispered before in his life, I began to think something was wrong. Or, if Danny was becoming poetic, something might be right. But anyway—something. Yes, I thought rather priggishly, Danny has probably never sat next to a good poetry-reading little girl in his life; my presence has probably opened the door to a whole new world of clean-smelling respectability.

It occurred to me that I might tame Danny and turn him into a star pupil, thus killing two birds with one stone and getting me a seat in Respectability too. Why, I could probably persuade Danny to take elocution lessons. Then he could learn to pronounce "th" and other things and Miss Malcolm would understand him. I had a little difficulty myself sometimes. And if I could convince his mother to get him some crisp white shirts and a tie. . . . Maybe my mother would iron them for him if Mrs. Tooey was busy.

Ronny, Harry, Alan and Jo-Jo, although they showed no immediate signs of conversion, might still follow their leader out of hood-hood and I would have a whole gang to my credit. I could learn to iron shirts myself. Soon I would walk down Destry Road to be pointed at and stared at by the citizenry. "There's the girl who saves hoods," ladies would say as they waited on line by the fruit counter at Willy's. "Can you come and talk to my boy after school?" "Dere's dat dame." The Avenue E Boys would scowl and lurk behind the gum machine in front of Harry's. "She's the one who's been takin' our best material. Why, Danny Tooey, he could've been the best hood in Brooklyn, he's studyin' for the ministry."

Yes, I would save Danny. I determined to bring my *Believe-It-Or-Not* Ripley book to school immediately so Danny could begin assimilating the mass of interesting facts so necessary to star pupils. We would sit in the first row, side by side.

Alas. While I had been making plans for reformation, I had overlooked the real reason for Danny's behavior, which was, of course, sex. Danny Tooey wanted me to be more than just a friend. On Friday morning, May 11, Danny asked me to go to the movies with him the next evening, May 12. Not in the afternoon. In the evening. It was a sword-fighting picture, he said, and I would like it. I was shocked. Respectable seventh-grade girls, especially me, didn't wear lipstick or go out with boys; eighth-grade girls could wear lipstick and go out, if they didn't make too much fuss about it. But no decent girl ever went anywhere, morning or evening, with a hood.

Oh, yes, there were a few. But they were scrawny and inky-haired and went to P.S. 293 and only appeared hanging around outside by the homogenized-bagel man at three o'clock. They weren't decent either. Because when the boys didn't show up, they would flirt with the homogenized-bagel man, and when he wasn't there they would go to Harry's and stand in front of the gum machine. And they would make remarks like "Look who's here," whenever someone passed. The Avenue E Dolls, an auxiliary of the Boys, set the fashion in this case, and any girl hood who didn't have long black hair had to grow it or dye it quick, or run the risk of not being à la mode hood. A la mode hood also meant doe eyes, ultrabright lipstick, gold bangle earrings, cheap, tight skirts and the black and white uniform: black bra and white sweater or white bra and black sweater. And no slip. These girls didn't need to wear bras and I did. Only I didn't, and always felt self-conscious when I passed Harry's Candy Store in my light lawn dresses.

No, I couldn't possibly go out with Danny. I might convert him, but I couldn't go out with him. He probably would want me to kiss him in the movies. I knew what went on in the Destry Theatre; I went every Saturday night with my mother and father; I knew. Those hoods. Surely Danny with all his hoodish savior-faire knew that a girl in a pinafore dress, long blond braids and well-fed expression was highly inappropriate for the leader of a gang. It was just the lure of the unknown, and was, of course, impossible.

I told Danny politely that I appreciated the thought but didn't think my mother would let me go out since I was only eleven years old. I had skipped several grades, I explained. Danny was very understanding about it and said I certainly looked older. At the end of the day I gave him my *Believe-It-Or-Not* Ripley book for keeps, saying that my mother had refused permission at lunchtime but that this was for him, blushing all the while, I suppose. Danny was very embarrassed. He didn't blush, at first only mumbled "Urghs," but later came over to me at the coatroom and said. "Tanks. I don't know how to make just retribution." He was sweet about the whole thing.

Actually, I hadn't told my mother about Danny's invitation at all. I doubted whether she'd think the connection savory. But I thought about this, my almost first date, all the way home from school and all weekend. In fact, I couldn't stop thinking about it. No sooner would I settle down with my favorite book than the name Tooey would intrude itself into my mental stream. I felt the iresistible urge to write Danny Tooey, Danny or just plain D. T. on all my clean book covers. Finally, in desperation, I wrote Yeoot Ynnad very small in the top of my stationery box. Such a thing had never happened to me before.

I decided to look up similar occurrences in my library, my highest source of wisdom. But mine proved an unprecedented occurrence. Heathcliff had been bad and Cathy had decided to be his girl friend, but he hadn't reformed and they had both died. That was the best I could find. But still . . . Jane Eyre wouldn't marry Mr. Rochester when he was already married to Bertha, so it didn't seem right for me to go out with Danny while he was still a hood. But after he reformed . . . it would probably take till eighth grade and then we could go out legitimately. Girls in the eighth grade not only went out, they could kiss too.

My mother noticed my mood of sorrowful melancholy, interspersed with come-hither glances and a slight puckering motion of the lips, and wrongly attributed my strange behavior to worry about the Middle Atlantic States. She instructed me to sue for Miss Malcolm's favor immediately or she would come up to school herself. Poor Mamma. How was she to know? After all, I had been a terrible bookworm, and I was only eleven years old.

When I went to the movies Saturday night with my parents I tried to reconstruct Danny's features. All that hair made it difficult; it was all I could reconstruct. Underneath Danny was handsome, I decided, and the features of the man on the screen melted, dimmed and turned Tooeyesque in the darkness. What if it had not been my father sitting next to me, wheezing slightly from the air conditioning? What if it had been . . . To this day I can give no accurate description of Danny. The years have blurred even that blurry face. No matter how handsome and hairy and suave the fifteen-year-old Danny may have been, I hardly think he could have looked as I still picture him today—the precise image of Clark Gable.

Coming out of the Destry after the show, I managed to walk into an embarrassing situation. There stood Alan Brodnik, leaning against the fire hydrant, his arms round a girl. Alan looked at me appealingly and removed his arms. I made no comment, walked by without turning my head. My heart was sad though, oh, sad. For what if it had been Yeoot Ynnad?

When I arrived at school Monday morning I found our back-seat idyl broken. No longer could we peruse the same book like lion and lamb. Danny and I breathed hard and stared in whatever direction was opposite; we both mumbled. At last I had enough courage to ask Danny if he had learned anything interesting from the *Believe-It-Or-Not* Ripley book. He only looked at me vaguely and mumbled "Urghs." He had retrogressed.

Danny continued shy all day and did not speak to me. But he gave long, piteous glances and drew girls' heads in ink on the backs of his hands. This was terrible. I decided to follow Danny after school and make him talk to me. It was only to find out something of his home life for future reform, I told myself. When three o'clock and Danny and Harry, Jo-Jo, Alan and Ronny broke upon the homogenized-bagel man, I was there too.

The boys looked at me curiously. All the other little girls were retreating away from school as fast as they could go, backs straight and heads held high. Was it true? Was it true? Jo-Jo winked at Harry. Danny said nothing but asked me if I wanted salt on my bagel. No, don't buy me bagels, don't, I felt like crying out. I don't *want* to be your girl friend. I just want to find out about your home life. However, I took one with salt.

Danny seemed relaxed and at ease now. He spoke animatedly, even vivaciously, and I could catch nearly every word he was saying. He took my arm and headed me, yes, toward Harry's Candy Store. The boys followed. I would not go to Harry's Candy Store, I told myself firmly, I would not under any conditions go to Harry's Candy Store. . . .

On the way to the candy store, Danny told me about his job as utility man, whatever that was, on a small fishing boat out of Sheepshead Bay. The boat and Danny left every day at three in the morning and didn't return till eight-thirty, just in time to drop Danny off for school. "Dat's why I'm so sleepy in da mornings," Danny explains.

When he was sixteen, next year, he wouldn't have to come to school any more and could be a full-time fisherman. How exciting, I thought, thinking of *Captains Courageous*, but then I remembered. If Danny left school, he'd never reach eighth grade, and what would happen to this "th's" and his white shirts and . . . our date for the movies. Even if he became a fisherman—? what if there were a fish famine or something? Without me Danny would have to go back to being a hood. I would not let that happen. I would persuade Danny not to leave school. I would go with him to Harry's Candy Store every day and stand around with him near the gum machine.

When we reached Harry's, there were no girls from 293 around, thank goodness. Danny did nothing worse than hitch himself up on the wooden rack that held the newspapers and let his feet dangle on the New York *Post*. He'd been working since he was ten, he said, and it was all right. Except when the weather was bad and he didn't get paid. Or just got paid in fish. His Aunt Bella didn't like fish he added a little glumly; she hated fish.

Aunt Bella's strong aversion to fish was all I ever found out about Danny Tooey's home life. "Look who's here," Danny said next, and when I looked, there stood Miss Malcolm.

"I want to talk to you, dear," she said.

Miss Malcolm and I walked home together. We had a long, intimate conversation on the way, though I couldn't imagine why. I still hadn't apologized, and I certainly wasn't going to. I suppose Miss Malcolm had come out of school at three and seen her ex-star pupil in informal conversation with a recognized hood. Poor Miss Malcolm. She thought she'd been responsible for starting me on a life of crime.

"You don't know it, dear, but I've been watching you," she said. I clutched my stationery box, but she only took my arm as we crossed the street as though I was her little girl.

"I've noticed how unhappy you've been at the back of the room. You've just been moping around and moping around, haven't you?"

I made no reply. I wondered what Miss Malcolm wanted me to do for not telling my mother about Harry's Candy Store. Yes, blackmail was on my mind. I had the makings of a first-class hood.

"You've been unhappy because you've wanted to come up to me and apologize for reading my note, haven't you?"

We were nearing my home. I thought about walking Miss Malcolm right past it and right on down to Sheepshead Bay. We could go down to the pier and watch the fishing boats come in. My Lord, I really was a fiendish child, now that I think of it.

"But you've been afraid. You've been afraid I was going to say something unkind, weren't you?"

She patted me kindly on the arm. I thought of how I had walked past her every morning on my way to the coatroom, my head held high.

"But you know, I wouldn't have said anything unkind. Because I like you, dear. I think you're my best pupil."

I still didn't say anything. I was her best pupil. I wondered what Miss Malcolm was planning to study next. It must be something harder than the Middle Atlantic, because three people had raised their hands that day and she didn't need me.

"And because I know you've wanted to apologize for a long time, tomorrow morning I am going to let you come back to the first seat, first row."

I couldn't stop the pleasure that I felt.

I didn't know why I had been reinstated but I was glad. Justice, as I had always maintained, does triumph. And oh, what I would do to all those schmoey kids. I was a nasty-good little girl.

Miss Malcolm came inside the house to meet my mother and we all had tea. I didn't mind taking the enemy inside. Danny would approve, I was sure. And from my influential position, what couldn't I do for my friends. Soon I would convince Miss Malcolm of Danny's merits—and then . . .

"Do you think seventh-grade girls are too young to go out?" I remember asking Miss Malcolm as Mamma poured tea.

Alas, again. All my plans were in vain. The end of the affair came next day.

As Miss Malcolm announced the happy news and I carried my books away from our scarred double seat to my honored one, Danny stared at me sullenly without saying a word. He didn't say good-by, but on my last trip to the front of the room he piled his *Believe-It-Or-Not* Ripley book on top of my grammar and the stationery box with the secret Yeoot Ynnad. He looked at me as though from across a million rows of double seats. Then he turned back to carving his name on the desk.

Hurt and bewildered, I couldn't understand Danny's heartlessness. I followed him out of the school building at three, lingered shyly by the homogenized-bagel man, but he just walked away. His back was slouched and his hair was no longer kempt. He was whistling.

After this I never went near Danny or any of the other boys again. And when Larry Dinhofer asked me for a date to the senior prom I pretended that he was the first. But I always kept track of the Destry Road Boys, secretly, ashamedly. I felt a strong sense of communion with them and liked to think that my short stay had done them all good. Alan and Ronny and Harry went on to high school with me, but were put in special RX classes where they could sit around all day and throw spitballs without being disturbed by anyone. They just had a happy, lazy time. Occasionally I'd glimpse them having refreshments in front of the school. It was a different, nonhomogenized-bagel man, but the same boys all right. When I passed they would stare but never make any sign of recognition.

Although none of the Destry Boys ever made Honor Society or anything like that, they never got any more delinquent than they were. As it turned out, only one boy from P.S. 333 ever ended up in jail, and that was Larry Dinhofer. He robbed a liquor store, and he had always worn white cuffs and sat in the first row, and no one I know has ever found a logical explanation. So Larry does belong among the hoods I've known after all. Alan Brodnik, bless him, was the only Destry Boy whose degenerate career I followed after high school. I've lost touch with him since, but the last I heard he'd turned up at Brooklyn College carrying *Tropic of Capricorn* and wearing a neat black goatee and a red velvet cummerbund. I never could quite understand that one either.

As for Danny, I never saw him after graduation. In fact, I don't think he stayed around that long but left after his sixteenth birthday sometime in March. I believe he gave the Destry Road Boys to Jo-Jo because he was the smartest. By that time my wounded feelings had healed, since I'd decided what had motivated him. It was all due to Danny's pure moral philosophy or something, I deduced, that was stronger than mere romance. Hoods didn't do anything but pledge allegiance to the flag. Star pupils sat in the first row. We just couldn't be friends. It was against all established codes, and Danny supported codes. I had to admire that.

Someone I know says she thinks she saw someone who looked like

Danny in a summer theatre production in Woodstock last year. She said that he was still big and had a lot of hair but that he spoke English perfectly. She said he was sweet and looked like Marlon Brando. Despite what my friend says, I don't like to think Danny became an actor. I don't like to think that at all. It makes me sad and a little embarrassed, for that would mean after all my seventh-grade heartbreak and eleven-year-old plans somebody else had reformed Danny after all. I'd rather have him be a fisherman. I'd rather have him be a hood.

THE IMAGINARY JEW
John Berryman

The second summer of the European war I spent in New York. I lived in a room just below street level on Lexington above Thirty-fourth, wrote a good deal, tried not to think about Europe, and listened to music on a small gramophone, the only thing of my own, except books, in the room. Haydn's London Symphony, his last, I heard probably fifty times in two months. One night when excited I dropped the pickup, creating a series of knocks at the beginning of the last movement where the oboe joins the strings which still, when I hear them, bring up for me my low dark long damp room and I feel the dew of heat and smell the rented upholstery. I was trying, as one says, to come back a little, uncertain and low after an exhausting year. Why I decided to do this in New York—the enemy in summer equally of soul and body, as I had known for years—I can't remember; perhaps I didn't, but we held on merely from week to week by the motive which presently appeared in the form of a young woman met the Christmas before and now the occupation of every evening not passed in solitary and restless gloom. My friends were away; I saw few other people. Now and then I went to the zoo in lower Central Park and watched with interest the extraordinary behavior of a female badger. For a certain time she quickly paced the round of her cage. Then she would approach the side wall from an angle in a determined, hardly perceptible, unhurried trot; suddenly, when an inch away, point her nose up it, follow her nose up over her back, turning a deft and easy somersault, from which she emerged on her feet moving swiftly and unconcernedly away, as if the action had been no affair of hers, indeed she had scarcely been present. There was another badger in the cage who never did this, and nothing else about her was remarkable; but this competent disinterested somersault she enacted once every five or ten minutes as long as I watched her—quitting the wall, by the way, always at an angle in fixed relation to the angle at which she arrived at it. It is no longer possible to experience the pleasure I knew each time she lifted her nose and I understood again that she would not fail me, or feel the mystery of her absolute disclaimer—she has been taken away or died.

The story I have to tell is no further a part of that special summer than a nightmare takes its character, for memory, from the phase of the moon one noticed on going to bed. It could have happened in another year and in another place. No doubt it did, has done, will do. Still, so weak is the talent of the mind for pure relation—immaculate apprehension of p alone—that everything helps us, as when we come to an unknown city:

architecture, history, trade practices, folklore. Even more anxious our approach to a city—like my small story—which we have known and forgotten. Yet how little we can learn! Some of the history is the lonely summer. Part of the folklore, I suppose, is which I now unwillingly rehearse, the character which experience has given to my sense of the Jewish people.

Born in a part of the South where no Jews had come, or none had stayed, and educated thereafter in states where they are not numerous, I somehow arrived at a metropolitan university without any clear idea of what in modern life a Jew was—without even a clear consciousness of having seen one. I am unable now to explain this simplicity or blindness. I had not escaped, of course, a sense that humans somewhat different from ourselves, called "Jews," existed as in the middle distance and were best kept there, but this sense was of the vaguest. From what it was derived I do not know; I do not recall feeling the least curiosity about it, or about Jews; I had, simply, from the atmosphere of an advanced heterogeneous democratic society, ingathered a gently negative attitude toward Jews. This I took with me, untested, to college, where it received neither confirmation nor stimulus for two months. I rowed and danced and cut classes and was political; by mid-November I knew most of the five hundred men in my year. Then the man who rowed Number Three, in the eight of which I was bow, took me aside in the shower one afternoon and warned me not to be so chatty with Rosenblum.

I wondered why not. Rosenblum was stroke, a large handsome amiable fellow, for whose ability in the shell I felt great respect and no doubt envy. Because the fellows in the house wouldn't like it, my friend said. "What have they against him?" "It's only because he's Jewish," explained my friend, a second-generation Middle European.

I hooted at him, making the current noises of disbelief, and went back under the shower. It did not occur to me that he could be right. But next day when I was talking with Herz, the coxswain, whom I knew very well, I remembered the libel with some annoyance, and told Herz about it as a curiosity. Herz looked at me oddly, lowering his head, and said after a pause, "Why Al *is* Jewish, didn't you know that?" I was amazed. I said it was absurd, he couldn't be! "Why not?" said Herz, who must have been as astonished as I was. "Don't you know I'm Jewish?"

I did not know, of course, and ignorance has seldom cost me such humiliation. Herz did not guy me; he went off. But greater than my shame at not knowing something known, apparently, without effort to everyone else, were my emotions for what I then quickly discovered. Asking careful questions during the next week, I learned that about a third of the men I spent time with in college were Jewish; that they knew it, and the others knew it; that some of the others disliked them for it, and they knew this also; that certain houses existed *only* for Jews, who were excluded from the rest; and that what in short I took to be an idiotic state was deeply established, familiar, and acceptable to everyone. This discovery was the beginning of my instruction in social life proper—construing social life as that from which political life issues like a somatic dream.

My attitude toward my friends did not alter on this revelation. I merely discarded the notion that Jews were a proper object for any special attitude; my old sense vanished. This was in 1933. Later, as word of German persecution filtered into this country, some sentimentality undoubtedly corrupted my no-attitude. I denied the presence of obvious defects in particular Jews, feeling that to admit them would be to side with the sadists and murderers. Accident allotting me close friends who were Jewish, their disadvantages enraged me. Gradually, and against my sense of impartial justice, I became the anomaly which only a partial society can produce, and for which it has no name known to the lexicons. In one area, not exclusively, "nigger-lover" is flung in a proximate way; but for a special sympathy and liking for Jews—which became my fate, so that I trembled when I heard one abused in talk—we have no term. In this condition I still was during the summer of which I speak. One further circumstance may be mentioned, as a product, I believe, of this curious training. I am spectacularly unable to identify Jews as Jews—by name, cast of feature, accent, or environment—and this has been true, not only of course before the college incident, but during my whole life since. Even names to anyone else patently Hebraic rarely suggest to me anything. And when once I learn that So-and-so is Jewish, I am likely to forget it. Now Jewishness—the religion or the race—may be a fact as striking and informative as someone's past heroism or his Christianity or his understanding of the subtlest human relations, and I feel sure that something operates to prevent my utilizing the plain signs by which such characters—in a Jewish man or woman—may be idenfitied, and prevent my retaining the identification once it is made.

So to the city my summer and a night in August. I used to stop on Fourteenth Street for iced coffee, walking from the Village home (or to my room rather) after leaving my friend, and one night when I came out I wandered across to the island of trees and grass and concrete walks raised in the center of Union Square. Here men—a few women, old—sit in the evenings of summer, looking at papers or staring off or talking, and knots of them stay on, arguing, very late; these the unemployed or unemployable, the sleepless, the malcontent. There are no formal orators, as at Columbus Circle in the nineteen-thirties and at Hyde Park Corner. Each group is dominated by serveral articulate and strong-lunged persons who battle each other with prejudices and desires, swaying with intensity, and take on from time to time the interrupters: a forum at the bottom of the pot—Jefferson's fear, Whitman's hope, the dream of the younger Lenin. It was now about one o'clock, almost hot, and many men were still out. I stared for a little at the equestrian statue, obscure in the night on top of its pedestal, thinking that misty Rider would sweep away again all these men at his feet, whenever he liked—what symbol for power yet in a mechanical age rivals the mounted man?—and moved to the nearest group; or I plunged to it.

The dictator to the group was old, with dark cracked skin, fixed eyes in an excited face, leaning forward madly on his bench toward the half-dozen men in semicircle before him. "It's bread! It's bread!" he was saying. "It's bittersweet. All the bitter and all the sweetness. Of an overture. What else do you want? When you ask for steak and potatoes, do you want pastry with it? It's bread! It's bread! Help yourself! Help yourself!"

The listeners stood expressionless, except one who was smiling with contempt and interrupted now.

"Never a happy minute, never a happy minute!" the old man cried. "It's good to be dead! Some men should kill themselves."

"Don't you want to live?" said the smiling man.

"Of course I want to live. Everyone wants to live! If death comes suddenly, it's better. It's better!"

With pain I turned away. The next group were talking diffusely and angrily about the mayor, and I passed to a third, where a frantic olive-skinned young man with a fringe of silky beard was exclaiming:

"No restaurant in New York had the Last Supper! No. When people sit down to eat they should think of that!"

"Listen," said a white-shirted student on the rail, glancing around for approbation, "listen, if I open a restaurant and put *The Last Supper* up over the door, how much money do you think I'd lose? Ten thousand dollars?"

The fourth cluster was larger and appeared more coherent. A savage argument was in progress between a man of fifty with an oily red face, hatted, very determined in manner, and a muscular fellow half his age with heavy eyebrows, coatless, plainly Irish. Fifteen or twenty men were packed around them, and others on a bench near the rail against which the Irishman was lounging were attending also. I listened for a few minutes. The question was whether the President was trying to get us into the war—or, rather, whether this was legitimate, since the Irishman claimed that Roosevelt was a goddamned warmonger whom all the real people in the country hated, and the older man claimed that we should have gone into the f—ing war when France fell a year before, as everybody in the country knew except a few immigrant rats. Redface talked ten times as much as the Irishman, but he was not able to establish any advantage that I could see. He ranted, and then Irish either repeated shortly and fiercely what he had said last, or shifted his ground. The audience were silent—favoring whom I don't know, but evidently much interested. One or two men pushed out of the group, others arrived behind me, and I was eddied forward toward the disputants. The young Irishman broke suddenly into a tirade by the man with the hat:

"You're full of s—. Roosevelt even tried to get us in with the communists in the Spanish war. If he could have done it we'd have been burning churches down like the rest of the Reds."

"No, that's not right," I heard my own voice, and pushed forward, feeling blood in my face, beginning to tremble. "No, Roosevelt, as a matter of fact, helped Franco by non-intervention, at the same time that Italians and German planes were fighting against the Government and arms couldn't get in from France.

"What's that? What are you, a Jew?" He turned to me contemptuously, and was back at the older man before I could speak. "The only reason we weren't over there four years ago is because you can only screw us so much. Then we quit. No New Deal bastard could make us go help the goddamned communists."

"That ain't the question, it's if we want to fight *now* or *later.* Them Nazis ain't gonna sit!" shouted the red-faced man. "They got Egypt practically, and then it's India if it ain't England first. It ain't a question of the communists, the communists are on Hitler's side. I tell ya we can wait and wait and chew and spit and the first thing you know they'll be in England, and then who's gonna help us when they start after us? Maybe Brazil? Get wise to the world! Spain don't matter now one way or the other, they ain't gonna help and they can't hurt. It's Germany and Italy and Japan, and if it ain't too late now it's gonna be. Get wise to yourself. We shoulda gone in—"

"What with?" said the Irishman with disdain. "Pop, pop. Wooden machine guns?"

"We were as ready a year ago as we are now. Defense don't mean nothing, you gotta have to fight!"

"No, we're much better off now," I said, "than we were a year ago. When England went in, to keep its word to Poland, what good was it to Poland? The German Army—"

"Shut up, you Jew," said the Irishman.

"I'm not a Jew," I said to him. "What makes—"

"Listen, Pop," he said to the man in the hat, "it's O.K. to shoot your mouth off, but what the hell have you got to do with it? You aren't gonna do any fighting."

"Listen," I said.

"You sit on your big ass and talk about who's gonna fight who. Nobody's gonna fight anybody. If we feel hot, we ought to clean up some of the sons of bitches here before we go sticking our nuts anywhere to help England. We ought to clean up the sons of bitches in Wall Street and

Washington before we take any ocean trips. You want to know something? You know why Germany's winning everything in this war? Because there ain't no Jews back home. There ain't no more Jews, first shouting war like this one here"—nodding at me—"and then skinning off to the synagogue with the profits. Wake up, Pop! You must have been around in the last war, you ought to know better."

I was too nervous to be angry or resentful. But I began to have a sense of oppression in breathing. I took the Irishman by the arm.

"Listen, I told you I'm not a Jew."

"I don't give a damn what you are." He turned his half-dark eyes to me, wrenching his arm loose. "You talk like a Jew."

"What does that mean?" Some part of me wanted to laugh. "How does a Jew talk?"

"They talk like you, buddy."

"That's a fine argument! But if I'm not a Jew, my talk only—"

"You probably are a Jew. You look like a Jew."

"I *look* like a Jew? Listen"—I swung around eagerly to a man standing next to me—"do I look like a Jew? It doesn't matter whether I do or not—a Jew is as good as anybody and better than this son of a bitch." I was not exactly excited, I was trying to adapt my language as my need for the crowd, and sudden respect for its judgment possessd me. "But in fact I'm not Jewish and I don't look Jewish. Do I?"

The man looked at me quickly and said, half to me and half to the Irishman, "Hell, I don't know. Sure he does."

A wave of disappointment and outrage swept me almost to tears. I felt like a man betrayed by his brother. The lamps seemed brighter and vaguer, the night large. Glancing 'round, I saw sitting on a bench near me a tall, heavy, serious-looking man of thirty, well dressed, whom I had noticed earlier, and appealed to him. "Tell me, do I look Jewish?"

But he only stared up and waved his head vaguely. I saw with horror that something was wrong with him.

"You look like a Jew. You talk like a Jew. You *are* a Jew," I heard the Irishman say.

I heard murmuring among the men, but I could see nothing very clearly. It seemed very hot. I faced the Irishman again helplessly, holding my voice from rising.

"I'm *not* a Jew," I told him. "I might be, but I'm not. You have no bloody reason to think so, and you can't make me a Jew by simply repeating like an idiot that I am."

"Don't deny it, son," said the red-faced man, "stand up to him."

"God damn it"—suddenly I was furious, whirling like a fool (was I afraid of the Irishman? had he conquered me?) on the red-faced man—"I'm *not* denying it! Or rather I am, but only because I'm not a Jew! I despise renegades, I hate Jews who turn on their people, if I were a Jew I would say so, I would be proud to be. What is the vicious opinion of a man like this to me if I were a Jew? But I'm not. Why the hell should I admit I am if I'm not?"

"Jesus, the Jew is excited," said the Irishman.

"I have a right to be excited, you son of a bitch. Suppose I call you a Jew. Yes, you're a Jew. Does that mean anything?"

"Not a damn thing." He spat over the rail past a man's head.

"Prove that you're not. I say you are."

"Now listen, you Jew. I'm a Catholic."

"So am I, or I was born one, I'm not one now. I was born a Catholic." I was a little calmer but goaded, obsessed with the need to straighten this out. I felt that everything for everyone there depended on my proving him wrong. If *once* this evil for which we have not even a name could be exposed to the rest of the men as empty—if I could *prove* I was not a Jew—it would fall to the ground, neither would anyone else be a Jew to be accused. Then it could be trampled on. Fascist America was at stake. I listened, intensely anxious for our fate.

"Yeah?" said the Irishman. "Say the Apostles' Creed."

Memory went swirling back. I could hear the little bell die as I hushed it and set it on the felt. Father Boniface looked at me tall from the top of the steps and smiled, greeting me in the darkness before dawn as I came to serve, the men pressed around me under the lamps, and I could remember nothing but *visibilium omnium, et invisibilium.*

"I don't remember it."

The Irishman laughed with his certainty.

The papers in my pocket; I thought them over hurriedly. In my wallet. What would they prove? Details of ritual. Church history: anyone could learn them. My piece of Irish blood. Shame, shame: shame for my ruthless people. I will not be his blood. I wish I were a Jew, I would change my blood, to be able to say *Yes* and defy him.

"I'm not a Jew." I felt a fool. "You only say so. You haven't any evidence in the world."

He leaned forward from the rail, close to me. "Are you cut?"

Shock, fear ran through me before I could make any meaning out of his words. Then they ran faster, and I felt confused.

From that point nothing is clear for me. I stayed a long time—it seemed impossible to leave, showing him victor to them—thinking of possible allies and new plans of proof, but without hope. I was tired to the marrow. The arguments rushed on, and I spoke often now but seldom was heeded except by an old fat woman, very short and dirty, who listened intently to everyone. Heavier and heavier appeared to me to press upon us in the fading night our general guilt.

In the days following, as my resentment died, I saw that I had not been a victim altogether unjustly. My persecutors were right: I was a Jew. The imaginary Jew I was was as real as the imaginary Jew hunted down, on other nights and days, in a real Jew. Every murderer strikes the mirror, the lash of the torturer falls on the mirror and cuts the real image, and the real and the imaginary blood flow down together.

Issues for Discussion

1. Bret Harte, in "The Outcasts of Poker Flat," nicely portrays the dynamics of the labeling process. Read the following quotations and relate how attaching the label of deviant to another is (a) largely dependent on the nature of the times and circumstances (i.e., fortuitous) and (b) a "holier than thou" (i.e., hypocritical) process.

   There was a Sabbath lull in the air, which, in a settlement [Poker Flat] unused to Sabbath influence, looked ominous. . . .
   In point of fact, Poker Flat was "after somebody." It had lately suffered the loss of two thousand dollars, two valuable horses, and a prominent citizen. It was experiencing a spasm of virtuous reaction, quite as lawless and ungovernable as any of the acts that had provoked it. A secret committee had determined to rid the town of all improper persons. . . . I regret to say that some of these were ladies. It was but due to the sex, however, to state that their impropriety was professional, and it was only in such easily established standards of evil that Poker Flat ventured to sit in judgement.
   Mr. Oakhurst was right in supposing that he was included in this category. A few of the committee had urged hanging him as a possible example and a sure method of reimbursing themselves from his pockets of the sums he had won from them. "It's agin justice," said Jim Wheeler, "to let this yer young man from Roaring Camp—an entire stranger—carry away our money." But a crude sentiment of equity residing in the breasts of those who had been fortunate enough to win from Mr. Oakhurst overruled this narrower local prejudice.

2. Cite evidence suggesting that "the outcasts" possessed many redeeming qualities.
3. Was Mr. Oakhurst a coward, or do you think there was an ulterior motive in his suicide?
4. Sondra Spatt Olsen's "Hoods I Have Known" and John Berryman's

ISSUES FOR DISCUSSION

"The Imaginary Jew" present excellent examples of the effects of the labeling process. In the second paragraph of her story, Olsen distinguishes a "hood" from a "juvenile delinquent." Discuss the distinction and analyze its significance.
5. What is the process and significance of the way one becomes a member of "the back of the class" (i.e., a hood)?
6. Relate how the labeling process affected the behavior of "the star pupil."
7. Discuss the concept of "the self-fulfilling prophecy" as it relates to the behavior of "the star pupil," Danny Tooey, and the rest of his gang.
8. Cite passages suggesting that once the boys were removed from the indignities of sitting in the back of the class (and for that matter, out of school), they acted in a manner demanded of them by their new role models and situations.
9. In Berryman's "The Imaginary Jew," the Jewish individual periodically denies he is Jewish. Relate how the labeling process compels the young man to deny his heritage.
10. Relate the following passage to the concept of the self-fulfilling prophecy:

The imaginary Jew I was was as real as the imaginary Jew hunted down [in Nazi Germany] on other nights and days, is a real Jew. Every murderer strikes the mirror, the lash of the torturer falls on the mirror and cuts the real image, and the real and the imaginary blood flow down together.

PART VII

Radical Criminology

A wealth of empirical studies exists suggesting that people of low socioeconomic status are significantly more likely to be arrested than are high-status persons.[1] The disadvantaged are also less likely to receive bail, more apt to go to trial and, if found guilty, usually receive harsher sentences. Statistics about class and the criminal justice system have been regularly used as "evidence" to support virtually every theory of crime causation. The most effective use of these data has been made by the radical theorists. Radical criminologists, sometimes called Marxist, socialist, or "new criminologists,"[2] perceive crime as the natural outgrowth of an inequitable economic order supported by an equally unjust political and legal system.[3] Contrary to the views of classicists and positivists, radicals do not believe that crime is the result of individual pathology.[4]

In *Das Kapital*, Karl Marx (1818-83) suggests that class distinctions are artificially erected and maintained by the capitalist system.[5] Inherent in capitalism is the exploitation of the working masses by the owners of the means of production. The state actively participates in this exploitation through its support of the status quo. Not until a system of socialism is

---

1. For an excellent collection of empirical studies on this point, see William J. Chambliss, *Criminal Law In Action* (Santa Barbara, Calif.: Hamilton, 1975).

2. See Robert F. Meir, "The New Criminology: Continuity in Criminological Theory," *Journal of Criminal Law and Criminology* 67 (December 1976): 461–69.

3. L. Alfanaszev et al., *The Political Economy of Capitalism* (Moscow: Progress Publishers, 1974), pp. 9–16.

4. See Seymour L. Halleck, *Politics of Therapy* (New York: Science House, 1971), p. 30.

5. New York: L. W. Schmidt Publishers, 1867.

instituted will the state, and its vestige, the class-structured society, wither away. In Marx's words, the masses

> enter into definite relations that are indispensable and independent of their will; these relations of production correspond to a definite stage of development of their material powers of production. The sum total of these relations of production constitutes the economic structure of society—the real foundation, on which rise legal and political superstructures and to which correspond definite forms of social consciousness. The mode of production in material life determines the general character of the social, political, and spiritual processes of life. It is not the consciousness of men that determines their existence, but on the contrary, their social existence determines their consciousness. At a certain stage of their development, the material forces of production in society come in conflict with the existing relations of production, or what is but a legal expression for the same thing—with the property relations within which they had been at work before. From forms of development of the forces of production these relations turn into their fetters.[6]

Marxist principles were originally applied to crime causation by Willem Bonger (1876-1940) in *Criminality and Economic Conditions*.[7] Bonger studied the social and economic systems of primitive societies and discovered that a sense of altruism existed there: man helped fellow man. In good times and bad, all members of the community received like treatment. Only in the more economically developed and nonsocialist societies were people inclined to behave in an egoistic or selfish fashion. Acting for the good of all was forsaken for individual betterment, even at the expense of community needs. Moreoever, criminality had nothing to do with individual pathology:

> From a biological point of view almost all crimes must be ranked as normal acts. The process which takes place in the brain of the gendarme when he kills a poacher who resists arrest is identical with that which takes place in the brain of the poacher killing the gendarme who pursues him. No anthropologist (evidently of the Lombrosian school) would maintain that a policeman clubbing a mob of strikers was performing a biologically abnormal act, or that the strikers were abnormal because they did not choose to let themselves be maltreated without defending themselves. It is only the social cir-

---

6. See *Critique of Political Economy* (New York: International Library, 1904), pp. 11–13.

7. Boston: Little, Brown, 1916.

cumstances which class this defense as a crime, and cause the action of the police to be considered otherwise.[8]

Bonger's attitude about crime and economic determinism can be illustrated in his comment that "upon the basis of what has gone before, we have a right to say that the part played by economic conditions in criminality is preponderant, even decisive."[9]

But capitalism cannot maintain itself. It is the political system, manifested in the *state*, that promotes and maintains the exploitation by the owners of the means of production. When necessary, the euphemism "law and order" is employed by officials like the police and the national guard, and their repressive behavior is legitimized by the courts and a prison system in order to perpetuate the status quo.[10] The most insidious method of assuring perpetuation of the status quo is through what Alan Wolfe refers to as "consciousness-manipulation," whereby society is conditioned by state representatives and state symbols to believe the existing political, social, and economic order is beneficial to all.

> The most important reproductive mechanism which does not involve the use of state violence is consciousness-manipulation. The liberal state has an enormous amount of violence at its disposal, but is often reluctant to use it. Violence may breed counter-violence, leading to instability. It may be far better to manipulate consciousness to such an extent that most people would never think of engaging in the kinds of action which could be repressed. The most perfectly repressive (though not violently so) capitalist system, in other words, would not be a police state, but the complete opposite, one in which there were no police because there was nothing to police, everyone having accepted the legitimacy of that society and all its daily consequences.[11]

---

8. Bonger, *Criminality and Economic Conditions*, p. 378.

9. J. M. Van Bemmelen, "William Adrian Bonger," in *Pioneers in Criminology*, ed. Hermann Mannheim (New Jersey: Patterson Smith Publishers, 1973), pp. 453–54. In Bonger's *Criminality and Economic Conditions*, he presents an interesting analysis relating the economic environment and egoism to women and crime, disruptive family life, prostitution, alcoholism, and a variety of economic crimes (e.g., robbery), adultery, rape, and indecent assault on children. More recently, the leading American spokesman for radical criminology, Richard Quinney, has systematically extended Marxist philosophy to the American criminal justice system in his *Critique of the Legal Order: Crime Control in Capitalist Society* (Boston: Little, Brown, 1974).

10. In support of this statement, Quinney notes that in 1976 nearly $20 billion was spent on the criminal justice system at all levels. See National Criminal Justice Information and Statistics Service, *Expenditure and Employment Data for the Criminal Justice System, 1976* (Washington, D.C.: U.S. Government Printing Office, 1978), p. 22.

11. "Political Repression and the Liberal State," *Monthly Review* 23 (December 1971): 20.

The extent of deviant behavior in lower-class neighborhoods is not solely attributable to the process of defining proper behavior and selective law enforcement. Criminogenic behavior is an expected reaction to the existing oppressive order. The informal and formal rules of the game make upward social and economic mobility unrealistically difficult. Frustration and anger develop. Tensions and animosity are further incubated by the highly visible police, symbol of the elite's vehicle for oppression. Not enjoying the established or lawful means of economic or social betterment, avenues of survival are sought through forbidden modes of conduct.

Radical criminologists also promote the *functional* effects of crime. The fear of victimization acts as a smokescreen, diverting the poor from the true sources of their exploitation. Also, society's impression about the deviant nature of the lower classes gains credence because crime thrives in the environment bequeathed the poor and powerless. Finally, the existing economic order is supported by capital generated from the worker through taxation of his wages. These monies are used to create and maintain such "law and order" institutions as police forces, courts, and prisons.[12]

Promoters of the radical school of criminology have made effective use of statistics suggesting disproportionate involvement in deviant behavior by the disadvantaged. They suggest that crime is a natural artifact of an unjust economic and social system. Laws are created and enforced by the ruling elite. Lawmakers naturally define as deviant those behaviors most likely to interfere with the existing order and, to a lesser extent, those activities not visibly engaged in by the ruling elite. The institutional support of the laws also explains the existence of crime. The police, courts, jurors, states' attorneys, and prison system are tools of the rule makers used to ensure perpetuation of the system. A disproportionate number of police are assigned to working-class precincts or, more to the point, away from the neighborhoods of the elite. More deviant behavior is discovered in these targeted areas. Following an arrest, the remaining instruments of the ruling class, such as the courts and prisons, are left to exact their expected and predictable retribution.

12. Much criticism about the relationship between the capitalist society and crime causation exists. See, for example, Don C. Gibbons, "Emerging Perspectives in Criminology," *Journal of Criminal Law and Criminology* 65 (June 1974): 206–13; and Paul Rock, "Feature Review Symposium," *Sociological Quarterly* 14 (Autumn 1973): 595. Perhaps the most often stated criticism involves the concept of "class conscious" criminality. Specifically, the primary difficulty with radical criminology is in its assumption that the disadvantaged are particularly likely to engage in criminal behavior because of the inequities of the social and economic system. Much evidence exists suggesting extensive criminal activity has been routinely engaged in by so-called white-collar criminals. The crimes involve those activities readily available to persons occupying prestigious occupational positions. Activities of the white-collar criminal, such as unfair trade practices, food adulteration, and alteration of the company books and the more visible lower-class crimes (e.g., robbery and assault) are probably more related to the *opportunity* of the miscreant than the effects of capitalism.

INTRODUCTION

James T. Farrell's portrayal of the home life of the boys in "Young Convicts" accurately depicts many central themes of crime causation espoused by radical criminologists. The plight of the boys appears predestined by forces they cannot understand, and certainly cannot control. The effects of economic determinism seem to be the controlling factors of their lives, and their future is indeed bleak. Finally, the criminal justice system seals their fate.

Heinrich Böll's "The Balek Scales" and Art Buchwald's "The Trial of Jack the Ripper" support the radical criminologists' claim that the legal milieu serves those persons who benefit from maintaining the status quo. In Böll's story an injustice has been uncovered, yet the persons against whom the crime has been perpetrated are powerless to act. Buchwald artfully uses the formal legal machinery in the form of a trial to illustrate that seemingly unconscionable attitudes and behavior can be legitimized at the expense of the politically impotent. The defendant receives due process of law by a trial of his peers, but there is no justice.

YOUNG CONVICTS
James T. Farrell

They were the children of Slavic immigrants and lived in the manufacturing district around Thirty-fifth and Morgan. Their fathers worked in the factories located in the area. Their sisters, even before they started to bloom and lose their gawky pre-puberty figures, also joined the ranks of those who trooped to the factories at six and seven in the morning. At six, seven, eight o'clock, rain or shine, morning after morning, their fathers, mothers, older brothers, sisters, all became a part of the long line plodding to work.

There were six kids in this gang. Tony, the eldest, was a boy of twelve, and Stanley, the youngest, was eight. They all liked candy. They liked to go to the movies, especially on Saturday afternoons, when the serial was shown. They liked serials and movies of that type best because there was danger and adventure, shooting, robbing, train wrecks, bandits, outlaws, Indians, Mexicans, battles. And they scarcely ever had money for candy or for movies.

But they liked candy and they liked movies. And they liked to do dangerous, brave things, to pull off stunts like those pulled off by the older fellows in the neighborhood. They wanted to fight and steal, and then brag about it, just as they heard their older brothers bragging. They could be heroes just like the older boys. And when they could steal, they could have money for candy and the movies.

Home to each of the kids in the gang was much the same. A wooden shack, one or two stories high, with an outside privy that smelled you out every time you wanted to take a leak. Three, four, five rooms, generally dirty, fulls of rags, papers, the smell of kerosene lamps. Dark bedrooms, old beds, dirty sheets, two, three, four, and five sleeping together in the same bed, and on cold nights there was always a fight for the blankets. A mother and a father who were generally overtired from work, and from raising a family. And the mother and father didn't speak English. They were greenhorns. And once every week, two weeks, three weeks, the mother and father would get drunk. They would curse and fight, throwing things at one another, shouting, even brandishing knives and cutting one another up, until the police came with a paddy wagon. These kids' homes were alike.

They didn't like school very much. They didn't like their studies, and in the classroom they groaned, twisted, squirmed, itched, dreamed of high deeds like those of the movie heroes and villains in the Saturday-afternoon serials, like those of the older fellows, like those of Al Capone. In school, they waited for the end of class. They were afraid of their teachers, and they neither liked nor trusted them. The teachers, some of them young girls from good families who were waiting until they found a husband, did not like the bad boys much either. Sometimes, in the hallways, the kids would hear one teacher tell another that she wished she would be transferred to another school where there was a better class of pupils than these incorrigible Polacks and Bohemians.

Often, they didn't learn their lessons. They bummed from school regularly, and went scavenging through vacant lots and streets, keeping their eyes peeled for the overworked truant officers. Or they went to the railroad yards with sacks and wagons for coal that was needed at home. In fact, they learned to steal in the railroad yards. The parents would send them out at night to get coal, and they'd go down to the yards and get it, one kid getting up in a car and throwing chunks down to the others. From the railroad yards they went to the stockyards, going over the fences and leaving with anything removable that could perhaps be sold. They stole everything they could, and finally stealing got to be a nightly occupation.

They knew about hold-ups. They knew that some of the older guys in the district had pulled off hold-ups, and that made them heroes. So they determined that they too would be heroes and pull hold-ups. That would get money for candy and movies. And they would be living like the heroes they saw in the movies. One night, Tony, the gang leader, picked out the Nation Oil filling station on Thirty-fifth Street. They played across the street from the station for two nights. They goofed about, ran, played tag by a closed factory, getting a line on what time the station closed and what time the cop on the beat passed by after it had closed. When they were sure of their time and their layout, they went to work. Young Stanley tossed a house brick through a side window. Tony then stood on a box, put his hand through the broken glass, and unlatched the window. He went in, followed by the others. The money was in the safe, and that could not be touched. So they tore the telephone box from the wall and scooted with it. They broke it open in a vacant lot and divided the nickels that were in it. The loot was three dollars, and, although it was to be divided evenly, Stanley was cheated out of a quarter.

Successful in their raid on the filling station, they made other raids. They robbed every filling station in the district, always running off with the telephone box, and they enjoyed the fruits of their robbery in candy, cigarettes, and movies. Tony liked it. He bossed his gang with an iron hand. Night after night he drove them in raid after raid. If they complained, he kicked them in the pants and slapped their faces. If they talked back to him, he cracked them. He saw himself as a young Al Capone. He dreamed of shootings, gang fights, submachine guns, robberies, money, automobiles, everything the gangsters had in the movies, everything Al

Capone had in real life. And he always planned out the raids, instructing each kid in what he should do, going to the place in advance to get the lay of the land. He always had money and gave some of it away to younger kids, to girls whom he would try to bribe in order to get them alone with him in basements. He hung around the corners and poolrooms late at night, watching the older fellows. He imitated them in walking, talking, gestures, held his cigarettes as they did, borrowed all their remarks. He pushed and pressed his gang constantly, always discovering new places to rob. One night they robbed a chain restaurant. Stanley threw a brick through the back window, and they entered and ran off with the cash in the till. Two nights later, they returned to the Nation Oil Company's filling station and again ran off with the telephone box full of nickels. This time they noticed that the attendant had gone home, leaving his safe open. In it, they saw bills, many of them, dollars and dollars, more money than they had ever seen before. They were so surprised by the sight of the money, so afraid, that they did not take it, satisfying themselves with only the small change in the safe. And on the night after this robbery they returned to the chain restaurant. They were caught by a watchman and a city policeman.

They were brought before Judge Katherine Henderson in the Juvenile Court; she was a woman jurist who was known beyond the city for her good work. The court was crowded with its usual array of young culprits and harassed, shamed parents. The boys had to wait their turn, and they sat with other boys, cowed and meek, and with their shabbily dressed immigrant parents. Nearly all those waiting to be tried were the children of working people, most of them immigrants. Some were released, some placed on probation, some sentenced to the Juvenile Detention Home. Judge Henderson spoke crisply, hastily, perfunctorily, often in a scolding tone. She hurried through case after case, disposed of it, making instant decisions, bawling out parents, often telling immigrant fathers and mothers that they were responsible for the delinquent conduct of their children.

Judge Henderson just didn't have the time. The cases had to be disposed of. Tomorrow there would be the same number. The juvenile problem was insoluble. There was no settlement of it. The same boys were warned, but they were brought back. Parents were warned, but they were helpless. There was nothing to do but rush through from case to case, let so many off, put so many on probation, send so many to the Detention Home. Day after day, this must go on. The law must be upheld. There was no time for her to delay, study, probe into the causes of these delinquencies. All she could do was reach out and try, and hope that a few boys would be rescued from crime, and a few girls from the life of a prostitute. That was what she did. Lectures, warnings, scoldings, questions, sentences. Next. Next. Next. All morning. Next. All afternoon. Next. Tomorrow. More. Next.

Tony and the gang were called up. The bailiff rounded them up and prodded them in the back, his language curt and sharp. He shoved them up to the bar of justice. Judge Henderson read the papers on the case, closed her lips as she read, nodded her gray head. She raised her brows. Her benign face showed worry. She seemed to be wondering and thinking. She looked down sharply at the six boys before her. Their heads dropped. They were afraid to look her in the eye, just as they feared looking teachers, or policemen, in the eye. Her gaze shifted. She stared at their parents, who stood silently behind the boys. She asked each of the boys what his name was. The first answered that he was Clement Comorosky. Where was his mother? He shook his head. Again she asked where his mother was. Again he shook his head. More stridently, she asked where his father and mother were. He said that both were working and could not come down. Stanley's mother then spoke in Polish. An interpreter was called, and she spoke to him. He told the judge that the woman had said that the father and mother of the Comorosky boy worked in a factory and were afraid to stay out because they were too poor, and needed the day's wages, and they were afraid that if they didn't report for work they might be laid off. Please, she would take their place.

"All right. Now, do you boys know what you did?" the judge asked.

None of them answered. They stood with averted eyes.

"Can any of you talk? Can you talk?" she asked, sweeping her eyes from one to another, fixing them on Clement, who was ten years old.

He nodded his head affirmatively.

"Do you know that it's a crime to break into other peoples' homes and stores and to take things that don't belong to you?"

"I'm sorry . . . ma'am," Clement said.

"How long have you been doing this?"

"Just this time," Clement said.

She looked through the papers before her and called out Stanley's name.

"You were here before, and I told you that I didn't want to see you brought back. And why don't you go to school?"

He looked at her with large-eyed awe.

"Are your parents here?"

A small Slavic woman said that she was his mother; her face was lined, and an old black shawl covered her head. The judge asked her if she ever tried to keep her boy in at night. She shook her head, and said that she tried, but that he went out anyway. The judge looked down at Stanley, glowering.

"And what did you do?"

"Me? I thrun the brick through de window."

Many who heard him smiled. The judge continued to question them in a brusque manner which inspired fear. Their answers came slowly. They were evasive. They did not understand all of her questions. She became more brusque. She seemed annoyed. She listened, with increasing irritation, while the watchman who caught the boys gave his testimony. Then the gas station attendant testified that twice the station had been broken into, and the telephone box had been ripped off the wall on each occasion. The restaurant manager gave testimony also.

"You boys have to learn that you can't go on breaking into places and stealing money. That is not right, and it is not permitted. Do you hear me?"

Six heads nodded.

"Well, why did you do it?"

Her additional questions brought out the fact that Tony was the leader and inspiration of the gang, that Stevie Lozminski was his lieutenant, and that the raids and burglaries had been committed under their direction. Both had been in the court before for truancy and burglary, and the truant officer testified that all her efforts to do anything that would keep them in the classroom, where they belonged, were fruitless. Their teachers and the principal of the school had turned in written reports describing them as incorrigible. The judge continued her brusque questioning, directing some of it at the parents, who stood in silent awe and fear. She lectured the parents about taking care of their offspring and insisted that the interpreter translate her remarks so that they would surely be understood. Tony, Stevie, and Clement were all sentenced to six months in the Juvenile Detention Home, and the others were put on probation. The mothers cried. They looked with bewildered grief at the judge, their pleading eyes almost like those of sick animals. The boys were pulled from their parents' arms and taken off. Two of the mothers cried.

The next case, that of a colored boy caught stealing, was called.

The mill of the court continued.

THE BALEK SCALES
Heinrich Böll

Where my grandfather came from, most of the people lived by working in the flax sheds. For five generations they had been breathing in the dust which rose from the crushed flax stalks, letting themselves be killed off by slow degrees, a race of long-suffering, cheerful people who ate goat cheese, potatoes, and now and then a rabbit; in the evening they would sit at home spinning and knitting; they sang, drank mint tea and were happy. During the day they would carry the flax stalks to the antiquated machines, with no protection from the dust and at the mercy of the heat which came pouring out of the drying kilns. Each cottage contained only one bed, standing against the wall like a closet and reserved for the parents, while the children slept all round the room on benches. In the morning the room would be filled with the odor of thin soup; on Sundays there was stew, and on feast days the children's faces would light up with pleasure as they watched the black acorn coffee turning paler and paler from the milk their smiling mother poured into their coffee mugs.

The parents went off early to the flax sheds, the housework was left to the children: they would sweep the room, tidy up, wash the dishes and peel the potatoes, precious pale-yellow fruit whose thin peel had to be produced afterwards to dispel any suspicion of extravagance or carelessness.

As soon as the children were out of school they had to go off into the woods and, depending on the season, gather mushrooms and herbs: woodruff and thyme, caraway, mint and foxglove, and in summer, when they had brought in the hay from their meager fields, they gathered hayflowers. A kilo of hayflowers was worth one pfennig, and they were sold by the apothecaries in town for twenty pfennigs a kilo to highly strung ladies. The mushrooms were highly prized: they fetched twenty pfennigs a kilo and were sold in the shops in town for one mark twenty. The children would crawl deep into the green darkness of the forest during the autumn when dampness drove the mushrooms out of the soil, and almost every family had its own places where it gathered mushrooms, places which were handed down in whispers from generation to generation.

The woods belonged to the Baleks, as well as the flax sheds, and in my grandfather's village the Baleks had a chateau, and the wife of the head of the family had a little room next to the dairy where mushrooms, herbs and hayflowers were weighed and paid for. There on the table stood the great Balek scales, an old-fashioned, ornate bronze-gilt contraption, which my grandfather's grandparents had already faced when they were children, their grubby hands holding their little baskets of mushrooms, their paper bags of hayflowers, breathlessly watching the number of weights Frau Balek had to throw on the scale before the swinging pointer came to rest exactly over the black line, that thin line of justice which had to be redrawn every year. Then Frau Balek would take the big book covered in brown leather, write down the weight, and pay out the money, pfennigs or ten-pfennig pieces and very, very occasionally, a mark. And when my grandfather was a child there was a big glass jar of lemon drops standing there, the kind that cost one mark a kilo, and when Frau Balek—whichever one happened to be presiding over the little room—was in a good mood, she would put her hand into this jar and give each child a lemon drop, and the children's faces would light up with pleasure, the way they used to when on feast days their mother poured milk into their coffee mugs, milk that made the coffee turn paler and paler until it was as pale as the flaxen pigtails of the little girls.

One of the laws imposed by the Baleks on the village was: no one was permitted to have any scales in the house. The law was so ancient that nobody gave a thought as to when and how it had arisen, and it had to be obeyed, for anyone who broke it was dismissed from the flax sheds, he could not sell his mushrooms or his thyme or his hayflowers, and the power of the Baleks was so far-reaching that no one in the neighboring villages would give him work either, or buy his forest herbs. But since the days when my grandfather's parents had gone out as small children to gather mushrooms and sell them in order that they might season the meat of the rich people of Prague or be baked into game pies, it had never occurred to anyone to break this law: flour could be measured in cups, eggs could be counted, what they had spun could be measured by the yard, and besides, the old-fashioned bronze-gilt, ornate Balek scales did not look as if there was anything wrong with them, and five generations had entrusted the swinging black pointer with what they had gone out as eager children to gather from the woods.

True, there were some among these quiet people who flouted the law, poachers bent on making more money in one night than they could earn in a whole month in the flax sheds, but even these people apparently never thought of buying scales or making their own. My grandfather was the first person bold enough to test the justice of the Baleks, the family who lived in the chateau and drove two carriages, who always maintained one boy from the village while he studied theology at the seminary in Prague, the family with whom the priest played taroc every Wednesday, on whom the local reeve, in his carriage emblazoned with the Imperial coat-of-arms, made an annual New Year's Day call and on whom the Emperor conferred a title on the first day of the year 1900.

My grandfather was hard-working and smart: he crawled farther into the woods than the children of his clan had crawled before him, he penetrated as far as the thicket where, according to legend, Bilgan the Giant was supposed to dwell, guarding a treasure. But my grandfather was not afraid of Bilgan: he worked his way deep into the thicket, even when he was quite little, and brought out great quantities of mushrooms; he even found truffles, for which Frau Balek paid thirty pfennigs a pound. Everything my grandfather took to the Baleks he entered on the back of a torn-off calendar page: every pound of mushrooms, every gram of thyme, and on the right-hand side, in his childish handwriting, he entered the amount he received for each item; he scrawled in every pfennig, from the age of seven to the age of twelve, and by the time he was twelve the year 1900 had arrived, and because the Baleks had been raised to the aristocracy by the Emperor, they gave every family in the village a quarter of a pound of real coffee, the Brazilian kind; there was also free beer and tobacco for the men, and at the chateau there was a great banquet; many carriages stood in the avenue of poplars leading from the entrance gates to the chateau.

But the day before the banquet the coffee was distributed in the little room which had housed the Balek scales for almost a hundred years, and the Balek family was now called Balek von Bilgan because, according to legend, Bilgan the Giant used to have a great castle on the site of the present Balek estate.

My grandfather often used to tell me how he went there after school to fetch the coffee for four families: the Cechs, the Weidlers, the Vohlas and his own, the Brüchers. It was the afternoon of New Year's Eve: there were the front rooms to be decorated, the baking to be done, and the families did not want to spare four boys and have each of them go all the way to the chateau to bring back a qurter of a pound of coffee.

And so my grandfather sat on the narrow wooden bench in the little room while Gertrud the maid counted out the wrapped four-ounce packages of coffee, four of them, and he looked at the scales and saw that the pound weight was still lying on the left-hand scale; Frau Balek von Bilgan was busy with preparations for the banquet. And when Gertrud was about to put her hand into the jar with the lemon drops to give my grandfather one, she discovered it was empty: it was refilled once a year, and held one kilo of the kind that cost a mark.

Gertrud laughed and said: "Wait here while I get the new lot," and my grandfather waited with the four four-ounce packages which had been wrapped and sealed in the factory, facing the scales on which someone had left the pound weight, and my grandfather took the four packages of coffee, put them on the empty scale, and his heart thudded as he watched the black finger of justice come to rest on the left of the black line: the scale with the pound weight stayed down, and the pound of coffee remained up in the air; his heart thudded more than if he had been lying behind a bush in the forest waiting for Bilgan the Giant, and he felt in his pocket for the pebbles he always carried with him so he could use his catapult to shoot the sparrows which pecked away at his mother's cabbage plants—he had to put three, four, five pebbles beside the packages of coffee before the scale with the pound weight rose and the pointer at last came to rest over the black line. My grandfather took the coffee from the scale, wrapped the five pebbles in his kerchief, and when Gertrud came back with the big kilo bag of lemon drops which had to last for another whole year in order to make the children's faces light up with pleasure, when Gertrud let the lemon drops rattle into the glass jar, the pale little fellow was still standing there, and nothing seemed to have changed. My grandfather only took three of the packages, then Gertrud looked in startled surprise at the white-faced child who threw the lemon drop onto the floor, ground it under his heel, and said: "I want to see Frau Balek."

"Balek von Bilgan, if you please," said Gertrud.

"All right, Frau Balek von Bilgan," but Gertrud only laughed at him, and he walked back to the village in the dark, took the Cechs, the Weidlers and the Vohlas their coffee, and said he had to go and see the priest.

Instead he went out into the dark night with his five pebbles in his kerchief. He had to walk a long way before he found someone who had scales, who was permitted to have them; no one in the villages of Blaugau and Bernau had any, he knew that, and he went straight through them till, after two hours' walking, he reached the little town of Dielheim where Honig the apothecary lived. From Honig's house came the smell of fresh pancakes, and Honig's breath, when he opened the door to the half-frozen boy, already smelled of punch, there was a moist cigar between his narrow lips, and he clasped the boy's cold hands firmly for a moment, saying: "What's the matter, has your father's lung got worse?"

"No, I haven't come for medicine, I wanted . . ." My grandfather undid his kerchief, took out the five pebbles, held them out to Honig and said: "I wanted to have these weighed." He glanced anxiously into Honig's face, but when Honig said nothing and did not get angry, or even ask him anything, my grandfather said: "It is the amount that is short of justice," and now, as he went into the warm room, my grandfather realized how wet his feet were. The snow had soaked through his cheap shoes, and in the forest the branches had showered him with snow which was now melting, and he was tired and hungry and suddenly began to cry because he thought of the quantities of mushrooms, the herbs, the flowers, which had been weighed on the scales which were short five pebbles' worth of justice. And when Honig, shaking his head and holding the five pebbles, called his wife, my grandfather thought of the generations of his parents, his grandparents, who had all had to have their mushrooms, their flowers, weighed on the scales, and he was overwhelmed by a great wave of injustice, and began to sob louder than ever, and, without waiting to be asked, he sat down on a chair, ignoring the pancakes, the cup of hot coffee which nice plump Frau Honig put in front of him, and did not stop crying till Honig himself came out from the shop at the back and, rattling the pebbles in his hand, said in a low voice to his wife: "Fifty-five grams, exactly."

My grandfather walked the two hours home through the forest, got a beating at home, said nothing, not a single word, when he was asked about the coffee, spent the whole evening doing sums on the piece of paper on which he had written down everything he had sold to Frau Balek, and when midnight struck, and the cannon could be heard from the chateau, and the whole village rang with shouting and laughter and the noise of rattles, when the family kissed and embraced all round, he said into the New Year silence: "The Baleks owe me eighteen marks and thirty-two pfennigs." And again he thought of all the children there were in the village, of his brother Fritz who had gathered so many mushrooms, of his sister Ludmilla; he thought of the many hundreds of children who had all gathered mushrooms for the Baleks, and herbs and flowers, and this time he did not cry but told his parents and brothers and sisters of his discovery.

When the Baleks von Bilgan went to High Mass on New Year's Day, their new coat-of-arms—a giant crouching under a fir tree—already emblazoned in blue and gold on their carriage, they saw the hard, pale faces of the people all staring at them. They had expected garlands in the village, a song in their honor, cheers and hurrahs, but the village was completely deserted as they drove through it, and in church the pale faces of the people were turned toward them, mute and hostile, and when the priest mounted the pulpit to deliver his New Year's sermon he sensed the chill in those otherwise quiet and peaceful faces, and he stumbled painfully through his sermon and went back to the altar drenched in sweat. And as the Baleks von Bilgan left the church after Mass, they walked through a lane of mute, pale faces. But young Frau Balek von Bilgan stopped in front of the children's pews, sought out my grandfather's face, pale little Franz Brücher, and asked him, right there in the church: "Why didn't you take the coffee for your mother?" And my grandfather stood up and said: "Because you owe me as much money as five kilos of coffee would cost." And he pulled the five pebbles from his pocket, held them out to the young woman and said: "This much, fifty-five grams, is short in every pound of your justice"; and before the woman could say anything the men and women in the church lifted up their voices and sang: "The justice of this earth, O Lord, hath put Thee to death. . . ."

While the Baleks were at church, Wilhelm Vohla, the poacher, had broken into the little room, stolen the scales and the big fat leatherbound book in which had been entered every kilo of mushrooms, every kilo of hayflowers, everything bought by the Baleks in the village, and all afternoon of that New Year's Day the men of the village sat in my great-grandparents' front room and calculated, calculated one tenth of everything that had been bought—but when they had calculated many thousands of talers and had still not come to an end, the reeve's gendarmes arrived, made their way into my great-grandfather's front room, shooting and stabbing as they came, and removed the scales and the book by force. My grandfather's little sister Ludmilla lost her life, a few men were wounded, and one of the gendarmes was stabbed to death by Wilhelm Vohla the poacher.

Our village was not the only one to rebel: Blaugau and Bernau did too, and for almost a week no work was done in the flax sheds. But a great many gendarmes appeared, and the men and women were threatened with prison, and the Baleks forced the priest to display the scales publicly in the school and demonstrate that the finger of justice swung to and fro accurately. And the men and women went back to the flax sheds—but no one went to the school to watch the priest: he stood there all alone, helpless and forlorn with his weights, scales, and packages of coffee.

And the children went back to gathering mushrooms, to gathering thyme, flowers and foxglove, but every Sunday, as soon as the Baleks entered the church, the hymn was struck up: "The justice of this earth, O Lord, hath put Thee to death," until the reeve ordered it proclaimed in every village that the singing of this hymn was forbidden.

My grandfather's parents had to leave the village, and the new grave of their little daughter; they became basket weavers, but did not stay long anywhere because it pained them to see how everywhere the finger of justice swung falsely. They walked along behind their cart, which crept slowly over the country roads, taking their thin goat with them, and passers-by could sometimes hear a voice from the cart singing: "The justice of this earth, O Lord, hath put Thee to death." And those who wanted to listen could hear the tale of the Baleks von Bilgan, whose justice lacked a tenth part. But there were few who listened.

THE TRIAL OF JACK THE RIPPER
Art Buchwald

After reading the accounts of the trial in Hayneville, Alabama, where a jury found a socially prominent citizen "not guilty" of killing a civil rights seminary student, one wonders how Jack the Ripper would have fared if he had been a citizen of Alabama and had been caught and tried in Lowndes County.

It might have gone something like this:

First, the grand jury would indict him for manslaughter instead of murder on the grounds that, although he killed five women, it was done without malice.

Then the trial takes place. An all-white jury made up of friends of the Ripper family is selected, and the judge, who is Jack's uncle, warns the prosecution to be brief and refrain from calling too many witnesses.

The county prosecutor reluctantly charges that Jack killed five women by slitting their throats and spreading their innards about. The people in the courtroom chuckle and several of Jack's cousins wave to him. The prosecutor produces the knife as evidence and then rests his case.

The defense attorney for Jack does not deny the charges, which causes members of the KKK in the courtroom to applaud. But he maintains Jack was acting in self-defense.

He calls his first witness. "Did you see the defendant stab his first victim?"

"Yes, sir, I did. Rip was walking down the street late at night when this here woman pulls a switchblade on him, and he had no choice but to slash out at her first. It was quick thinking on his part, because that woman meant to do him harm."

The second witness, Zeke Ripper, is called.

"Zeke, eight days after Rip defended himself, he ran into another woman on the street. What was her name?"

"Dark Annie Chapman."

"Would you repeat that again?"

"Dark Annie Chapman."

"What happened, Zeke?"

"Wal, Rip is just strolling along and suddenly Dark Annie comes up to him with a pistol in her hand like she's going to kill him, so Jack pulls out his knife and slits her throat."

"Where's the pistol now, Zeke?"

"Some nigra rushed up and took it away 'fore the police came."

"Thank you, Zeke. Now, ladies and gentlemen of the jury, I'm not even going to call any witnesses in regards to the killings of 'Long Liz' Stride and Kate Edowes, because there is no need to. Jack saw both these women kissing nigras and he went up to them and told them to stop it and when they didn't Jack did what any Hayneville gentleman would do and stabbed them both in the abdomen.

"As for the killing of Black Mary Kelly, I'd like to call Jefferson Lingo Ripper. Jefferson, what happened, in your own words?"

"This here Black Mary, she comes up to Rip and she said something to him that I can't repeat here in court and poor Rip followed her to her room and cut her up. I've known Rip since he was a boy and he wouldn't hurt a fly, but that woman provoked him something awful."

Laughter from the court.

"Are these Black Mary's clothes?"

"Yes, sir."

"Ladies and gentlemen of the jury, I ask, you, what kind of woman would wear clothes like this and bring shame and world-wide publicity to the good people of Lowndes County? No white man will be safe on the streets of Hayneville if you find Jack the Ripper guilty of defending himself. Put yourself in his place. Wouldn't you have done the same thing?"

The judge asks the jury to file out and decide a verdict.

The foreman says, "No need for that, judge. We find the defendant not guilty and we wish to take this opportunity to nominate Jack the Ripper for sheriff of this God-fearing community."

Issues for Discussion

1. Explain how the family life of the immigrants in James T. Farrell's "Young Convicts" is, from a radical criminologist's perspective, conducive to criminality.
2. The radical criminologist argues that the inequitable economic system is maintained and legitimized by an equally unjust legal system. What characteristics of the courtroom scene described by Farrell illustrate that Judge Henderson did not, and could not, dispense justice?
3. What is the significance of Farrell's title "Young Convicts"?
4. Compare and contrast the working conditions of the characters in Heinrich Böll's "The Balek Scales" with the immigrant parents in "Young Convicts." Then relate how the concept of "consciousness manipulation" serves to explain the lack of criminality among Böll's characters.
5. Explain how the Balek scales fortify the statements of the radical criminologist.
6. How do the Balek scales represent "respectable" or "white collar" crime?
7. Who was punished more severely, the owner of the Balek scales, or the grandfather who discovered the fraud? Why?
8. How would the radical criminologist analogize the Balek scales to the American symbol of justice, the blindfolded woman holding the scales of justice?
9. What is the significance of the phrase sung at the church service, "The justice of this earth, O Lord, hath put Thee to death. . . .?
10. Explain the significance of Böll's closing words: "And those who wanted to listen could hear the tale of the Baleks van Bilgan, whose justice lacked a tenth part. But there were few who listened."
11. The courtroom scene in Art Buchwald's "The Trial of Jack the Ripper" initially seems to refute the radical criminologists' claims that the common man cannot receive justice. Specifically, the "average citizen" has a voice in the process because he now sits on the jury. And, in fact, the disservice appears to have been perpetrated against the

state. How are "the people" once again victimized by the legal system?
12. Who does Jack the Ripper represent, and why is his trial held in Alabama in the early 1960s?
13. Discuss from a radical criminologist's perspective the common characteristics of Farrell's immigrants, Böll's farmers, and Buchwald's victims.

PART VIII

Differential Association

The theory of differential association was developed by Edwin Hardin Sutherland (1883–1950) and presented in his *Principles of Criminology*.[1] Sutherland's theory rejects the positivist belief that behavior results from biological determinism: "I reached the general conclusion that a concrete condition [e.g., genetic defect] cannot be a cause of crime, and that the only way to get a causal explanation of criminal behavior is by extracting from the varying concrete conditions things that are universally associated with crime."[2] Sutherland contends that all behavior (criminal and noncriminal) is learned: [T]he principles of the process of association by which criminal behavior develops are the same as the principles of the process by which lawful behavior develops."[3]

The process by which people come to behave in a deviant manner can be outlined as follows:

> 1. *Criminal behavior is learned.* Negatively, this means that criminal behavior is not inherited, as such; also, the person who is not already trained in crime does not invent criminal behavior, just as a

---

1. Philadelphia: Lippincott, 1939. Slight modifications appear in the 1947 edition of this textbook.

2. Albert K. Cohen et al., *The Sutherland Papers* (Bloomington: Indiana University Press, 1956), p. 19.

3. Sutherland, *Principles of Criminology*, p. 5.

person does not make mechanical inventions unless he has had training in mechanics.

2. *Criminal behavior is learned in interaction with other persons in a process of communication.* This communication is verbal in many respects but includes also "the communication of gestures."

3. *The principal part of the learning of criminal behavior occurs within intimate personal groups.* Negatively, this means that the impersonal agencies of communication, such as movies and newspapers, play a relatively unimportant part in the genesis of criminal behavior.

4. *When criminal behavior is learned, the learning includes (a) techniques of committing the crime, which are sometimes very complicated, sometimes very simple; (b) the specific direction of motives, drives, rationalizations, and attitudes.*

5. *The specific direction of motives and drives is learned from definitions of the legal codes as favorable or unfavorable.*

6. *A person becomes delinquent because of an excess of definitions favorable to violation of law.* This is the principle of differential association. It refers to both criminal and anticriminal associations and has to do with counteracting forces. When persons become criminal, they do so because of contacts with criminal patterns and also because of isolation from anticriminal patterns.

7. *Differential associations may vary in frequency, duration, priority, and intensity.* This means that associations with criminal behavior and also associations with anticriminal behavior vary in those respects. Frequency and duration as modalities of associations are obvious and need no explanation. Priority is assumed to be important in the sense that lawful behavior developed in early childhood may persist throughout life, and also that delinquent behavior developed in early childhood may persist throughout life.

8. *The process of learning criminal behavior by association with criminal and anticriminal patterns involves all of the mechanisms that are involved in any other learning.* Negatively, this means that the learning of criminal behavior is not restricted to the process of imitation.

9. *While criminal behavior is an expression of general needs and values, it is not explained by those general needs and values, since noncriminal behavior is an expression of the same needs and values.* Thieves generally steal in order to secure money, but likewise honest laborers work in order to secure money. The attempts by many scholars to explain criminal behavior by general drives and values, such as the happiness principle, striving for social status, the money

motive, or frustration, have been, and must continue to be, futile, since they explain lawful behavior as completely as they explain criminal behavior. They are similar to respiration, which is necessary for any behavior, but which does not differentiate criminal from non-criminal behavior.[4]

An example may help clarify Sutherland's statements. An armed robber kills a liquor store clerk. He is caught, convicted, and sentenced to death. An executioner is paid to assist in the termination of the murderer's life. The killing of the clerk is labeled as first-degree murder, whereas the execution of the murderer is considered to be justifiable homicide. In both cases the actors voluntarily selected a method of financial aggrandizement. Even though both actors' vocations involve extinguishing human life, the murderer's job is legally impermissible. Differential association theorists assert it is relatively unimportant that socially acceptable conduct and, in this case, homicide, is the result of two seemingly different kinds of behavior. Nor should one become bogged down with the notion that one behavior is legal, the other illegal. The test is to view both actors' conduct as involving acting out roles voluntarily engaged in. Both actors behaved in a particular manner. The behavior conforms to, and was probably reinforced by, attitudes and expectations of both individuals' reference groups. The only difference between good (socially acceptable) and bad (socially unacceptable) behavior is in the adjectives "good" and "bad." The basis of acquiring either good or bad behavior habits is the same: *Behavior is learned.*

Accepting the premise that behavior is learned does not explain why one person learns and acts out socially acceptable behavior while another chooses an unacceptable course. Advocates of differential association theory suggest that the answer lies in understanding the process of man's socialization into, or in the case of the deviant, away from, the cultural mainstream. Just as one becomes socialized politically, so one becomes socialized criminally. The primary task in understanding criminality is the assessment of the impact of the array of effective stimuli on behavior patterns. These stimuli include the nature and direction of influence from family, peer groups, educational mentors, and occupational colleagues. The quality and quantity of a person's differential associations must then be ascertained. Criteria include the *frequency, duration, priority,* and *intensity* of contact with these associations. An excess of definitions favorable

---

4. Ibid., 10th ed., pp. 80–82.

to deviance over definitions favorable to socially acceptable behavior is what produces deviant behavior.[5]

Hugh Allyn Hunt's "Acme Rooms and Sweet Marjorie Russell" and James T. Farrell's "Young Convicts" (in Part VII) support Sutherland's contention that behavior is learned. In both stories the boys need money to accomplish their ends. Both groups form a gang. But the gangs accomplish their goals in radically different ways. The key to the differential behaviors seems to be the boys' primary reference groups—their parents and the examples of behavior of other adolescents. These intimate personal groups clearly communicate their attitudes to the boys, and the boys respond to the cues.

A bizarre annual ritual is described in Shirley Jackson's "The Lottery." The lottery itself is steeped in tradition and is accepted, even welcomed, by participants. The outcome of the drawing may seem strange, if not illegal. That is the point: acceptable behavior is conduct supported by the community in which we live. When the values of the community are strongly and consistently reinforced by our primary and secondary reference models, those values are likely to be supported.

---

5. As with earlier theories, criticisms of the current theory have been lodged. Sutherland and Cressey (1978) cite, discuss, and occasionally defend most of the criticisms. See ibid., pp. 83–95. See also Daniel Glasser, "The Differential Association Theory of Crime," in *Human Behavior and Social Process*, ed. Arnold M. Rose (Boston: Houghton Mifflin, 1962), pp. 435–42. Sheldon Glueck faults the theory for being unclear when it attributes criminality to the environment generally, making measurement and testing impossible. See his "Theory and Fact in Criminology: A Criticism of Differential Association," *British Journal of Delinquency* 7 (October 1956): 92–109.

Also, the theory generally ignores the effects of personality or psychological factors on behavior. Sutherland acknowledges this flaw in "Development of the Theory," in *Edwin H. Sutherland on Analyzing Crime*, ed. Karl Schuessler (Chicago: University of Chicago Press, 1973), p. 21. In addition, phrases like "definitions favorable to criminality versus unfavorable to criminality" are too vague to be quantified and measured. See James F. Short, Jr., "Differential Association and Delinquency," *Social Problems* 4 (1957): 233–39. Finally, the theory oversimplifies the process of learning deviant behavior, ignoring the fact that some people simply choose a life of crime with no apparent prior criminal associations. See David Matza, *Becoming Deviant* (Englewood Cliffs, N.J.: Prentice-Hall, 1969), p. 107.

ACME ROOMS AND SWEET MARJORIE RUSSELL
Hugh Allyn Hunt

A puce romance, this is. Small towners hover round, for this romantic message comes to you straight from the hinterland heart of fields, farm houses and gentle, leafy communities of less than 20,000. These words figure to be nostalgia-laden, memory-aimed. Youth and love, those ever-warm states of being and mind, are about to be reheated. Sit down and prepare an indulgent smile for rural, boyish things recalled.

My town has exactly 16,548 easy-going, rather unanxious folk in it at the time all this takes place. It's bigger now, but this was faraway in the days of my youth, four thousand years ago in 1949. We're not, of course, going to deal with *all* those people. Just about a dozen or so.

For a helpful point of identification, I'm the long, skinny, flax-headed kid hinching his shoulders nervously over there at the drugstore counter. Notice this is not the usual adolescent cliché: I am *not* plagued by acne; beneath my straw sloshes a green river, *not* a Coke; my Levi's, *not* corduroys or khakis, are hooked lethally low, the belt loops sliced off and the bottoms carefully cut the right length with a razor blade. I do have to admit to a letter sweater, but there's a switchblade knife in my pocket to offset this. The sweater and the blade, incidentally, more or less typify a division of opinion within myself at this time. With normal high school aplomb, I am supporting two opposing and totally unintegrated points of view of the world. It is the co-presence of these two incompatible attitudes that, I think, I sincerely hope, will provide the dramatic tension of this purple-hued reminiscence.

Around me, in similar stagged pants, sweaters and lazily-drooping cigarettes, stand my fellow adolescents. There are six of us, all of different sizes, everyone an eleventh grader and to a man sixteen.

If our sallow and fatigued features seem to indicate that we are plotting unspeakable degradations, good. For after all, the most significant and exciting hours of the day are just commencing: after school. Moments given completely over to teen-age evil. We are here at this particular hour—four o'clock in the afternoon—too, because it is between the end of the basketball season and the beginning of track season. All of us at this counter attend Catholic high school and in this Protestant town we fish-eaters are known as deadly, fanatical competitors—not especially good, but competitive. At the moment, our six pallid faces are open testimony to the dissolute relief we're taking from months of tendon-stretching athletic combat. In a very brief time we've worked hard to relax, getting little sleep, losing our spending money at the poolhall, breathing numberless cigarettes and doing other things.

In plotting our boyish iniquities we have, naturally, come across such unimaginative things as getting into fights and stealing automobiles. But such things are not it; not what we are after. What we are seeking with undeviating single-mindedness, has to do with girls. We call it many things, most of them fanciful and extravagant. It is, of course, *sex*. Mysterious, furtive, condemned and immeasurably fascinating.

At sixteen, all of us have had our initial and incomplete little grapplings in cramped back seats. It is, in fact, this minor kind of experimentation that emboldens several of us (me, for instance) to keep an old American myth alive—that we are rampant swordsmen, that we've "gone all the way" with this or that girl, long ago last month—carefully selecting for these lies older females, usually recently graduated from public high school, who possess well-known reputations and who are totally removed from the possibility of knowing any of us. Against this unsatisfactory behavior and this unsurprising dishonesty, we relentlessly prepare and verbally rehearse keen teen orgies. What we impatiently seek now is the raw, unclothed act, fact, confrontation, the great entwined spasm. We are at the counter, behind our emerald drinks, waiting—nervously.

One other community of municipal (if you will) fact should be pointed out here. My home town is at the time of this story a division point for a Midwestern railroad and as such possesses the remarkable total of thirteen whorehouses. There's really little more to add about this at the moment, except that ours is no sin city. The houses, regulated by the mayor and the city council, are quite sedate and rather spectacularly unobvious.

"Look," I tell Jerry Donovan, working hard to keep my cigarette balanced at the side of my lip and grab the position of chief evil-artist of the group at the same time, "what we'll do is pool all our loot, get two cases of beer, go up, ask for a big room and for as many girls for as long as we can afford." It is a long sentence for me and I am confused. I end by nodding rapidly, persuasively.

Jerry, who tries to be swift and clever, but is really good-natured and kind of slow, quickly wags his broad head and grins. "Yeah, yeah. Two blondes, a brunette and three redheads." He rubs his hands together hungrily. When and how he has worked out this ratio, I don't know, but every time girls are mentioned lately he offers this ambitious numerical proportion. Since he's agreeing with me, I agree with him.

"Sure," I tell him, trying to sound authoritative. "If we've got enough money. Now, how much loot do we all have?" The five prematurely worn faces around me turn childishly reticent and doubtful at this. Like small grade-schoolers they tug hesitantly, almost shyly at their pockets.

Tom Murray finally flips out fifty cents and suggests cockily: "How about making up a pot and I'll go down to the poolhall and double it, huh?"

"Not my money, by God," Jerry squeezes his fist shut. Tom Murray is our school's hotshot football player, really pretty good, and this leads him to believe he's the world's greatest everything. Actually, he's an erratic pool player who usually loses all his money if he plays very long. Usually, he loses to Don Brandon or me. Now, belligerently, Brandon reaches over and punches Tom on the arm with wicked force.

"You couldn't win a game of slop from a blind, back-busted whore." Don has a thin, prisoner's face with a slit mouth. The first time I met him, I was immediately frightened. At eight years old, he was the only child I'd ever seen who looked as if he might at any moment, coldly, premeditatively, murder a close relative—his mother, say. He wasn't that tough at all, though he worked awfully hard to live up to that grim face of his.

Between the six of us, we place on the counter an unpromisingly small pile of gritty coins and a single faded bill. Acting as temporary treasurer, I count it. "Four dollars and seventy-three cents. Not even a buck apiece. God. What a bunch of duds." I shake my head. "What the hell do you think this is going to be anyway—a sodality meeting, for Christ's sake? We need . . . , well. . . ." I don't really know how much we need. "At least five bucks apiece for the whorehouse," I say recklessly, immediately appalled by the vast fortune that must be mounted to bring this orgy off.

"Damn," murmurs Curly Franklin. "That's . . . that's thirty dollars." Curly is the mathematician in our group. There is a long silence as the monumentality of this sum sinks in.

"OK, how many want to chicken out? Say so now, before we get started," I challenge them, abruptly able to do so for the first time in the many years of our boyhood lives together. Compulsively, I am pushed to this exceptional brashness, this ferocity, by the dazzling, lustful visions writhing in my imagination, refusing to be dimmed or stilled by something so minor as thirty dollars. I sneer at my companions so unpleasantly that no one says a word. We all order another green river and ponder how we're going to get more money.

"A dice game," announces Tom Murray who has never been in one.

"You're nuts," says Jerry fretfully.

"We could steal it," Don Brandon grins, trying to be evil.

"Crap," Curly Franklin tells him. "Crap. We'll have to work for it." This announcement depresses us even more and silence wades through our ranks.

"Work," someone murmurs incredulously. "Wow."

"We could borrow it," says Franky Shea suddenly.

"Sure," Curly nods. "Just walk up to the bank teller and say 'We want thirty dollars to go to the whorehouse, how much is the interest on that?'"

"Yeah," says Frank disheartenedly. "I don't know anybody that'd lend it to us."

"Look, it's about five bucks apiece. Now each of us ought to be able to scrounge up that much some way." I'm still flexing my newly discovered and unfamiliar organizational abilities. "What things can we do to make money?" I ask. "That's the way to approach it." But unfortunately that's a hard question to answer. It's mid-school year and most of the after-class and weekend kind of jobs are already in the anemic grip of creeps that don't go out for sports. Then too, there is the fact that we are in a terrible hurry, both because we're impatient and sweaty to get to those simmering, purchasable female bodies, and because track season will start next week.

"Let's cop something to sell," says Don Brandon, still trying to live up to his face. His unlipped mouth smiles criminally, but we know he'll do nothing unless we all tag along to help.

"Look," says Curly, pretending to be smart and logical and, I think, maybe trying to ace me out of my just-gained foothold on temporary leadershp. "Look," he says solemnly and I've already got three good reasons why whatever it is he says is wrong. "There are little things like, let's see. . . ." He's playing it big, pretending to think. "Like collecting bottles and selling them—"

"Oh, man, man," both Jerry and Don moan in unison. "You're kidding."

That's good, that's practical, I think. Maybe Curly and I can make a team. "Fine, fine," I declare with as much superiority as I can master in a hurry. "What else?" Generously giving him the lead, but thinking fast now that there's a challenger. "Maybe hook a job as a grocery boy after school this week," I say before anybody else can get it out. "Or mow lawns, do lawn work." Here I lose momentum because the grass isn't growing that fast yet; it's just spring, not summer. But my brain joggles and spins out a better one: "Con your parents into paying you to do something around home. Clean the garage, the basement, something."

Curly nods his head in admiration. The challenge dies and I suck noisily at my straw, then calmly light a butt. "This is Monday," I snap in a company commander's voice, imitating the infantry captain in the movie I've seen over the weekend. "Friday is five days away. By then we should have it. That means we've got to come up with a buck a day. All right?"

"No sweat," declares Tom Murray, easing his fifty-cent piece out of the sandy pile on the counter.

"Anybody showing up without a full five dollars is out. Right?" I glare at them like a two-star general. They all agree: "Sure, sure." After that, I don't really know of anything else to say and neither does anybody else. Silently, we wonder about the money, chew the melting ice in our glasses and then, finally, split up, each going his acquisitive way, elaborate financial schemes sprouting in his head.

Skating with infinitely lewd dreams jerking my limbs toward the rear door of the drugstore, I spy blond and pink Marjorie Russell snuggled in a back booth with other public high school girls. I slow my pace, lecherous hopes losing their evil focus, changing to something I can't quite grasp. My pulse and breath maintain the same rambling race, but some hidden mechanism has shifted ever so slightly. My speed diminishes, my path wavers and I casually lope over to Marjorie Russell's booth, draping myself with careful ease across the back of it. "Hi," I grin with the sensible face of an idiot since the presence of a lot of girls confuses me. "Hi, Marjorie." I want to let the others know they don't exist, not for squishy emotional reasons, I think, but for convenience.

Marjorie is sipping a cherry phosphate demurely and can only nod. To fill the silence, I snarl at her companions and sardonically light a cigarette.

"Hi," she says at last. "How are you?"

I mumble rudely and blow smoke at her. For a moment I grit my teeth. Marjorie's nice, I like her and am anxious to do things with her, but she often says these very formal, stupid type things that drive me nutty. Like "How are you?" For Christ's sake, I just saw her last night. I'm fine and whatever trouble I've got she knows it.

Sawing my head up and down, I try to signal her out of the crowded booth, but she just giggles a little and blinks. The other girls laugh and I flinch at their pitched syllables. Behind a fog of smoke, I poke Margie's shoulder and growl: "Hey, I want to talk to you." At this she glares and turns away. Irritably, I flick ashes on the splotch-faced girl next to her. "Come on, Marjorie," I plead, weary already. "Please. Just a minute."

At this, signaling her friends she has won, she simpers, smirks into her phosphate and considers my request. In my private presence, she is not like this at all, and while she makes me wait for my answer, I puzzle this curious adolescent warfare of the sexes. Finally, slowly, she comes out of the booth, sighing wearily as if it were costing her dearly, plopping books down, asking friends to stand up, at last stepping into the aisle with a very public expression of condescension on her girlish features. At the moment, I could easily strangle her and wish wildly for Don Brandon's cruel face with which to frighten them all. Instead, I grab her hand and stalk to the telephone booth for our intimate exchange. At once, dumped unceremoniously onto the booth seat, she is demure, quiet, no longer simpering. Such changes jostle me, and I stand in the doorway squinting, my brow undoubtedly doubled, for she asks: "What's wrong, honey?"

"Jesus, Jesus," I say to that pretty face and blond hair, abruptly unable to explain why I'm angry. Marjorie is wearing the soft, pale pink sweater I like so much and within it her small, round breasts press gently outward. That is Marjorie: small and round and smooth. My alternate opinion of the world: soft, poignant, immeasurably emotional, infinitely hushed and gentle—Marjorie. My other astigmatic affliction. "Marjorie," I say, neither beginning nor ending a sentence. Then: "Look, let's walk home, huh?"

I wait at the telephone booth as she goes back and picks up her books, laughs at someone's joke and says good-bye to her friends. Outside in the street, I take her school things and put my hand around her plump, childish fingers. This is my girl, and as I ramble on about school and tease her easily, now that we are alone, I am troubled by the contrast between my whorehouse plotting and the dreams I have for Marjorie. Though I know intimately how Marjorie's small breasts feel, I do not know what they look like and I have never made successful explorations elsewhere. Though we are not going "steady," we date no one else and I believe we have ambitious plans for one another, romantically. Marjorie's present physical reticence does not offend me outrageously, really, I'm infatuated with her, I cherish her and am trusting the future—tonight, tomorrow, the next night—to provide the opportunity, the right responses so that our romance may be consummated. I am young and incorrigibly American. I have little real evidence how she feels about our sexual destiny, nor am I clearly positive how I feel about it at this exact second, but nervously, jerkily, I believe we both think it's a certainty. I want to believe that, need to. As we stroll along, I saunter and strut, grimace and boast, entertaining her. I nip her ear and tell her how much I love her. On her porch, I've become so nervous that I kiss her and hug her quickly even though her mother stands watching in the doorway. Then, embarrassed, I run off shouting back that I'll call her later. Instead of seeing her after dinner tonight, I will be busy launching my fund for carnal purposes.

All week long opposing instincts within me cut across each other. I dream of Marjorie in soft colors: pinks, faint blues, lavender—and she is cuddly, vulnerable, innocent yet passionate. In my other, darker dreams, I ruthlessly, coldly drive with abandon into the faceless, twitching bodies of dark-haired women, my passion there as close to rage as my unwieldly love for my dreamt Marjorie is to a kind of physical prayer. During the long hours of emptying the family garage of five years' of accumulated junk, of running endless errands for my mother, for neighbors, of doing fifty odd little jobs, these two warring fantasies clash behind my sweaty brow. And diminish only slightly each night as I count the dimes and quarters. By Wednesday I am determined to get enough for a case of beer. My own. And Thursday afternoon I rush away from school and begin cleaning the back yard of a neighbor, bruising my sore hands with rakes, shovels, hoes, brooms. Then from that yard I go on to the next, pocketing with secret greedy glee the money these women pay me. From female to female these coins will pass, I think with exultant cynicism.

That night, after a hurried and rattled call to Margie, I count my money. I know, almost to the penny, how much is there, but I must count it, nonetheless. All the dimes I arrange in careful columns, side by side, the nickels, quarters, fifty-cent pieces, the few pennies. I smooth out the bills, turning them all green side up. There are ten amazing, potent dollars marching in little totem rows across my desk. I gloat. I giggle and clutch my sides and glee hiccups loose. At the locked door, my mother knocks and asks what's wrong, am I sick? Painfully suppressing my bouncing spirits, I gasp as calmly as I can: "No. No. Everything's fine." Indeed, it's glorious, uproarious. Troubled by my sniggering and gurgling, she stands outside my door as if waiting for prolonged cries of illness. But finally, with a sigh, she leaves and I topple onto the bed, burying my hysterical head in the pillow.

The endless moments of sunny Friday morning crawl by with incredible slowness. By ten o'clock, I've fretted and fidgeted myself into a state of near exhaustion. At the break, we feverishly confer, interrupting each other, demanding to know if everyone's brought their money. But the really big question is, where's Don Brandon? He isn't in school. Is he chickening out? He can't. We'll go to his home and get him, pull him out of bed if he's pretending to be sick. Nobody cops out. Standing in the crowded school hallway, squirting down Cokes and peanuts, we curse Brandon for his cowardice. Then, we count the money. I put down my five. Everyone has theirs, except Franky Shea. He has only three dollars and twenty cents. I curse him and then Tom Murray slugs him, starts slapping him, venting his rage at Don on Franky.

"Hey, hey," I yell. "Maybe the girls are cheaper than we think. Anyway, if he needs some more money, I'll loan it to him." This surprises all of us, especially Franky and me. We both know I don't really like Franky that well. But at times like this, I dislike Tom more than enough. So. . . .

Gravely then, with uneasy glances flickering between us, we recount the money and speculate on exactly how much we'll really need. That's the unknown quantity—how much does a girl cost? A whore? Standing in the close hallway of this Catholic high school, we can think of no one who knows such facts.

Then, evil-leader of them all, I announce: "Hell, I'll call them. They've got a phone, haven't they?" I grin smugly, proud to have thought of it first. But the bell rings and we have to wait until lunch time to call.

At noon, across the street from the school, I sit in a service station telephone booth, carefully looking up the number of Acme Rooms—all such places of business hide behind this ingenious disguise. I find the number, write it neatly in my palm, open the door slightly and murmur to my friends: "Bless you my sons. When was your last confession?" They all grin and I close the door and theatrically dial.

An indifferent feminine voice answers and replies to my question. "All rooms here are five dollars, mister." There is a click as the connection is cut.

"Five," I announce solemnly as I climb out of my confessional. The remainder of the afternoon, we plot vengence against Brandon and wish time, time, time would hurry. We are not going to the Acme until after dark, seven o'clock. As I listen to talk about parallelograms and side-angle-side, I wonder doubtfully how we'll ever last until seven. My muscles are fluttering and jumping.

At three-thirty, we race with relieved shouts and ragged laughter out of school, Don Brandon is waiting for us across the street, a patronizing smirk fixed on his thin lips. Before we can grab him, accuse him, he waves a five-dollar bill at us. He's got more, he declares. Since six this morning he's been driving a truck for a dollar an hour. As soon as he'd earned eight dollars, he'd quit. He has a total of ten, he brags, and is not going to lend *any* of it to *any*body. "Beer," he grins thirstily. "Beer and broads, bring them on." And all of us, wrestling and punching one another, chant "yes, yes." Passersby stare at us. We leap down the street, pent excitement jerking our limbs, voices, thoughts. We are anxious for the Big Game.

At the drugstore we swarm into a booth, crowding each other, smoking, arguing, ordering, sipping, hoping time will disappear. Behind our bright, agitated eyes we are all planning just how we're going to act with the girl we'll buy at seven o'clock. Cool and steady, I direct myself. And unrushed. Get your money's worth, is my basic consideration.

As other students come and take booths about us, we eye them with open superiority. They instantly become objects of our scorn, pitifully unsophisticated and innocent. Dull, unimaginably clean-minded, they sit around us mindlessly munching their Cokes and sundaes. We laugh outrageously and they look up, puzzled by our outbursts and this drives us to further hilarity. Those pathetically sinless, bewildered expressions. The manager comes back and asks us to please be a little quieter and we grin false obedience at him.

Then I see Marjorie. As I stand up my companions hoot and yell, kidding me, warning me in merciless, loud voices to be careful, not to become too exhausted before we meet at six-thirty. Luckily, Marjorie doesn't understand any of this as I hurry off to the counter in front. There, I buy her a phosphate, and smile with exaggerated innocence. "Margie, uhn, the track team has a meeting tonight at about seven at the gym, so I guess I can't make it over." Intently, I concentrate on my drink.

"What about after?" she asks. For a week I have devised elaborate excuses for not seeing her. By now she is becoming hurt and distrustful. I can't blame her. I just hope she holds on until after tonight.

"Sure, if it's not too late." I try to be positive, yet vague.

Solemnly, she finishes her drink. Then, with exceptional quiet, she watches me. Doesn't say anything, merely looks at me steadily. Immediately, I begin hitching my shoulders and scratching and wiggling.

Pretty soon, Marjorie breaks the silence: "Are you going to come over tonight or not?" That's all, just that simple question.

"Yes. Yes, I am," I promise—both her and myself. "But it might be kind of late."

"Are you *really* going to a track team meeting?"

"Yes, I am," I lie and grit my teeth. In spite of my recent desire to be sinister, I dislike lying to Marjorie. Once more, she gazes silently at me with her smooth, little girl's face. Scratching my ear, I grin back, senselessly. After a moment, she picks up her books.

"I'll walk you home," I tell her.

"No, I'm meeting Mom over at the dime store. I'll see you tonight. OK?"

"Sure." I grab her hand and squeeze those small, doll-like fingers.

Six-thirty, six-thirty. six-thirty, I tell myself giddily. By the clock at the back of the drugstore, it now is six-thirty—rendezvous hour for the Sinister Six. Cleverly, I have fortified myself for the ravages of this evening with a healthy supper and eight multi-vitamin pills . . . which make me belch. Presently, I am watching the clock and holding my breath, hoping to cure the belches.

Spang. In burst my fellow evildoers, shouting. They are practically rubbing their hands in anticipation. Spilling nervous excitement all about us, we huddle and count the money again. Don has relented and contributes part of his ten dollars for the beer, as do I.

When we arrive at the Acme Rooms, we scurry almost soundlessly up the steps to the door and, as chief evil-one, I press the buzzer. A little nervously, I set myself for this first, peripheral encounter. For tonight's occasion, I have carefully dressed in my adventurous best: a blue and white polka-dotted, long-sleeved shirt, pressed Levi's, white sweat socks and newly shined shoes. With a clever flair for the needs of the evening, I have worn no underwear. The polished door before me opens slightly and a woman stares at me. "Just a minute," she says and I can hear her trundle away.

"What the hell," mutters Curly Franklin impatiently. "What's going on?"

Then the door swings wide and a plump, henna-haired woman of about forty-five or so, examines us. "Well, boys, what can I do for you?"

"Girls," cries Brandon. "Girls, girls."

The woman chuckles. "How old are you boys, anyway?"

"Old enough," I tell her with ingenious brashness and move into the doorway. My companions hoot and laugh approvingly at this.

"Looks like you've come prepared." She flicks a red fingernail at the case of beer under my arm.

"Did you bring any money?" she asks with a smile.

We all wave dollar bills at her and she stands back, inviting us in with a generous gesture. Like eager children, I'm afraid, we crowd in, gawking around with immense, unrestrained curiosity.

"Hey, hey," chants Jerry Donovan, pushing past me, snapping his fingers in time to some personally heard music. "Hey, hey."

With an amused expression, the woman takes us into a parlor-like room furnished with a couch, several chairs and a jukebox. "Hey, hey," Jerry cries and pushes a quarter into the machine.

There is no one in the amber-lit room and we all look at each other a little nervously, disappointedly. To indicate we mean business, I slap the case of beer down on the couch and tear it open.

"Girls," Tom Murray says. "We'd like to see some girls, huh?"

Nodding, the woman counts us and hurries out.

Then, as Jerry's quarter begins to work and music comes bouncing out of the jukebox, we hear spiked heels in the hallway and swing around in a single, intent group. The girls—they are women, to my surprise—are all dressed in short, fluffly costumes. Like chorus girls; I think dimly. But the material is awfully thin and you can easily see their breasts through it. We stare. We stare with great intensity. Here it is. This is *sex*. The women we'll possess in a few moments. The confrontation threatens for an instant to become almost grim. Then, thumb and forefinger clicking nervously, Jerry whispers: "Hey, heaayh." And we all grin at the lightly clad women across the room.

For a moment, I wish the lights were just a little dimmer, that we were each alone with a girl, that it was more . . . more romantic, I guess. But the long-checked lust coiling hungrily in my stomach, rapping impatiently at the base of my skull, overcomes all hesitations and I leer eagerly at the women. For an instant, I vaguely remember our plans for a mass orgy, my particular aim to select the best-looking, most gorgeous, most appealing whore in the world. But these are misty, evanescent thoughts, vanishing as one of the young ladies steps toward me and, with rather candid charm, smiles and administers a pleasant, professional caress. That is it—all my planning, my careful considerations disapear. There is really nothing at all in my mind, just the clotted web of blank desire. That's all. Sensation, but no thought. Laughing gently, she leads me from the parlor and, two doors down a carpeted hall, into a small room.

The room, I vaguely notice, has a table, a lamp and a single straight chair. Plus the bed, of course. The girl is quite merry and whispers something appealingly obscene in my ear. I don't really understand her, but I grin anyway and comment that the light is awfully bright.

"All the better to see you with, honey," she smiles and touches me again. As she unbuttons me, I ask what her name is.

"Shirley," she says and with warm water swabs me off. Squinting with embarrassment, I watch her pink-nailed fingers move efficiently over my skin.

"OK. Now, if you'll give me the money, I'll be right back, sweetie."

"Uh," I shrug uneasily. "How much is it?"

"What? Oh, haven't you been here before? My, my," she grins and squeezes my arm. "It's five dollars a round, sweetie. More, if you stay longer."

Rather blankly, I blink at her, wondering if she's overcharging me. Then automatically, I nod and hand her the money.

"Just take off your pants, baby. I'll be right back."

All these cold, directional remarks are reviving me from my trance and I stomp resolutely back down the hall into the now empty parlor and get a couple of beers. Back in the room, I take off all my clothes, draping my polka dotted shirt over the lamp, dimming it provocatively, I think. Then, naked, I open a beer and lay back on the bed, momentarily in command of myself.

"Hey," Shirley exclaims when she comes in. "You've got all your clothes off." Unzipping her dress, kicking off her shoes, she grins at me. "You're not bad looking, for a kid."

"I'm not a kid," I correct her. "You want a beer?"

"Well say, you know if you're in here too long, it's going to cost you more."

"Fine."

"OK, I'll take one." She gets a glass off the table and sits down beside me. She has rather long, pale brown hair and a wide, friendly mouth. Opening the beer for her, I stare at her breasts. They seem nice—I really have few comparisons, books, primarily. And below her navel her hair is black. This seems disturbingly incongruous to me and I realize that her long, light hair is dyed.

She takes the beer and, with a slim hand on my thigh, drinks.

"Humm, that's nice." Quickly, she finishes her glass and leans over me. "Come on, honey, let's go," she purrs roughly.

And then, then, with a deft, practiced movement, she runs her tongue from my ear downward, downward . . . I'm sure I groan, at least, for I'm close to crying out in surprise. Sensations totally unexpected break in on me and after a moment she skillfully pulls me over on top of her. Desperately trying to clear my head, to refocus my vision, I blink against the red, clogged web of turbulence and amazement—totally without result. And then, easily, still smiling, she eases me off and steps away from the bed. Quite numbly, quite bereft of any feeling at all now, I blankly study the ceiling above me. What has happened? I ask myself. What has really taken place? What did I really do—I mean, feel? I don't know. I haven't the slightest idea. A stirring numbness is the only impression reaching my mind.

"OK, honey. Better get up and into your clothes," Shirley announces with that ever-present grin in her voice. Did she experience anything? I wonder. No. Whores aren't supposed to. Then, in spite of her indifferent, abrupt instructions, I have a difficult time believing Shirley is really a whore. I have the impression that she'll now get dressed in street clothes and we'll walk out of this place together, preferably hand in hand. She's become my girl—even if I haven't felt anything, nothing I can remember, at least. This fact and the money I gave her doesn't matter. The act does. That makes her my girl. Watching as she stoops, picking up her little dress, I see her breasts sag and as she bends beside the lamp, wiggling a foot into a shoe, the light cuts unbecoming lines beneath her eyes and all at once I understand that she is older than I, much older. She is, well, maybe almost my mother's age.

"How old are you, Shirley?"

Frowning, she glances at me, then shrugs carelessly. "Oh, about twenty-seven."

Eleven years older than I am, maybe even more. Slowly, I get up and dress. In the hallway I pull myself along despondently, wearily. From the parlor comes the clatter of my friends' noisy banter and as we enter, I put my hand on Shirley's loose flank, wondering silently if I'll ever see her again.

Laughing at the girls, patting them familiarly, we tumble with our beer down the stairs. On the street, we exultantly brag to one another, replacing old lies with new ones. Elaborately, we gesture and giggle how it was with the whore we had. Confidently, we tell each other we're coming back as soon as we have another five dollars. Great, it's absolutely great, we all declare, agree.

Then, as we approach the corner, I unaccountably, fiercely, feel I must see Marjorie—immediately. Handing the remaining beer to my companions, I leave them, offering no explanation and their jeers echo down the sidewalk as I hurry away.

In the front room, she is waiting for me. As I say hello to her parents I am certain they can see the stain of my lechery, my wantonness, my new strangeness on my face, hands. Insistently, I pull Marjorie out onto the porch, away from her parent's eyes.

"Margie," I say with a big breath. "It's good to see you." And I try to kiss her.

"Is your meeting over already?" she asks coolly.

"Yes." I hunch my shoulders and look out at the lawn. "Margie, uh, you know . . . that I like you. You know that, don't you?"

Her blond hair swings softly and I want to touch it.

"After last week," she says crossly, "I don't know anything. I mean," her voice arches unhappily, "I mean, what's going on, anyway?"

"Nothing." I want to reassure her. "Nothing at all. Really. Just this track thing. It's all over now." At this moment, I am ready to tell her any fantastic lie I can think of. Now, close beside me, the warm scent of her floating around us, she's infinitely more real, more *possible* than ever before; both abruptly close and very far from tonight's experience. "Margie, I love you. I really do." This is not a lie, I realize at once. Yet, I am not sure it is the truth. It is something I feel, a lush unstoppable longing reaching my limbs, startling my fingertips. It is something, something absolutely new. For an instant I possess a totally unfamiliar confidence that I know much more about her than she can possibly know about me. In that moment, as our bodies lightly touch, I understand what it is I desire; that portion of her, of me, is no longer frightening and thoroughly dangerous. I want to share my total physical discovery, the immense freedom of it with Margie. And tell her much, more more. How this emotion I feel for her now is a gift of the *instructive*, nerveless lust that broke over me in that room at the Acme. That there is no longer any reason to be afraid of one another.

Immediately, I sense that these things will only frighten her. Besides, I have no truly accurate words for it. Instead of saying any of this, I touch her velvet hair, the deep curve of her cheek and whisper the word love, love, love, helplessly, happily—my alternating dual dreams of the world narrowed, abruptly, to one.

THE LOTTERY
Shirley Jackson

The morning of June 27th was clear and sunny, with the fresh warmth of a full-summer day; the flowers were blossoming profusely and the grass was richly green. The people of the village began to gather in the square, between the post office and the bank, around ten o'clock; in some towns there were so many people that the lottery took two days and had to be started on June 26th, but in this village, where there were only about three hundred people, the whole lottery took less than two hours, so it could begin at ten o'clock in the morning and still be through in time to allow the villagers to get home for noon dinner.

The children assembled first, of course. School was recently over for the summer, and the feeling of liberty sat uneasily on most of them; they tended to gather together quietly for a while before they broke into boisterous play, and their talk was still of the classroom and the teacher, of books and reprimands. Bobby Martin had already stuffed his pockets full of stones, and the other boys soon followed his example, selecting the smoothest and roundest stones; Bobby and Harry Jones and Dickie Delacroix—the villagers pronounced this name "Dellacroy"—eventually made a great pile of stones in one corner of the square and guarded it against the raids of the other boys. The girls stood aside, talking among themselves, looking over their shoulders at the boys, and the very small children rolled in the dust or clung to the hands of their older brothers or sisters.

Soon the men began to gather, surveying their own children, speaking of planting and rain, tractors and taxes. They stood together, away from the pile of stones in the corner, and their jokes were quiet and they smiled rather than laughed. The women, wearing faded house dresses and sweaters, came shortly after their menfolk. They greeted one another and exchanged bits of gossip as they went to join their husbands. Soon the women, standing by their husbands, began to call to their children, and the children came reluctantly, having to be called four or five times. Bobby Martin ducked under his mother's grasping hand and ran, laughing, back to the pile of stones. His father spoke up sharply, and Bobby came quickly and took his place between his father and his oldest brother.

The lottery was conducted—as were the square-dances, the teen-age club, the Halloween program—by Mr. Summers, who had time and energy to devote to civic activities. He was a round-faced, jovial man and he ran the coal business, and people were sorry for him, because he had no children and his wife was a scold. When he arrived in the square, carrying the black wooden box, there was a murmur of conversation among the villagers, and he waved and called, "Little late today, folks." The postmaster, Mr. Graves, followed him, carrying a three-legged stool, and the stool was put in the center of the square and Mr. Summers set the black box down on it. The villagers kept their distance, leaving a space between themselves and the stool, and when Mr. Summers said, "Some of you fellows want to give me a hand?" there was a hesitation before two men, Mr. Martin and his oldest son, Baxter, came forward to hold the box steady on the stool while Mr. Summers stirred up the papers inside it.

The original paraphernalia for the lottery had been lost long ago, and the black box now resting on the stool had been put into use even before Old Man Warner, the oldest man in town, was born. Mr. Summers spoke frequently to the villagers about making a new box, but no one liked to upset even as much tradition as was represented by the black box. There was a story that the present box had been made with some pieces of the box that had preceded it, the one that had been constructed when the first people settled down to make a village here. Every year, after the lottery, Mr. Summers began talking again about a new box, but every year the subject was allowed to fade off without anything's being done. The black box grew shabbier each year; by now it was no longer completely black but splintered badly along one side to show the original wood color, and in some places faded or stained.

Mr. Martin and his oldest son, Baxter, held the black box securely on the stool until Mr. Summers had stirred the papers thoroughly with his hand. Because so much of the ritual had been forgotten or discarded, Mr. Summers had been successful in having slips of paper substituted for the chips of wood that had been used for generations. Chips of wood, Mr. Summers had argued, had been all very well when the village was tiny, but now that the population was more than three hundred and likely to keep on growing, it was necessary to use something that would fit more easily into the black box. The night before the lottery, Mr. Summers and Mr. Graves made up the slips of paper and put them in the box, and it was then taken to the safe of Mr. Summers' coal company and locked up until Mr. Summers was ready to take it to the square next morning. The rest of the year, the box was put away, sometimes one place, sometimes another: it had spent one year in Mr. Graves's barn and another year underfoot in the post office, and sometimes it was set on a shelf in the Martin grocery and left there.

There was a great deal of fussing to be done before Mr. Summers declared the lottery open. There were the lists to make up—of heads of families, heads of households in each family, members of each household in each family. There was the proper swearing-in of Mr. Summers by the postmaster, as the official of the lottery; at one time, some people remembered, there had been a recital of some sort, performed by the official of the lottery, a perfunctory, tuneless chant that had been rattled off duly each year; some people believed that the official of the lottery used to stand just so when he said or sang it, others believed that he was supposed to walk among the people, but years and years ago this part of the ritual had been allowed to lapse. There had been, also, a ritual salute, which the official of the lottery had had to use in addressing each person who came up to draw from the box, but this also changed with time, until now it was felt necessary only for the official to speak to each person approaching. Mr. Summers was very good at all this; in his clean white shirt and blue jeans, with one hand resting carelessly on the black box, he seemed very proper and important as he talked interminably to Mr. Graves and the Martins.

Just as Mr. Summers finally left off talking and turned to the assembled villagers, Mrs. Hutchinson came hurriedly along the path to the square, her sweater thrown over her shoulders, and slid into place in the back of the crowd. "Clean forgot what day it was," she said to Mrs. Delacroix, who stood next to her, and they both laughed softly. "Thought my old man was out back stacking wood," Mrs. Hutchinson went on, "and then I looked out the window and the kids was gone, and then I remembered it was the twenty-seventh and came a-running." She dried her hands on her apron, and Mrs. Delacroix said, "You're in time though. They're still talking away up there."

Mrs. Hutchinson craned her neck to see through the crowd and found her husband and children standing near the front. She tapped Mrs. Delacroix on the arm as a farewell and began to make her way through the crowd. The people separated good-humoredly to let her through; two or three people said, in voices just loud enough to be heard across the crowd, "Here comes your Missus, Hutchinson," and "Bill, she made it after all." Mrs. Hutchinson reached her husband, and Mr. Summers, who had been waiting, said cheerfully, "Thought we were going to have to get on without you, Tessie." Mrs. Hutchinson said, grinning, "Wouldn't have me leave m'dishes in the sink, now, would you, Joe?," and soft laughter ran through the crowd as the people stirred back into position after Mrs. Hutchinson's arrival.

"Well, now," Mr. Summers said soberly, "guess we better get started, get this over with, so's we can go back to work. Anybody ain't here?"

"Dunbar," several people said. "Dunbar, Dunbar."

Mr. Summers consulted his list. "Clyde Dunbar," he said. "That's right. He's broke his leg, hasn't he. Who's drawing for him?"

"Me, I guess," a woman said, and Mr. Summers turned to look at her. "Wife draws for her husband," Mr. Summers said. "Don't you have a grown boy to do it for you, Janey?" Although Mr. Summers and everyone else in the village knew the answer perfectly well, it was the business of the official of the lottery to ask such questions formally. Mr. Summers waited with an expression of polite interest while Mrs. Dunbar answered.

"Horace's not but sixteen yet," Mrs. Dunbar said regretfully. "Guess I gotta fill in for the old man this year."

"Right," Mr. Summers said. He made a note on the list he was holding. Then he asked, "Watson boy drawing this year?"

A tall boy in the crowd raised his hand. "Here," he said. "I'm drawing for m'mother and me." He blinked his eyes nervously and ducked his head as several voices in the crowd said things like "Good fellow, Jack," and "Glad to see your mother's got a man to do it."

"Well," Mr. Summers said, "guess that's everyone. Old Man Warner make it?"

"Here," a voice said, and Mr. Summers nodded.

A sudden hush fell on the crowd as Mr. Summers cleared his throat and looked at the list. "All ready?" he called. "Now, I'll read the names—heads of families first—and the men come up and take a paper out of the box. Keep the paper folded in your hand without looking at it until everyone has had a turn. Everything clear?"

The people had done it so many times that they only half listened to the directions; most of them were quiet, wetting their lips, not looking around. Then Mr. Summers raised one hand high and said, "Adams." A man disengaged himself from the crowd and came forward. "Hi, Steve," Mr. Summers said, and Mr. Adams said, "Hi, Joe." They grinned at one another humorlessly and nervously. Then Mr. Adams reached into the black box and took out a folded paper. He held it firmly by one corner as he turned and went hastily back to his place in the crowd, where he stood a little apart from his family, not looking down at his hand.

"Allen," Mr. Summers said. "Anderson . . . Bentham."

"Seems like there's no time at all between lotteries any more," Mrs. Delacroix said to Mrs. Graves in the back row. "Seems like we got through with the last one only last week."

"Time sure goes fast," Mrs. Graves said.

"Clark. . . . Delacroix."

"There goes my old man," Mrs. Delacroix said. She held her breath while her husband went forward.

"Dunbar," Mr. Summers said, and Mrs. Dunbar went steadily to the box while one of the women said, "Go on, Janey," and another said, "There she goes."

"We're next," Mrs. Graves said. She watched while Mr. Graves came around from the side of the box, greeted Mr. Summers gravely, and selected a slip of paper from the box. By now, all through the crowd there were men holding the small folded papers in their large hands, turning them over and over nervously. Mrs. Dunbar and her two sons stood together, Mrs. Dunbar holding the slip of paper.

"Harburt. . . . Hutchinson."

"Get up there, Bill," Mrs. Hutchinson said, and the people near her laughed.

"Jones."

"They do say," Mr. Adams said to Old Man Warner, who stood next to him, "that over in the north village they're talking of giving up the lottery."

Old Man Warner snorted. "Pack of crazy fools," he said: "Listening to the young folks, nothing's good enough for *them*. Next thing you know, they'll be wanting to go back to living in caves, nobody work any more, live *that* way for a while. Used to be a saying about 'Lottery in June, corn be heavy soon.' First thing you know, we'd all be eating stewed chickweed and acorns. There's *always* been a lottery," he added petulantly. "Bad enough to see young Joe Summers up there joking with everybody."

"Some places have already quit lotteries," Mrs. Adams said.

"Nothing but trouble in *that*," Old Man Warner said stoutly. "Pack of young fools."

"Martin." And Bobby Martin watched his father go forward. "Overdyke. . . . Percy."

"I wish they'd hurry," Mrs. Dunbar said to her older son. "I wish they'd hurry."

"They're almost through," her son said.

"You get ready to run tell Dad," Mrs. Dunbar said.

Mr. Summers called his own name and then stepped forward precisely and selected a slip from the box. Then he called, "Warner."

"Seventy-seventh year I been in the lottery," Old Man Warner said as he went though the crowd. "Seventy-seventh time."

"Watson." The tall boy came awkwardly through the crowd. Someone said, "Don't be nervous, Jack," and Mr. Summers said, "Take your time, son."

"Zanini."

After that, there was a long pause, a breathless pause, until Mr. Summers, holding his slip of paper in the air, said, "All right, fellows." For a minute, no one moved, and then all the slips of paper were opened. Suddenly, all the women began to speak at once, saying, "Who is it?" "Who's got it?" "Is it the Dunbars?" "Is it the Watsons?" Then the voices began to say, "It's Hutchinson. It's Bill." "Bill Hutchinson's got it."

"Go tell your father," Mrs. Dunbar said to her older son.

People began to look around to see the Hutchinsons. Bill Hutchinson was standing quiet, staring down at the paper in his hand. Suddenly, Tessie Hutchinson shouted to Mr. Summers, "You didn't give him time enough to take any paper he wanted. I saw you. It wasn't fair!"

"Be a good sport, Tessie," Mrs. Delacroix called, and Mrs. Graves said, "All of us took the same chance."

"Shut up, Tessie," Bill Hutchinson said.

"Well, everyone," Mr. Summers said, "that was done pretty fast, and now we've got to be hurrying a little more to get done in time." He consulted his next list. "Bill," he said, "you draw for the Hutchinson family. You got any other households in the Hutchinsons?"

"There's Don and Eva," Mrs. Hutchinson yelled. "Make *them* take their chance!"

"Daughters draw with their husbands' families, Tessie," Mr. Summers said gently. "You know that as well as anyone else."

"It wasn't *fair*," Tessie said.

"I guess not, Joe," Bill Hutchinson said regretfully. "My daughter draws with her husband's family, that's only fair. And I've got no other family except the kids."

"Then, as far as drawing for families is concerned, it's you," Mr. Summers said in explanation, "and as far as drawing for households is concerned, that's you, too. Right?"

"Right," Bill Hutchinson said.

"How many kids, Bill?" Mr. Summers asked formally.

"Three," Bill Hutchinson said. "There's Bill, Jr., and Nancy, and little Dave. And Tessie and me."

"All right, then," Mr. Summers said. "Harry, you got their tickets back?"

Mr. Graves nodded and held up the slips of paper. "Put them in the box, then," Mr. Summers directed. "Take Bill's and put it in."

"I think we ought to start over," Mrs. Hutchinson said, as quietly as she could. "I tell you it wasn't *fair*. You didn't give him time enough to choose. Everybody saw that."

Mr. Graves had selected the five slips and put them in the box, and he dropped all the papers but those onto the ground, where the breeze caught them and lifted them off.

"Listen, everybody," Mrs. Hutchinson was saying to the people around her.

"Ready, Bill?" Mr. Summers asked, and Bill Hutchinson, with one quick glance around at his wife and children, nodded.

"Remember," Mr. Summers said, "take the slips and keep them folded until each person has taken one. Harry, you help little Dave." Mr. Graves took the hand of the little boy, who came willingly with him up to the box. "Take a paper out of the box, Davy," Mr Summers said. Davy put his hand into the box and laughed. "Take just *one* paper," Mr. Summers said. "Harry, you hold it for him." Mr. Graves took the child's hand and removed the folded paper from the tight fist and held it while little Dave stood next to him and looked up at him wonderingly.

"Nancy next," Mr. Summers said. Nancy was twelve, and her school friends breathed heavily as she went forward, switching her skirt, and took a slip daintily from the box. "Bill, Jr.," Mr. Summers said, and Billy, his face red and his feet overlarge, nearly knocked the box over as he got a paper out. "Tessie," Mr. Summers said. She hesitated for a minute, looking around defiantly, and then set her lips and went up to the box. She snatched a paper out and held it behind her.

"Bill," Mr. Summers said, and Bill Hutchinson reached into the box and felt around, bringing his hand out at last with the slip of paper in it.

The crowd was quiet. A girl whispered, "I hope it's not Nancy," and the sound of the whisper reached the edges of the crowd.

"It's not the way it used to be," Old Man Warner said clearly. "People ain't the way they used to be."

"All right," Mr. Summers said. "Open the papers. Harry, you open little Dave's."

Mr. Graves opened the slip of paper and there was a general sigh through the crowd as he held it up and everyone could see that it was blank. Nancy and Bill, Jr., opened theirs at the same time, and both beamed and laughed, turning around to the crowd and holding their slips of paper above their heads.

"Tessie," Mr. Summers said. There was a pause, and then Mr. Summers looked at Bill Hutchinson, and Bill unfolded his paper and showed it. It was blank.

"It's Tessie," Mr. Summers said, and his voice was hushed. "Show us her paper, Bill."

Bill Hutchinson went over to his wife and forced the slip of paper out of her hand. It had a black spot on it, the black spot Mr. Summers had made the night before with the heavy pencil in the coal-company office. Bill Hutchinson held it up, and there was a stir in the crowd.

"All right, folks," Mr. Summers said. "Let's finish quickly."

Although the villagers had forgotten the ritual and lost the original black box, they still remembered to use stones. The pile of stones the boys had made earlier was ready; there were stones on the ground with the blowing scraps of paper that had come out of the box. Mrs. Delacroix selected a stone so large she had to pick it up with both hands and turned to Mrs. Dunbar. "Come on," she said. "Hurry up."

Mrs. Dunbar had small stones in both hands, and she said, gasping for breath, "I can't run at all. You'll have to go ahead and I'll catch up with you."

The children had stones already, and someone gave little Davy Hutchinson a few pebbles.

Tessie Hutchinson was in the center of a cleared space by now, and she held her hands out desperately as the villagers moved in on her. "It isn't fair," she said. A stone hit her on the side of the head.

Old Man Warner was saying, "Come on, come on, everyone." Steve Adams was in the front of the crowd of villagers, with Mrs. Graves beside him.

"It isn't fair, it isn't right," Mrs. Hutchinson screamed, and then they were upon her.

Issues for Discussion

1. Edwin H. Sutherland declares that deviant behavior, like nondeviant behavior, is learned; it is not the product of individual pathology. Moreover, one engages in criminal activity as a result of an excess of definitions favorable to law violation. The group of boys in Hugh Allyn Hunt's "Acme Rooms and Sweet Marjorie Russell" are determined to live out their sexual fantasies. What illegal options for fulfilling their desires could the boys choose?
2. Go back to Part VII and reread Farrell's "Young Convicts." Compare and contrast the social and economic environments of Farrell's gang with Hunt's gang. Account for the radically different behavior of the two groups, using the assumptions proposed by the differential associations theorists.
3. Who were the most important role models for the boys in Farrell's gang and Hunt's gang? Explain how these models encouraged or discouraged criminal activity.
4. The activities of the gang members in Farrell's and Hunt's stories were affected by the lawmaking bodies of their communities. Compare the legal systems in both communities and explain what the boys would learn from each system.
5. Marjorie Russell appears to be instrumental in confirming to her boy friend the mores of their town. What are these seemingly contradictory rules of moral conduct, and what is Marjorie's role in enforcing them?
6. In Shirley Jackson's "The Lottery," the townspeople willingly engage in a strange ritual. Jackson writes, "The lottery was conducted—as were the square dances, the teen-age club, the Halloween program—by Mr. Summers, who had time and energy to devote to civic activities." What was the purpose of this bizarre "civic activity"?
7. Using the statements about differential association theory, explain why the lottery has such strong support from the townspeople.
8. What do the black box, the stones, Mr. Summers, Old Man Warner, and the lottery represent?

ISSUES FOR DISCUSSION

9. Discuss the significance of the following dialogue:

   "They do say," Mr. Adams said to Old Man Warner, who stood next to him, "that over in the north village they're talking of giving up the lottery."
   Old Man Warner snorted. "Pack of crazy fools," he said. "Listening to the young folks, nothing's good enough for *them*. Next thing you know, they'll be wanting to go back to living in caves, nobody work any more, live *that* way for a while. Used to be a saying about 'Lottery in June, corn be heavy soon.' First thing you know, we'd all be eating stewed chickweed and acorns. There's *always* been a lottery," he added petulantly. "Bad enough to see young Joe Summers up there joking with everybody."

10. A traditional taboo of society has been the unjustified killing of another human being. Does the outcome of the lottery serve to "legalize" murder?

PART IX

Predicting Deviant Behavior

Over the past two hundred years many scholars have attempted to inform us of the causes of criminal behavior. Indicators of crime causation have included body structure; inherited genetic defects; psychoses; the social, economic, and political structure; demons; and the effects of labeling. Most theories have enjoyed relatively brief periods of acceptance before being subjected to well-reasoned and often fatal criticism. The criticism has occasionally been pointed. For example, one critic of the somatology (body type) school sarcastically stated that this system of identifying persons likely to be deviant was a "new Phrenology in which the bumps on the buttocks take the place of the bumps of the head."[1] A critic of the school of endocrinology wrote: "The fact is that as far as the endocrine system and its relation to personality behavior are concerned, we are still almost completely in a world of the unknown, and to resort to that system for an explanation of criminality is merely to attempt to explain the known by the unknown."[2]

Even those who supported a particular theory have not always escaped the wrath of critics: "It [phrenology] finally succumbed and is accepted today only by those who have a flair for exploiting the gullible and ignorant who accept and even crave oversimplified explanation of character."[3] The

1. See S. L. Washburn, "Review of W. H. Sheldon, *Varieties of Delinquent Youth*," *American Anthropologist* 53 (July 1951): 561–63.

2. Quoted by M. F. Ashley Montagu, "The Biologist Looks at Crime," *Annals of the American Academy of Political and Social Science*, September 1941, p. 55, from Hopkins, *Endocrinology* (New York: Norton, 1941), p. 348.

3. Harry Elmer Barnes and Negley K. Teeters, *New Horizons in Criminology* (Englewood Cliffs, N.J.: Prentice-Hall, 1945), p. 161.

currently popular theory of differential association which suggests that criminal behavior depends on the length and intensity of exposure to negative influences, has received extensive criticism for being vague, myopic, too comprehensive, anemic, and the like. Sheldon Glueck notes that if becoming deviant depends on an excess of definitions favoring deviance, then the "biggest criminals of all would be professors of criminology, prison guards, and prison chaplains."[4]

Yet the controversy rages. No one theory (or statement) explains all deviance. Currently, enough speculation about why crime exists to allow the researcher to "explain" every single criminal act. But many explanations emerge after the fact. For example, persons raised in essentially the same environment, even in the same families, exhibit different behavior. The theory of differential association informs us that in these cases one individual learned to be deviant because of his association with a strong role-model group that was deviant. But the question remains, Why did one person in the family choose to associate with the "bad" group, and the others in the family with the "good" group? Does the process of association, and the behavior that is allegedly dependent on that association, occur completely by chance? If so, then indeed we will continue to explain deviance *ex post facto*, straining to make the circumstances fit the theory.

A potentially more trying problem exists. The task of criminologists has been to isolate qualities that are indicators of deviant behavior. These criteria are separable into qualities inherent in the individual (e.g., genetic or psychological impairment, external qualities) and qualities relating to the environment (e.g., social class, unemployment, peer groups). Early studies, such as those typical of the classical school, attempted to isolate these qualities by studying persons *convicted* of criminal behavior. More sophisticated researchers began using control groups to compare the individual and environmental differences between criminals and noncriminals. When it became obvious no statistically significant differences existed between the populations, new explanations of criminality were needed, and provided.

Unfortunately, the use of control groups has not dispelled the suspicion that we are mystified about who is likely to become a law violator. We remain mystified about the cause of crime primarily because we do not know the extent of crime in society. The data base is muddled because (1) not all crime is reported; (2) not all people who commit crimes are apprehended; (3) not all persons who are apprehended are arrested; (4) not all persons who are arrested are charged with a crime by the prosecutor or grand jury; (5) of those charged, only a limited number of suspects are

---

4. "Theory and Fact in Criminology: A Criticism of Differential Association," *British Journal of Delinquency* 7 (October 1956): 92–109.

indicted at the preliminary hearing by the judge; and (6) not all persons, even those who are guilty, are declared guilty by judge or jury.

In order to develop a more accurate picture of who has been deviant so that comparisons with nondeviants could be made, researchers conducted studies sampling populations previously believed to be relatively free of criminal activity.[5] The results have uncovered some fascinating data. Virtually every college student surveyed admitted to having engaged in some form of criminal conduct, but remained free from any official charge. Moreover, in a sample of 1600 adults, 91 percent admitted committing one or more of 49 violations presented to them. Males committed an average of 18 offenses, and females 11 offenses. Forty-six percent of the males admitted committing at least one felony, as compared with 27 percent of the females.[6] Studies of so-called white-collar criminals reveal equally surprising high rates of "respectable" citizen participation in crime.[7] These studies raise the horrifying thought that no crime theory is accurate because crime theories are predicated on the notion that criminality varies among individuals in different social, economic, and political environments. If it is true that almost all of us are law violators, the next generation of criminologists may have to narrow the focus of their work to ascertaining why some people engage in sporadic deviance while others are habitual law violators.

Stated simply, no adequate theory of crime causation exists, just as no theory of why people refrain from criminal activity exists. Most studies immediately miss the mark by examining deviance in a general manner. The feeling is that "deviance is deviance is deviance." But recent data inform us that the professional criminal tends to engage in a narrow range of illegal activity. A professional burglar becomes a murderer only accidentally, not by choice. Professional killers do not ordinarily rob or rape, and so on. Consequently, we remain either uninformed or misinformed about why specific people commit specific crimes.

The problem of predicting deviance is further compounded by our ignorance about the relationship between deviance and the effects of formal (i.e., legal) codes. The law has been society's primary official vehicle to order behavior. The efficacy of prescribing acceptable or deviant behavior, however, has yet to be determined. Statistics are available informing the social scientist whether the extent and type of criminal behavior have

---

5. See J. S. Wallenstein and C. J. Wyle, "Our Law-Abiding, Law Breakers," *Probation* 25 (March–April 1947): 107–12; and Sophia Rubinson, *Can Delinquency Be Measured* (New York: Columbia University Press, 1976).

6. See Wallenstein and Wyle, "Law-Abiding, Law Breakers," pp. 107–12.

7. For an excellent collection of articles relating to white-collar crime, see Gilbert Creis and Robert F. Meier, eds., *White-Collar Crime: Offenses in Business, Politics, and the Professions* (New York: Free Press, 1977).

increased or decreased over particular periods of time. But these data measure only "official" crime. Criminal activity that is undetectable, or for which arrests are not made, confounds the data's accuracy. Nor are statistics informative as to how many persons are unaffected by formal law. For example, if murder or the use of heroin were decriminalized, how many more people would commit murder or use the drug? Do existing laws prevent to any significant degree fornication or the use of marijuana? The fact is, we do not know the impact of the formal law because we do not know the extent to which informal codes (folkways, mores, customs) order behavior.

The efficacy of formal law is only partially obscured by incomplete data and the effect of informal constraints on behavior. The alleged ordering effects of law lie in the threat or actual use of various retributive techniques. Nevertheless, it is questionable whether punishment is a reliable behavior modification tool. Few criminals ply their trade believing they will be arrested and convicted. It seems that definitive statements about the efficacy of law cannot be made as long as we remain mystified as to why laws are violated, or not violated.

It is perhaps too much to expect that a foolproof theory of deviant behavior will ever emerge. The researcher is confronted with countless confounding variables when studying human beings in their natural environment. We are simply too uninformed about such important intangibles as cognition, motiviation, and perception. A review of the state of the art leaves the impression that we are somehow nearer a viable theory than were our forefathers, but also that much work remains to be done.

The true account depicted in the court case of *The Queen* v. *Dudley and Stephens* illustrates one of the difficulties of consistently and accurately predicting deviant behavior. The behavior of the seamen would ordinarily offend the sensibilities of civilized people, including the seamen. Here, existing circumstances mandate and control their actions. And, in these situations, the uncharacteristic behavior is not susceptible to the predictive theories of the criminologist.

Nathaniel Hawthorne's "The Minister's Black Veil" also illustrates the difficulties inherent in predicting who is likely to act in a deviant manner. This story serves to challenge the notion that certain individuals are innately "criminaloid." Rather, the story demonstrates that we all may be capable of criminal conduct under certain extenuating circumstances.

THE QUEEN v. DUDLEY AND STEPHENS

Queen's Bench Division, 1884.
L.R. 14 Q.B.D. 273.

INDICTMENT for the murder of Richard Parker on the high seas within the jurisdiction of the Admiralty.

At the trial before Huddleston, B. . . . November 7, 1884, the jury, at the suggestion of the learned judge, found the facts of the case in a special verdict which stated "that on July 5, 1884, the prisoners, Thomas Dudley and Edward Stephens, with one Brooks, all able-bodied English seamen, and the deceased also an English boy, between seventeen and eighteen years of age, the crew of an English yacht, a registered English vessel, were cast away in a storm on the high seas 1600 miles from the Cape of Good Hope, and were compelled to put into an open boat belonging to the said yacht. That in this boat they had no supply of water and no supply of food, except two 1 lb. tins of turnips, and for three days they had nothing else to subsist upon. That on the fourth day they caught a small turtle, upon which they subsisted for a few days, and this was the only food they had up to the twentieth day when the act now in question was committed. That on the twelfth day the remains of the turtle were entirely consumed, and for the next eight days they had nothing to eat. That they had no fresh water, except such rain as they from time to time caught in their oilskin capes. That the boat was drifting on the ocean, and was probably more than 1000 miles away from land. That on the eighteenth day, when they had been seven days without food and five without water, the prisoners spoke to Brooks as to what should be done if no succour came, and suggested that some one should be sacrificed to save the rest, but Brooks dissented, and the boy, to whom they were understood to refer, was not consulted. That on the 24th of July, the day before the act now in question, the prisoner Dudley proposed to Stephens and Brooks that lots should be cast who should be put to death to save the rest, but Brooks refused to consent, and it was not put to the boy, and in point of fact there was no drawing of lots. That on that day the prisoners spoke of their having families, and suggested it would be better to kill the boy that their lives should be saved, and Dudley proposed that if there were no vessel in sight by the morrow morning the boy should be killed. That next day, the 25th of July, no vessel appearing, Dudley told Brooks that he had better go and have a sleep, and made signs to Stephens and Brooks that the boy had better be killed. The prisoner Stephens agreed to the act, but Brooks dissented from it. That the boy was then lying at the bottom of the boat quite helpless, and extremely weakened by famine and by drinking sea water, and unable to make any resistance, nor did he ever assent to his being killed. The prisoner Dudley offered a prayer asking forgiveness for them all if either of them should be tempted to commit a rash act, and that their souls might be saved. That Dudley, with the assent of Stephens, went to the boy, and telling him that his time was come, put a knife into his throat and killed him then and there; that the three men fed upon the body and blood of the boy for four days; that on the fourth day after the act had been committed the boat was picked up by a passing vessel, and the prisoners were rescued, still alive, but in the lowest state of prostration. That they were carried to the port of Falmouth, and committed for trial at Exeter. That if the men had not fed upon the body of the boy they would probaby not have survived to be so picked up and rescued, but would within the four days have died of famine. That the boy, being in a much weaker condition, was likely to have died before them. That at the time of the act in question there was no sail in sight, nor any reasonable prospect of relief. That under these circumstances there appeared to the prisoners every probability that unless they then fed or very soon fed upon the boy or one of themselves they would die of starvation. That there was no appreciable chance of saving life except by killing some one for the others to eat. That assuming any necessity to kill anybody, there was no greater necessity for killing the boy than any of the other three men. But whether upon the whole matter by the jurors found the killing of Richard Parker by Dudley and Stephens be felony and murder the jurors are ignorant, and pray the advice of the Court there upon, and if upon the whole matter the Court shall be of opinion that the killing of Richard Parker be felony and murder, then the jurors say that Dudley and Stephens were each guilty of felony and murder as alleged in the indictment." . . .

LORD COLERIDGE, C.J. . . . There remains to be considered the real question in the case—whether killing under the circumstances set forth in the verdict be or be not murder. The contention that it could be anything else was, to the minds of us all, both new and strange, and we stopped the Attorney General in his negative argument in order that we might hear what could be said in support of a proposition which appeared to us to be at once dangerous, immoral, and opposed to all legal principle and analogy. All, no doubt, that can be said has been urged before us, and we are now to consider and determine what it amounts to. First it is said that it follows from various definitions of murder in books of authority, which definitions imply, if they do not state, the doctrine, that in order to save your own life you may lawfully take away the life of another when that other is neither attempting nor threatening yours, nor is guilty of any illegal act whatever towards you or any one else. But if these definitions be looked at they will not be found to sustain this contention. The earliest in point of date is the passage cited to us from Bracton, who lived in the reign of Henry III. . . . But in the very passage as to necessity, on which reliance has been placed, it is clear that Bracton is speaking of necessity in the ordinary sense—the repelling of violence, violence justified so far as it was necessary for the object, any illegal violence used towards oneself. If, says Bracton, the necessity be *"evitabilis, et evadere posset absque occisone, tunc erit reus homicidii"*—words which shew clearly that he is thinking of physical danger from which escape may be possible, and that the *"inevitabilis necessitas"* of which he speaks as justifying homicide is a necessity of the same nature.

It is, if possible, yet clearer that the doctrine contended for receives no support from the great authority of Lord Hale. It is plain that in his view the necessity which justified homicide is that only which has always been and is now considered a justification. "In all these cases of homicide by necessity," says he, "as in pursuit of a felon, in killing him that assaults to rob, or comes to burn or break a house, or the like, which are in themselves no felony" (1 Hale's Pleas of the Crown, p. 491). . . .

"If a man be desperately assaulted and in peril of death, and cannot otherwise escape unless, to satisfy his assailant's fury, he will kill an innocent person then present, the fear and actual force will not acquit him of the crime and punishment of murder, if he commit the fact, for he ought rather to die himself than kill an innocent; but if he cannot otherwise save his own life the law permits him in his own defense to kill the assailant, for by the violence of the assault, and the offence committed upon him by the assailant himself, the law of nature, and necessity, hath made him his own protector *cum debito moderamine inculpatae tutelae.*" (Hale's Pleas of the Crown, vol. i. 51.)

But, further still, Lord Hale in the following chapter deals with the position asserted by the casuists, and sanctioned, as he says, by Grotius and Puffendorf, that in a case of extreme necessity, either of hunger or clothing; "theft is no theft, or at least not punishable as theft, as some even of our own lawyers have asserted the same." "But," says Lord Hale, "I take it that here in England, that rule, at least by the laws of England, is false; and therefore, if a person, being under necessity for want of victuals or clothes, shall upon that account clandestinely and *amino furandi* steal another man's goods, it is felony, and a crime by the laws of England punishable with death." (Hale, Pleas of the Crown, i. 54.) If, therefore, Lord Hale is clear—as he is—that extreme necessity of hunger does not justify larceny, what would he have said to the doctrine that it justified murder? . . .

Is there, then, any authority for the proposition which has been presented to us? Decided cases there are none. . . .

The American case cited by my Brother Stephen in his Digest, from Wharton on Homicide, in which it was decided, correctly indeed, that sailors had no right to throw passengers overboard to save themselves, but on the somewhat strange ground that the proper mode of determining who was to be sacrificed was to vote upon the subject by ballot, can hardly as my Brother Stephen says, be an authority satisfactory to a court in this country. . . .

The one real authority of former time is Lord Bacon, who, in his commentary on the maxim, *"necessitas inducit privilegium quoad jura privata,"* lays down the law as follows:—"Necessity carrieth a privilege in itself. Necessity is of three sorts—necessity of conservation of life, necessity of obedience, and necessity of the act of God or of a stranger. First of conservation of life; if a man steal viands to satisfy his present hunger, this is no felony nor larceny. So if divers be in danger of drowning by the casting away of some boat or barge, and one of them get to some plank, or on the boat's side to keep himself above water, and another to save his life thrust him from it, whereby he is drowned, this is neither *se defendendo* nor by misadventure, but justifiable." On this it is to be observed that Lord Bacon's propositon that stealing to satisfy hunger is no larceny . . . and is expressly contradicted by Lord Hale in the passage already cited. And for the proposition as to the plank or boat, it is said to be derived from the canonists. At any rate he cites no authority for it, and it must stand upon his own. Lord Bacon was great even as a lawyer; but it is permissible to much smaller men, relying upon principle and on the authority of others, the equals and even the superiors of Lord Bacon as lawyers, to question the soundness of his dictum. There are many conceivable states of things in which it might possibly be true, but if Lord Bacon meant to lay down the broad proposition that a man may save his life by killing, if necessary, an innocent and unoffending neighbour, it certainly is not law at the present day. . . .

Now, except for the purpose of testing how far the conservation of a man's own life is in all cases and under all circumstances, an absolute, unqualified, and paramount duty, we exclude from our consideration all the incidents of war. We are dealing with a case of private homicide, not one imposed upon men in the sevice of their Sovereign and in defence of their country. Now it is admitted that the deliberate killing of this unoffending and unresisting boy was clearly murder, unless the killing can be justified by some well-recognised excuse admitted by the law. It is further admitted that there was in this case no such excuse, unless the killing was justified by what has been called "necessity." But the temptation to the act which existed here was not what the law has ever called necessity. Nor is this to be regretted. Though law and morality are not the same, and many things may be immoral which are not necessarily illegal, yet the absolute divorce of law from morality would be of fatal consequence; and such divorce would follow if the temptation to murder in this case were to be held by law an absolute defence of it. It is not so. To preserve one's life is generally speaking a duty, but it may be the plainest and the highest duty to sacrifice it. War is full of instances in which it is a man's duty not to live, but to die. The duty, in case of shipwreck, of a captain to his crew, of the crew to the passengers, of soldiers to women and children, as in the noble case of the *Birkenhead;* these duties impose on men the moral necessity, not of the preservation, but of the sacrifice of their lives for others, from which in no country, least of all, it is to be hoped, in England, will men ever shrink, as indeed, they have not shrunk. It is not correct, therefore, to say that there is any absolute or unqualified necessity to preserve one's life. *"Necesse est ut eam, non ut vivan,"* is a saying of a Roman officer quoted by Lord Bacon himself with high eulogy in the very chapter on necessity to which so much reference has been made. It would be a very easy and cheap display of commonplace learning to quote from Greek and Latin authors, from Horace, from Juvenal, from Cicero, from Euripides, passage after passage, in which the duty of dying for others has been laid down in glowing and emphatic language as resulting from the principles of heathen ethics; it is enough in a Christian country to remind ourselves of the Great Example whom we profess to follow. It is not needful to point out the awful danger of admitting the principle which has been contended for. Who is to be the judge of this sort of necessity? By what measure is the comparative value of lives to be measured? Is it to be strength, or intellect, or what? It is plain that the principle leaves to him who is to profit by it to determine the necessity which will justify him in deliberately taking another's life to save his own. In this case the weakest, the youngest, the most unresisting, was chosen. Was it more necessary to kill him than one of the grown men? The answer must be "No" —

> "So spake the Fiend, and with necessity,
> The tyrant's plea, excused his devilish deeds."

It is not suggested that in this particular case the deeds were "devilish," but it is quite plain that such a principle once admitted might be made the legal cloak for unbridled passion and atrocious crime. There is no safe path for judges to tread but to ascertain the law to the best of their ability and to declare it according to their judgment; and if in any case the law appears to be too severe on individuals, to leave it to the sovereign to exercise that prerogative of mercy which the Constitution has intrusted to the hands fittest to dispense it.

It must not be supposed that in refusing to admit temptation to be an excuse for crime it is forgotten how terrible the temptation was; how awful the suffering; how hard in such trials to keep the judgment straight and the conduct pure. We are often compelled to set up standards we cannot reach ourselves, and to lay down rules which we could not ourselves satisfy. But a man has no right to declare temptation to be an excuse, though he might himself have yielded to it, nor allow compassion for the criminal to change or weaken in any manner the legal definition of the crime. It is therefore our duty to declare that the prisoners' act in this case was wilful murder, that the facts as stated in the verdict are no legal justification of the homicide; and to say that in our unanimous opinion the prisoners are upon this special verdict guilty of murder.[1]

The COURT then proceeded to pass sentence of death upon the prisoners.[2]

---

1. My brother Grove has furnished me with the following suggestion too late to be embodied in the judgment but well worth preserving: "If the two accused men were justified in killing Parker, then if not rescued in time, two of the three survivors would be justified in killing the third, and of the two who remained the stronger would be justified in killing the weaker, so that three men might be justifiably killed to give the fourth a chance of surviving."—C.

2. This sentence was afterwards commuted by the Crown to six months' imprisonment.

THE MINISTER'S BLACK VEIL
Nathaniel Hawthorne

The sexton stood in the porch of Milford meeting-house, pulling busily at the bell-rope. The old people of the village came stooping along the street. Children, with bright faces, tripped merrily beside their parents or mimicked a graver gait, in the conscious dignity of their Sunday clothes. Spruce bachelors looked sidelong at the pretty maidens, and fancied that the Sabbath sunshine made them prettier than on week days. When the throng had mostly streamed into the porch, the sexton began to toll the bell, keeping his eye on the Reverend Mr. Hooper's door. The first glimpse of the clergyman's figure was the signal for the bell to cease its summons.

"But what has good Parson Hooper got upon his face?" cried the sexton in astonishment.

All within hearing immediately turned about, and beheld the semblance of Mr. Hooper, pacing slowly his meditative way towards the meeting-house. With one accord they started, expressing more wonder than if some strange minister were coming to dust the cushions of Mr. Hooper's pulpit.

"Are you sure it is our parson?" inquired Goodman Gray of the sexton.

"Of a certainty it is good Mr. Hooper," replied the sexton. "He was to have exchanged pulpits with Parson Shute, of Westbury; but Parson Shute sent to excuse himself yesterday, being to preach a funeral sermon."

The cause of so much amazement may appear sufficiently slight. Mr. Hooper, a gentlemanly person, of about thirty, though still a bachelor, was dressed with due clerical neatness, as if a careful wife had starched his band, and brushed the weekly dust from his Sunday's garb. There was but one thing remarkable in his appearance. Swathed about his forehead, and hanging down over his face, so low as to be shaken by his breath, Mr. Hooper had a black veil. On a nearer view it seemed to consist of two folds of crape, which entirely concealed his features, except the mouth and chin, but probably did not intercept his sight, further than to give a darkened aspect to all living and inanimate things. With this gloomy shade before him, good Mr. Hooper walked onward, at a slow and quiet pace, stooping somewhat, and looking on the ground, as is customary with abstracted men, yet nodding kindly to those of his parishioners who still waited on the meeting-house steps. But so wonder-struck were they that his greeting hardly met with a return.

"I can't really feel as if good Mr. Hooper's face was behind that piece of crape," said the sexton.

"I don't like it," muttered an old woman, as she hobbled into the meeting-house. "He has changed himself into something awful, only by hiding his face."

"Our parson has gone mad!" cried Goodman Gray, following him across the threshold.

A rumor of some unaccountable phenomenon had preceded Mr. Hooper into the meeting-house, and set all the congregation astir. Few could refrain from twisting their heads towards the door; many stood upright, and turned directly about; while several little boys clambered upon the seats, and came down again with a terrible racket. There was a general bustle, a rustling of the women's gowns and shuffling of the men's feet, greatly at variance with that hushed repose which should attend the entrance of the minister. But Mr. Hooper appeared not to notice the perturbation of his people. He entered with an almost noiseless step, bent his head mildly to the pews on each side, and bowed as he passed his oldest parishioner, a white-haired great grandsire, who occupied an arm-chair in the centre of the aisle. It was strange to observe how slowly this venerable man became conscious of something singular in the appearance of his pastor. He seemed not fully to partake of the prevailing wonder, till Mr. Hooper had ascended the stairs, and showed himself in the pulpit, face to face with his congregation, except for the black veil. That mysterious emblem was never once withdrawn. It shook with his measured breath, as he gave out the psalm; it threw its obscurity between him and the holy page, as he read the Scriptures; and while he prayed, the veil lay heavily on his uplifted countenance. Did he seek to hide it from the dread Being whom he was addressing?

Such was the effect of this simple piece of crape, that more than one woman of delicate nerves was forced to leave the meeting-house. Yet perhaps the pale-faced congregation was almost as fearful a sight to the minister, as his black veil to them.

Mr. Hooper had the reputation of a good preacher, but not an energetic one: he strove to win his people heavenward by mild, persuasive influences, rather than to drive them thither by the thunders of the Word. The sermon which he now delivered was marked by the same characteristics of style and manner as the general series of his pulpit oratory. But there was something, either in the sentiment of the discourse itself, or in the imagination of the auditors, which made it greatly the most powerful effort that they had ever heard from their pastor's lips. It was tinged, rather more darkly than usual, with the gentle gloom of Mr. Hooper's temperament. The subject had reference to secret sin, and those sad mysteries which we hide from our nearest and dearest, and would fain conceal from our own consciousness, even forgetting that the Omniscient can detect them. A subtle power was breathed into his words. Each member of the congregation, the most innocent girl, and the man of hardened breast, felt as if the preacher had crept upon them, behind his awful veil, and discovered their hoarded iniquity of deed or thought. Many spread their clasped hands on their bosoms. There was nothing terrible in what Mr. Hooper said, at least, no violence; and yet, with every tremor of his melancholy voice, the hearers quaked. An unsought pathos came hand in hand with awe. So sensible were the audience of some unwonted attribute in their minister, that they longed for a breath of wind to blow aside the veil, almost believing that a stranger's visage would be discovered, though the form, gesture, and voice were those of Mr. Hooper.

At the close of the services, the people hurried out with indecorous confusion, eager to communicate their pent-up amazement, and conscious of lighter spirits the moment they lost sight of the black veil. Some gathered in little circles, huddled closely together, with their mouths all whispering in the centre; some went homeward alone, wrapt in silent meditations; some talked loudly, and profaned the Sabbath day with ostentatious laughter. A few shook their sagacious heads, intimating that they could penetrate the mystery; while one or two affirmed that there was no mystery at all, but only that Mr. Hooper's eyes were so weakened by the midnight lamp, as to require a shade. After a brief interval, forth came good Mr. Hooper also, in the rear of his flock. Turning his veiled face from one group to another, he paid due reverence to the hoary heads, saluted the middle aged with kind dignity as their friend and spiritual guide, greeted the young with mingled authority and love, and laid his hands on the little children's heads to bless them. Such was always his custom on the Sabbath day. Strange and bewildered looks repaid him for his courtesy. None, as on former occasions, aspired to the honor of walking by their pastor's side. Old Squire Saunders, doubtless by an accidental lapse of memory, neglected to invite Mr. Hooper to his table, where the good clergyman had been wont to bless the food, almost every Sunday since his settlement. He returned, therefore, to the parsonage, and, at the moment of closing the door, was observed to look back upon the people, all of whom had their eyes fixed upon the minister. A sad smile gleamed faintly from beneath the black veil, and flickered about his mouth, glimmering as he disappeared.

"How strange," said a lady, "that a simple black veil, such as any woman might wear on her bonnet, should become such a terrible thing on Mr. Hooper's face!"

"Something must surely be amiss with Mr. Hooper's intellects," observed her husband, the physician of the village. "But the strangest part of the affair is the effect of this vagary, even on a sober-minded man like myself. The black veil, though it covers only our pastor's face, throws its influence over his whole person, and makes him ghostlike from head to foot. Do you feel it so?"

"Truly do I," replied the lady; "and I would not be alone with him for the world. I wonder he is not afraid to be alone with himself!"

"Men sometimes are so," said her husband.

The afternoon service was attended with similar circumstances. At its conclusion, the bell tolled for the funeral of a young lady. The relatives and friends were assembled in the house and the more distant acquaintances stood about the door, speaking of the good qualities of the deceased, when their talk was interrupted by the appearance of Mr. Hooper, still covered with his black veil. It was now an appropriate emblem. The clergyman stepped into the room where the corpse was laid, and bent over the coffin, to take a last farewell of his deceased parishioner. As he stooped, the veil hung straight down from his forehead, so that, if her eyelids had not been closed forever, the dead maiden might have seen his face. Could Mr. Hooper be fearful of her glance, that he so hastily caught back the black veil? A person who watched the interview between the dead and living, scrupled not to affirm, that, at the instant when the clergyman's features were disclosed, the corpse had slightly shuddered, rustling the shroud and muslin cap, though the countenance retained the composure of death. A superstitious old woman was the only witness of this prodigy. From the coffin Mr. Hopper passed into the chamber of the mourners, and thence to the head of the staircase, to make the funeral prayer. It was a tender and heart-dissolving prayer, full of sorrow, yet so imbued with celestial hopes, that the music of a heavenly harp, swept by the fingers of the dead, seemed faintly to be heard among the saddest accents of the minister. The people trembled, though they but darkly understood him when he prayed that they, and himself, and all of mortal race, might be ready, as he trusted this young maiden had been, for the dreadful hour that should snatch the veil from their faces. The bearers went heavily forth, and the mourners followed, saddening all the street, with the dead before them, and Mr. Hooper in his black veil behind.

"Why do you look back?" said one in the procession to his partner.

"I had a fancy," replied she, "that the minister and the maiden's spirit were walking hand in hand."

"And so had I, at the same moment," said the other.

That night, the handsomest couple in Milford village were to be joined in wedlock. Though reckoned a melancholy man, Mr. Hooper had a placid cheerfulness for such occasions, which often excited a sympathetic smile where livelier merriment would have been thrown away. There was no quality of his disposition which made him more beloved than this. The company at the wedding awaited his arrival with impatience, trusting that the strange awe, which had gathered over him throughout the day, would now be dispelled. But such was not the result. When Mr. Hooper came, the first thing that their eyes rested on was the same horrible black veil, which had added deeper gloom to the funeral, and could portend nothing but evil to the wedding. Such was its immediate effect on the guests that a cloud seemed to have rolled duskily from beneath the black crape, and dimmed the light of the candles. The bridal pair stood up before the minister. But the bride's cold fingers quivered in the tremulous hand of the bridegroom, and her deathlike paleness caused a whisper that the maiden who had been buried a few hours before was come from her grave to be married. If ever another wedding were so dismal, it was that famous one where they tolled the wedding knell. After performing the ceremony, Mr. Hooper raised a glass of wine to his lips, wishing happiness to the new-married couple in a strain of mild pleasantry that ought to have brightened the features of the guests, like a cheerful gleam from the hearth. At that instant, catching a glimpse of his figure in the looking-glass, the black veil involved his own spirit in the horror with which it overwhelmed all others. His frame shuddered, his lips grew white, he spilt the untasted wine upon the carpet, and rushed forth into the darkness. For the Earth, too, had on her Black Veil.

The next day, the whole village of Milford talked of little else than Parson Hooper's black veil. That, and the mystery concealed behind it, supplied a topic for discussion between acquaintances meeting in the street, and good women gossiping at their open windows. It was the first item of news that the tavern-keeper told to his guests. The children babbled of it on their way to school. One imitative little imp covered his face with an old black handkerchief, thereby so affrighting his playmates that the panic seized himself, and he well-nigh lost his wits by his own waggery.

It was remarkable that of all the busybodies and impertinent people in the parish, not one ventured to put the plain question to Mr. Hooper, wherefore he did this thing. Hitherto, whenever there appeared the slightest call for such interference, he had never lacked advisers, nor shown himself averse to be guided by their judgment. If he erred at all, it was by so painful a degree of self-distrust, that even the mildest censure would lead him to consider an indifferent action as a crime. Yet, though so well acquainted with this amiable weakness, no individual among his parishioners chose to make the black veil a subject of friendly remonstrance. There was a feeling of dread, neither plainly confessed nor carefully concealed, which caused each to shift the responsibility upon another, till at length it was found expedient to send a deputation of the church, in order to deal with Mr. Hooper about the mystery, before it should grow into a scandal. Never did an embassy so ill discharge its duties. The minister received them with friendly courtesy, but became silent, after they were seated, leaving to his visitors the whole burden of introducing their important business. The topic, it might be supposed, was obvious enough. There was the black veil swathed round Mr. Hooper's forehead, and concealing every feature above his placid mouth, on which, at times, they could perceive the glimmering of a melancholy smile. But that piece of crape, to their imagination, seemed to hang down before his heart, the symbol of a fearful secret between him and them. Were the veil but cast aside, they might speak freely of it, but not till then. Thus they sat a considerable time, speechless, confused, and shrinking uneasily from Mr. Hooper's eye, which they felt to be fixed upon them with an invisible glance. Finally, the deputies returned abashed to their constituents, pronouncing the matter too weighty to be handled, except by a council of the churches, if, indeed, it might not require a general synod.

But there was one person in the village unappalled by the awe with which the black veil had impressed all beside herself. When the deputies returned without an explanation, or even venturing to demand one, she, with the calm energy of her character, determined to chase away the strange cloud that appeared to be settling round Mr. Hooper, every moment more darkly than before. As his plighted wife, it should be her privilege to know what the black veil concealed. At the minister's first visit, therefore, she entered upon the subject with a direct simplicity, which made the task easier both for him and her. After he had seated himself, she fixed her eyes steadfastly upon the veil, but could discern nothing of the dreadful gloom that had so overawed the multitude: it was but a double fold of crape, hanging down from his forehead to his mouth, and slightly stirring with his breath.

"No," said she aloud, and smiling, "there is nothing terrible in this piece of crape, except that it hides a face which I am always glad to look upon. Come, good sir, let the sun shine from behind the cloud. First lay aside your black veil: then tell me why you put it on."

Mr. Hooper's smile glimmered faintly.

"There is an hour to come," said he, "when all of us shall cast aside our veils. Take it not amiss, beloved friend, if I wear this piece of crape till then."

"Your words are a mystery, too," returned the young lady. "Take away the veil from them, at least."

"Elizabeth, I will," said he, "so far as my vow may suffer me. Know, then, this veil is a type and a symbol, and I am bound to wear it ever, both in light and darkness, in solitude and before the gaze of multitudes, and as with strangers, so with my familiar friends. No mortal eye will see it withdrawn. This dismal shade must separate me from the world: even you, Elizabeth, can never come behind it!"

"What grievous affliction hath befallen you," she earnestly inquired, "that you should thus darken your eyes forever?"

"If it be a sign of mourning," replied Mr. Hooper, "I, perhaps, like most other mortals, have sorrows dark enough to be typified by a black veil."

"But what if the world will not believe that it is the type of an innocent sorrow?" urged Elizabeth. "Beloved and respected as you are, there may be whispers that you hide your face under the consciousness of secret sin. For the sake of your holy office, do away this scandal!"

The color rose into her cheeks as she intimated the nature of the rumors that were already abroad in the village. But Mr. Hooper's mildness did not forsake him. He even smiled again—that same sad smile, which always appeared like a faint glimmering of light, proceeding from the obscurity beneath the veil.

"If I hide my face for sorrow, there is cause enough," he merely replied; "and if I cover it for secret sin, what mortal might not do the same?"

And with this gentle, but unconquerable obstinacy did he resist all her entreaties. At length Elizabeth sat silent. For a few moments she appeared lost in thought, considering, probably, what new methods might be tried to withdraw her lover from so dark a fantasy, which, if it had no other meaning, was perhaps a symptom of mental disease. Though of a firmer character than his own, the tears rolled down her cheeks. But, in an instant, as it were a new feeling took the place of sorrow: her eyes were fixed insensibly on the black veil, when, like a sudden twilight in the air, its terrors fell around her. She arose, and stood trembling before him.

"And do you feel it then, at last?" said he mournfully.

She made no reply, but covered her eyes with her hand, and turned to leave the room. He rushed forward and caught her arm.

"Have patience with me, Elizabeth!" cried he, passionately. "Do not desert me, though this veil must be between us here on earth. Be mine, and hereafter there shall be no veil over my face, no darkness between our souls! It is but a mortal veil—it is not for eternity! O! you know not how lonely I am, and how frightened, to be alone behind my black veil. Do not leave me in this miserable obscurity forever!"

"Lift the veil but once, and look me in the face," said she.

"Never! It cannot be!" replied Mr. Hooper.

"Then farewell!" said Elizabeth.

She withdrew her arm from his grasp, and slowly departed, pausing at the door, to give one long shuddering gaze, that seemed almost to penetrate the mystery of the black veil. But, even amid his grief, Mr. Hooper smiled to think that only a material emblem had separated him from happiness, though the horrors, which it shadowed forth, must be drawn darkly between the fondest of lovers.

From that time no attempts were made to remove Mr. Hooper's black veil, or, by a direct appeal, to discover the secret which it was supposed to hide. By persons who claimed a superiority to popular prejudice, it was reckoned merely an eccentric whim, such as often mingles with the sober actions of men otherwise rational, and tinges them all with its own semblance of insanity. But with the multitude, good Mr. Hooper was irreparably a bugbear. He could not walk the street with any peace of mind, so conscious was he that the gentle and timid would turn aside to avoid him, and that others would make it a point of hardihood to throw themselves in his way. The impertinence of the latter class compelled him to give up his customary walk at sunset to the burial ground; for when he leaned pensively over the gate, there would always be faces behind the gravestones, peeping at his black veil. A fable went the rounds that the stare of the dead people drove him thence. It grieved him, to the very depth of his kind heart, to observe how the children fled from his approach, breaking up their merriest sports, while his melancholy figure was yet afar off. Their instinctive dread caused him to feel more strongly than aught else, that a preternatural horror was interwoven with the threads of the black crape. In truth, his own antipathy to the veil was known to be so great, that he never willingly passed before a mirror, nor stooped to drink at a still fountain, lest, in its peaceful bosom, he should be affrighted by himself. This was what gave plausibility to the whispers, that Mr. Hooper's conscience tortured him for some great crime too horrible to be entirely concealed, or otherwise than so obscurely intimated. Thus, from beneath the black veil, there rolled a cloud into the sunshine, an ambiguity of sin or sorrow, which enveloped the poor minister, so that love or sympathy could never reach him. It was said that ghost and fiend consorted with him there. With self-shudderings and outward terrors, he walked continually in its shadow, groping darkly within his own soul, or gazing through a medium that saddened the whole world. Even the lawless wind, it was believed, respected his dreadful secret, and never blew aside the veil. But still good Mr. Hooper sadly smiled at the pale visages of the worldly throng as he passed by.

Among all its bad influences, the black veil had the one desirable effect of making its wearer a very efficient clergyman. By the aid of his mysterious emblem—for there was no other apparent cause—he became a man of awful power over souls that were in agony for sin. His converts always regarded him with a dread peculiar to themselves, affirming, though but figuratively, that, before he brought them to celestial light, they had been with him behind the black veil. Its gloom, indeed, enabled him to sympathize with all dark affections. Dying sinners cried aloud for Mr. Hooper, and would not yield their breath till he appeared; though ever, as he stooped to whisper consolation, they shuddered at the veiled face so near their own. Such were the terrors of the black veil even when Death had bared his visage! Strangers came long distances to attend service at his church, with the mere idle purpose of gazing at his figure, because it was forbidden them to behold his face. But many were made to quake ere they departed! Once, during Governor Belcher's administration, Mr. Hooper was appointed to preach the election sermon. Covered with his black veil, he stood before the chief magistrate, the council, and the representatives, and wrought so deep an impression, that the legislative measures of that year were characterized by all the gloom and piety of our earliest ancestral sway.

In this manner Mr. Hooper spent a long life, irreproachable in outward act, yet shrouded in dismal suspicions; kind and loving, though unloved, and dimly feared; a man apart from men, shunned in their health and joy, but ever summoned to their aid in mortal anguish. As years wore on, shedding their snows above his sable veil, he acquired a name throughout the New England churches, and they called him Father Hooper. Nearly all his parishioners, who were of mature age when he was settled, had been borne away by many a funeral: he had one congregation in the church, and a more crowded one in the churchyard; and having wrought so late into the evening, and done his work so well, it was now good Father Hooper's turn to rest.

Several persons were visible by the shaded candlelight, in the death chamber of the old clergyman. Natural connections he had none. But there was the decorously grave, though unmoved physician, seeking only to mitigate the last pangs of the patient whom he could not save. There were the deacons, and other eminently pious members of his church. There, also, was the Reverend Mr. Clark, of Westbury, a young and zealous divine, who had ridden in haste to pray by the bedside of the expiring minister. There was the nurse, no hired handmaiden of death, but one whose calm affection had endured thus long in secrecy, in solitude, amid the chill of age, and would not perish, even at the dying hour. Who, but Elizabeth! And there lay the hoary head of good Father Hooper upon the death pillow, with the black veil still swathed about his brow, and reaching down over his face, so that each more difficult gasp of his faint breath caused it to stir. All through life that piece of crape had hung between him and the world: it had separated him from cheerful brotherhood and woman's love, and kept him in that saddest of all prisons, his own heart; and still it lay upon his face, as if to deepen the gloom of his darksome chamber, and shade him from the sunshine of eternity.

For some time previous, his mind had been confused, wavering doubtfully between the past and the present, and hovering forward, as it were, at intervals, into the indistinctness of the world to come. There had been feverish turns, which tossed him from side to side, and wore away what little strength he had. But in his most convulsive struggles, and in the wildest vagaries of his intellect, when no other thought retained its sober influence, he still showed an awful solicitude lest the black veil should slip aside. Even if his bewildered soul could have forgotten, there was a faithful woman at this pillow, who, with averted eyes, would have covered that aged face, which she had last beheld in the comeliness of manhood. At length the death-stricken old man lay quietly in the torpor of mental and bodily exhaustion, with an imperceptible pulse, and breath that grew fainter and fainter, except when a long, deep, and irregular inspiration seemed to prelude the flight of his spirit.

The minister of Westbury approached the bedside.

"Venerable Father Hooper," said he, "the moment of your release is at hand. Are you ready for the lifting of the veil that shuts in time from eternity?"

Father Hooper at first replied merely by a feeble motion of his head; then, apprehensive, perhaps, that his meaning might be doubted, he exerted himself to speak.

"Yea," said he, in faint accents, "my soul hath a patient weariness until that veil be lifted."

"And is it fitting," resumed the Reverend Mr. Clark, "that a man so given to prayer, of such a blameless example, holy in deed and thought, so far as mortal judgment may pronounce; is it fitting that a father in the church should leave a shadow on his memory, that may seem to blacken a life so pure? I pray you, my venerable brother, let not this thing be! Suffer us to be gladdened by your triumphant aspect as you go to your reward. Before the veil of eternity be lifted, let me cast aside this black veil from your face!"

And thus speaking, the Reverend Mr. Clark bent forward to reveal the mystery of so many years. But, exerting a sudden energy, that made all the beholders stand aghast, Father Hooper snatched both his hands from beneath the bedclothes, and pressed them strongly on the black veil, resolute to struggle, if the minister of Westbury would contend with a dying man.

"Never!" cried the veiled clergyman. "On earth, never!"

"Dark old man!" exclaimed the affrighted minister, "with what horrible crime upon your soul are you now passing to the judgment?"

Father Hooper's breath heaved; it rattled in his throat; but, with a mighty effort, grasping forward with his hands, he caught hold of life, and held it back till he should speak. He even raised himself in bed; and there he sat, shivering with the arms of death around him, while the black veil hung down, awful, at that last moment, in the gathered terrors of a lifetime. And yet the faint, sad smile, so often there, now seemed to glimmer from its obscurity, and linger on Father Hooper's lips.

"Why do you tremble at me alone?" cried he, turning his veiled face round the circle of pale spectators. "Tremble also at each other! Have men avoided me, and women shown no pity, and children screamed and fled, only for my black veil? What, but the mystery which it obscurely typifies, has made this piece of crape so awful? When the friend shows his inmost heart to his friend; the lover to his best beloved; when man does not vainly shrink from the eye of his Creator, loathsomely treasuring up the secret of his sin; then deem me a monster, for the symbol beneath which I have lived, and die! I look around me, and, lo! on every visage a Black Veil!"

While his auditors shrank from one another, in mutual affright, Father Hooper fell back upon his pillow, a veiled corpse, with a faint smile lingering on the lips. Still veiled, they laid him in his coffin, and a veiled corpse they bore him to the grave. The grass of many years has sprung up and withered on that grave, the burial stone is moss-grown, and good Mr. Hooper's face is dust; but awful is still the thought that it mouldered beneath the Black Veil!

Issues for Discussion

1. Briefly outline the facts and the courts's ruling in *The Queen* v. *Dudley and Stephens*. Discuss the deficiences of the following theories in explaining or predicting the murder and acts of cannibalism by Dudley and Stephens:
   a. anomie
   b. culture conflict
   c. radical
   d. differential association
2. Which, if any, of the theories of crime causation you have studied best explains the seamen's deviance?
3. The boy who was murdered did not consent to have his life taken. Nor did Dudley and Stephens conduct a lottery, as was orginally planned. Do you think the decision of the court would have been different if the above two conditions had been met? Use the rationale of Lord Coleridge, the chief justice, to support your answer.
4. Try to devise hypothetical situations in which otherwise deviant behaviors would be justified because of the circumstances in which they were performed for the following acts:
   a. robbery
   b. murder
   c. assault and battery
   d. arson
   e. rape
5. Why is it difficult to develop a justifying hypothetical situation for rape? Does the same problem exist for the so-called willing-victim crimes (e.g., adultery, fornication, homosexual or heterosexual sodomy)?
6. The criminologist is confronted with the extremely difficult task of ascertaining criteria for predicting criminality. Explain how the statement by Chief Justice Coleridge illustrates the process by which the lawmaker virtually assures everyone that criminal behavior is almost impossible to avoid: "We are often compelled to set up standards we cannot reach ourselves, and to lay down rules which we could not ourselves satisfy."

ISSUES FOR DISCUSSION

7. In Nathaniel Hawthorne's "The Minister's Black Veil," the Reverend Mr. Hooper suddenly decides to wear a black veil over his face. What is the significance of the veil, and how does it illustrate the suspicision that statistics about criminal behavior are often misleading?
8. Explain the difficulties of establishing criteria for predicting deviance, which are illustrated by Hawthorne's statement, "The people trembled, though they but darkly understood him when he prayed that they, and himself, and all of mortal race, might be ready, as he trusted this young maiden had been, for the dreadful hour that should snatch the veil from their faces."

Bibliography

Articles

ABRAHAMSEN, D. "Psychodynamics in Criminal Behavior." *Journal of Nervous and Mental Disease* 102 (1945): 65–75.
———. "Motivation of Crime: Forces of Motivation in Primitive Society." *Boston University Law Review* 26 (1946): 91–118.
———. "Family Tension: Basic Cause of Criminal Behavior." *Journal of Criminal Law and Criminology* 40 (1949): 330–43.
———. "Psychiatric Aspects of Delinquency." *Journal of Educational Sociology* 24 (1950): 40–44.
———. "Study of 102 Sex Offenders at Sing Sing." *Federal Probation* 14 (1950): 26–32.
ADLER, A. "Some Psychiatric Aspects of Female Offenders in the Women's House of Detention." *Journal of Social Therapy* 1 (1955): 199–202.
BLOOM, D.M., and C.E. REASONS. "Ideology and Crime: A Study in the Sociology of Knowledge." *International Journal of Criminology and Penology* 6 (London, 1978): 19–30.
CHAMBLISS, W. J. "The Deterrent Influence of Punishment." *Crime and Delinquency* 12 (1966): 70–75.
———. "Types of Deviance and the Effectiveness of Legal Sanctions." *Wisconsin Law Review* (1967): 703–19.
———. "On the Validity of Official Statistics: A Comparative Study of White, Black, and Japanese High School Boys." *Journal of Research in Crime and Delinquency* 6 (1969): 71–77.
———. "Vice, Corruption, Bureaucracy and Power." *Wisconsin Law Review* 1 (1971): 1150–73.
CLARK, J. P. "Socio-Economic Class and Area as Correlates of Illegal Behavior among Juveniles." *American Sociological Review* 27 (1962): 826–34.
———. "Age and Sex Roles of Adolescents and Their Involvement in Misconduct. A Reappraisal." *Sociology and Social Research* 50 (1966): 495–508.

———. "Polygraph and Interview Validation of Self-Reported Deviant Behavior." *American Sociological Review* 31 (1966): 516–23.
CLINARD, M. B. "Criminal Behavior is Human Behavior." *Federal Probation* 13 (1949): 21–27.
———. "Research Frontiers in Criminology." *Research Frontiers in Criminology* 7 (1956): 110–22.
———. "Areas for Research in Deviant Behavior." *Sociology and Social Research* 42 (1957): 415–19.
———. "Contributions of Sociology to Understanding Deviant Behaviour." *British Journal of Criminology* 3 (1962): 110–29.
CLOWARD, R. A. "Illegitimate Means, Anomie, and Deviant Behavior." *American Sociological Review* 24 (1959): 164–76.
COHEN, A. K. "Sociological Research in Juvenile Delinquency." *American Journal of Ortho-Psychiatry* 27 (1957): 781–88.
———. "The Sociology of the Deviant Act: Anomie Theory and Beyond." *American Sociological Review* 30 (1965): 5–14.
CONKLIN, J. E. "Criminal Environment and Support for the Law." *Law and Social Review* 6 (1971): 247–59.
———. "Dimensions of Community Response to the Crime Problem." *Social Problems* 18 (1971): 373–85.
CRESSEY, D. R. "The Criminal Violation of Financial Trust." *American Sociological Review* 15 (1950): 738–43.
———. "Criminological Research and the Definition of Crimes." *American Journal of Sociology* 56 (1951): 546–51.
———. "Application and Verification of the Differential Association Theory." *Journal of Criminal Law and Criminology* 43 (1952): 43–52.
———. "The Differential Association Theory and Compulsive Crimes." *Journal of Criminal Law, Criminology and Police Science* 45 (1954): 43–52.
———. "Changing Criminals: The Application of the Theory of Differential Association." *American Journal of Sociology* 61 (1955): 116–20.
———. "The State of Criminal Statistics." *National Probation Association Yearbook* 3 (1957): 230–41.
———. "The Respectable Criminal: Why Some of Our Best Friends Are Crooks." *Transaction* 03/00 (1965): 12–15.
———. "The Language of Set Theory and Differential Association." *Journal of Research in Crime Delinquency* 3 (1966): 22–26.
———. "Methodological Problems in the Study of Organized Crime as a Social Problem." *Annals of the American Academy of Political and Social Science* 374 (1967): 101–12.
GAROFALO, J. "Radical Criminology and Criminal Justice: Points of Divergence and Contact." *Crime and Social Justice* 10 (1978): 17–27.

GEIS, G. "Pioneers in Criminology: Jeremy Bentham, 1748–1832." *Criminal Law, Criminology and Police Science* 46 (1955): 159–71.
———. "Sociology, Criminology and Criminal Law." *Social Problems* 7 (1959): 40–47.
———. "Toward a Delineation of White Collar Offenses." *Sociological Inquiry* 32 (1962): 160–71.
———. "Statistics Concerning Race and Crime." *Crime and Delinquency* 11 (1965): 142–50.
———. "Violence in American Society." *Current History* 52 (1967): 354–58.
———. "Charles Manson and His Girls: Notes on a Durkheimian Theme." *Criminology* 9 (1971): 342–53.
GIBBONS, D. C. "Some Suggestions for the Development of Etiological and Treatment Theory in Criminology." *Sociological Forecast* 38 (1959): 51–58.
———. "Definition and Analysis of Certain Criminal Types." *Journal of Criminal Law, Criminology, and Police Science* 53 (1962): 27–35.
———. "Some Critical Notes on Current Definitions of Deviance." *Pacific Social Review* 7 (1964): 20–37.
———. "Problems of Causal Analysis in Criminology. A Case Illustration." *Journal of Research in Crime Delinquency* 3 (1966): 47–52.
———. "Observations on the Study of Crime Causation." *American Journal of Sociology* 77 (1971): 262–78.
GIBBS, J. P., and JAMES F. SHORT, JR. "Criminal Differentiation and Occupational Differentiation." *Journal of Research in Crime Delinquency* 11 (1974): 89–100.
GLUECK, E. T. "Spotting Potential Delinquents: Can It Be Done?" *Federal Probation* 20 (1956): 7–13.
———. "Status of Glueck Prediction Studies." *Journal of Criminal Law, Criminology, and Police Science* 47 (1956): 18–32.
———. "Body Build in the Prediction of Delinquency." *Journal of Criminal Law, Criminology, and Police Science* 48 (1958): 577–79.
———. "Role of the Family in the Etiology of Delinquency." *British Int. Soc. Crim.* (1960): 1–11.
———. "A More Discriminative Instrument for the Identification of Potential Delinquents at School Entrance." *Journal of Criminal Law, Criminology, and Police Science* 57 (1966): 27–30.
———. "Identification of Potential Delinquents at 2–3 Years of Age." *International Journal of Social Psychology* 12 (1966): 5–16.
HARRIS, A. R. "Sex and Theories of Deviance: Toward a Functional Theory of Deviant Type-Scripts." *American Sociological Review* 42 (1977): 3–16.

JEFFERY, C. R. "Pioneers in Criminology: The Historical Development of Criminology." *Journal of Criminal Law, Criminology, and Police Science* 50 (May–June 1959): 3–19.

KAMISAR, Y. "How to Use, Abuse—and Fight Back with—Crime Statistics." *Oklahoma Law Review* 25 (May 1972): 239–58.

KESSLER, S. "The XYY Karyotype and Criminality: A Review." *Journal of Psychological Research* 7 (1970): 153–70.

KITSUSE, J. I., and AARON V. CICOUREL. "A Note on the Uses of Official Statistics." *Social Problems* 11 (Fall 1963): 131–39.

KITTRIE, N. N. "Will the XYY Syndrome Abolish Guilt?" *Federal Probation* 35 (1971): 26–31.

KLEIN, D. "Some Applications of Delinquency Theory to Childhood Accidents." *Pediatrics* 44 (1969): 805–10.

———. "The Etiology of Female Crime: A Review of the Literature." *Issues in Criminology* 8 (1973): 3–30.

MANKOFF, M. "On the Responsibility of Marxist Criminologists: A Reply to Quinney." *Contemporary Issues* 2 (1978): 293–301.

MERTON, R. K. "Social Structure and Anomie." *American Sociological Review* 3 (October 1938): 672–82.

MILLER, W. B. "Lower Class Culture as a Generating Milieu of Gang Delinquency." *Journal of Sociological Issues* 14 (1958): 5–19.

———. "Violent Crimes in City Gangs." *Annals of the American Academy of Political and Social Science* 364 (1966): 96–112.

———. "White Gangs" *Transaction* 09/00 (1969): 11–26.

MORAN, R. "Biomedical Research and the Politics of Crime Control: A Historical Perspective." *Contemporary Issues* 2 (1978): 335–57.

NIEBURG, H. L. "Violence, Law, and the Social Process." *American Journal of Behavioral Science* 11 (1968): 17–19.

QUINNEY, R. "Crime, Delinquency and Social Areas." *Journal of Research in Crime Delinquency* 1 (1964): 149–54.

———. "A Conception of Man and Society for Criminology." *Sociological Quarterly* 6 (1965): 119–27.

———. "Is Criminal Behaviour Deviant Behaviour?" *British Journal of Criminology* 5 (1965): 132–42.

———. "The Production of a Marxist Criminology." *Contemporary Issues* 2 (1978): 277–92.

RECKLESS, W. C. "Self-Concept as an Insulator Against Delinquency." *American Sociological Review* 21 (1956): 744–46.

———. "Female Criminality." *National Probation and Parole Association Journal* 3 (1957): 1–6.

———. "A New Theory of Delinquency and Crime." *Federal Probation* 25 (1961): 42–46.

———. "American Criminology." *Criminology* 8 (1970): 4.
REISS, A. J. "An Empirical Test of Differential Association Theory." *Journal of Research in Crime Delinquency* 1 (1964): 5–18.
ROBISON, S. "A Critical View of the Uniform Crime Reports." *Michigan Law Review* 64 (April 1966): 1031–54.
SCHUR, E. M. "Theory Planning and Pathology." *Social Problems* 6 (1958): 221–29.
———. "Reactions to Deviance: A Critical Assessment." *American Journal of Sociology* 75 (1969): 305–22.
SELLIN, T. "The Sociological Study of Criminality." *Journal of Criminal Law and Criminology* 41 (1950): 406–22.
———. "The Uniform Criminal Statistics Act." *Journal of Criminal Law and Criminology* 40 (1950): 679–700.
———. "Recidivism and Maturation." *National Probation and Parole Association Journal* 4 (1958): 241–50.
———. "Crime and Delinquency in the United States: An Over-All View." *Annals of the American Academy of Political and Social Science* 339 (1962): 11–23.
———. "International Criminal Statistics." *Criminologica* 5 (1967): 2–11.
SHORT, J. F. "Differential Association with Delinquent Friends and Delinquent Behavior." *Pacific Sociological Review* 1 (1958): 20–25.
SZASZ, T. S. "The Role of the Counterphobic Mechanism in Addiction." *Journal of the American Psychological Association* 6 (1958): 309–25.
———. "The Ethics of Addiction." *American Journal of Psychology* 128 (1971): 541–46.
TOBY, J. "Criminal Motivation. A Sociocultural Analysis." *British Journal of Criminology* 2 (1962): 317–36.
———. "Violence and the Masculine Ideal: Some Qualitative Data." *Annals of the American Academy of Political and Social Science* 364 (1966): 19–27.
TURK, A. T. "The Mythology of Crime in America." *Criminology* 8 (February 1971): 397–411.
WATTENBERG, W. W. "A Phenomenon in Search of a Cause." *Journal of Criminal Law and Criminology* 48 (1957): 54–58.
WERKENTIN, F.; MICHAEL HOFFERBERT; and MICHAEL BAURMANN. "Criminology as a Police Science or: 'How Old is the New Criminology?' " *Crime and Social Justice* 2 (Fall–Winter 1974): 24–41.
WOLFGANG, M. E. "Pioneers in Criminology: Cesare Lombroso (1835–1909)." *Journal of Criminal Law, Criminology, and Police Science* 52 (November–December 1961): 361–69.
———. "A Sociological Analysis of Criminal Homicide." *Federal Probation* 25 (1961): 48–55.
———. "Comparison of the Executed and the Commuted Among Admis-

sions to Death Row." *Journal of Criminal Law, Criminology, and Police Science* 53 (1962): 301–11.
―――. "Criminology and the Criminologist." *Journal of Criminal Law, Criminology, and Police Science* 54 (1963): 155–62.
―――. "Uniform Crime Reports: A Critical Appraisal." *University of Pennsylvania Law Review* 111 (1963): 708–38.
―――. "Mathematical Methods in Criminology." *International Social Science Journal* 18 (1966): 200–223.
―――. "A Preface to Violence." *Annals of the American Academy of Political and Social Science* 364 (1966): 1–7.
―――. "Who Kills Whom?" *Psychology Today* 3 (1969): 55–75.

Books

ABRAHAMSEN, DAVID. *The Psychology of Crime.* New York: Columbia University Press, 1960.
ADLER, FREDA. *Sisters in Crime: The Rise of the New Female Criminal.* New York: McGraw-Hill, 1975.
BECCARIA, CESARE B. *On Crimes and Punishments.* Translated by Henry Paolucci. Indianapolis: Bobbs-Merrill, 1968.
BECKER, HOWARD S. *Outsiders: Studies in the Sociology of Deviance.* New York: Free Press, 1963.
BONGER, W. A. *Race and Crime.* Translated by Margaret M. Horduk. New York: Columbia University Press, 1943.
CHAMBLISS, WILLIAM. *Crime and the Legal Process.* New York: McGraw-Hill, 1969.
―――. *Functional and Conflict Theories of Crime.* New York: MSS Modular Publications, 1974.
―――. *Criminal Law in Action.* Santa Barbara, Calif.: Hamilton, 1975.
COHEN, ALBERT K. *Delinquent Boys: The Culture of the Gang.* New York: Free Press, 1955.
DE REUCH, A. S., and R. PORTER, eds. *The Mentally Abnormal Offender.* Boston: Little, Brown, 1968.
DUGALE, RICHARD, *The Jukes: A Study in Crime, Pauperism, and Heredity.* New York: Putnam, 1877.
DURKHEIM, EMILE. *The Division of Labor in Society.* 1893.
―――. *Suicide.* New York: Free Press, 1951.
―――. *The Rules of Sociological Method.* New York: Free Press, 1964.
ESTABROOK, A. H. *The Jukes in 1915.* Washington D.C.: Carnegie Institution, 1916.
EYSENCK, H. J. *Crime and Personality.* Boston: Houghton Mifflin, 1964.
FERDINAND, THEODORE N. *Typologies of Delinquency: A Critical Analysis.* New York: Random House, 1966.

FERRI, ENRICO. *Criminal Sociology*. Translated by. J. I. Kelly and John Lisle. Boston: Little, Brown, 1917.

FINGARETTE, HERBERT. *The Meaning of Criminal Insanity*. Berkeley: University of California Press, 1972.

FINK, ARTHUR E. *Causes of Crime: Biological Theories in the United States, 1800-1915*. Philadelphia: University of Pennsylvania Press, 1938.

FREUD, SIGMUND. *A General Introduction to Psychoanalysis*. New York: Liveright, 1948.

GAROFALO, RAFFAELE. *Criminology*. Translated by Robert Wyness. Boston: Little, Brown, 1914.

GEIS, GILBERT, and ROBERT G. MEIER, eds. *White-Collar Crime: Offenses in Business, Politics, and the Professions*. New York: Free Press, 1977.

GLASER, DANIEL, ed. *Handbook of Criminology*. Chicago: Rand McNally, 1974.

GORING, CHARLES. *The English Convict*. London: H. M. Stationery Office, 1913.

GRUPP, STANLEY E. *The Positive School of Criminology: Three Lectures by Enrico Ferri*. Pittsburgh: University of Pittsburgh Press, 1968.

GUZE, SAMUEL B. *Criminality and Psychiatric Disorders*. New York: Oxford University Press, 1976.

HALLECK, SEYMOUR L. *Psychiatry and the Dilemma of Crime*. New York: Harper & Row, 1967.

HARE, R. D. *Psychopathy: Theory and Research*. New York: Wiley, 1970.

HEATH, JAMES, ed. *Eighteenth Century Penal Theory*. New York: Oxford University Press, 1963.

HIPPCHEN, LEONARD J., ed. *Ecologic-Biochemical Approaches to Treatment of Delinquents and Criminals*. New York: Van Nostrand-Reinhold, 1978.

HOOTON, ERNEST A. *Crime and the Man*. Cambridge, Mass.: Harvard University Press, 1939.

KITTRIE, NICHOLAS N. *The Right to Be Different*. Baltimore: Johns Hopkins University Press, 1971.

LEMERT, EDWIN M. *Human Deviance, Social Problems, and Social Control*. 2nd ed. Englewood Cliffs, N. J.: Prentice-Hall, 1972.

LOPEZ-REY, MANUEL. *Crime: An Analytic Appraisal*. New York: Praeger, 1970.

MAESTRO, MARCELLO T. *Voltaire and Beccari as Reformers of Criminal Law*. New York: Columbia University Press, 1942.

MANNHEIM, HERMANN, ed. *Pioneers in Criminology*. Montclair, N.J.: Patterson Smith, 1973.

MARX, KARL. *Critique of Political Economy*. New York: International Library, 1904.

MATZA, DAVID. *Becoming Deviant*. Englewood Cliffs, N. J.: Prentice-Hall, 1969.
MCCAGHY, CHARLES. *Deviant Behavior: Crime, Conflict, and Interest Groups*. New York: Macmillan, 1976.
MEDNICK, SARNOFF A., and KARL O. CHRISTIANSEN, eds. *Biosocial Bases of Criminal Behavior*. New York: Gardner, 1977.
PARMELEE, MAURICE. *Criminology*. New York: Macmillan, 1918.
PARSONS, TALCOTT. *The Social System*. New York: Free Press, 1951.
PHILLIPSON, COLMAN. *Three Criminal Law Reformers: Beccari, Bentham, and Romilly*. New York: Dutton, 1923.
QUINNEY, RICHARD. *The Social Reality of Crime*. Boston: Little, Brown, 1970.
―――. *Critique of Legal Order: Crime Control in Capitalist Society*. Boston: Little, Brown, 1974.
ROEBUCK, JULIAN B. *Criminal Typology: The Legalistic, Physical-Constitutional-Heredity, Psychological-Psychiatric and Sociological Approaches*. Springfield, Ill.: Charles C Thomas, 1967.
SCHAFER, STEPHEN. *Theories of Criminology*. New York: Random House, 1969.
SCHEFF, THOMAS J. *Being Mentally Ill*. Chicago: Aldine, 1966.
SELLIN, THORSTEN. *Culture Conflict and Crime*. New York: Social Science Research Council, 1938.
SHELDON, WILLIAM. *The Varieties of Human Physique: An Introduction to Constitutional Psychology*. New York: Harper & Row, 1940.
SCHUR, EDWIN M. *Labeling Deviant Behavior*. New York: Harper & Row, 1971.
SZASZ, THOMAS S. *The Myth of Mental Illness: Foundations of a Theory of Personal Conduct*. New York: Hoeber-Harper, 1961.
―――. *Law, Liberty, and Psychiatry*. New York: Macmillan, 1963.
TANNENBAUM, FRANK. *Crime and the Community*. New York: Columbia University Press, 1938.
TAYLOR, IAN; PAUL WALTON; and JACK YOUNG. *The New Criminology: For a Social Theory of Deviance*. New York: Harper & Row, 1973.
TURK, AUSTIN. *Criminality and Legal Order*. Chicago: Rand McNally, 1969.
VOLD, GEORGE B. *Theoretical Criminology*. New York: Oxford University Press, 1958.
YOCKELSON, SAMUEL, and STANTON E. SAMENOW. *The Criminal Personality*. New York: Jason Aronson, 1977.